Things That Go Bump In The Night

How to Help Children Resolve Their Natural Fears

Dr. Paul Warren
Dr. Frank Minirth
with Sandy Dengler

A JANET THOMA BOOK

THOMAS NELSON PUBLISHERS
Nashville

This book is dedicated to all children, young and old, who grow from their fear experiences.

Dr. Warren extends special thanks to his parents, Robert and Pauline Warren, who taught him the strength to face fear.

We also express loving appreciation to our wives, Mary Alice Minirth and Vicky Warren, and to our children, Rachel, Renee, Carrie, and Alicia Minirth and Matthew Warren. They encourage us daily.

May the glory be to God, our loving heavenly Father, who makes all growth possible through His love and grace.

Published in Nashville, Tennessee, by Thomas Nelson, Inc., and distributed in Canada by Lawson Falle, Ltd., Cambridge, Ontario.

Printed in the United States of America.

Unless otherwise noted, the Bible version used in this publication is THE NEW KING JAMES VERSION OF THE BIBLE. Copyright © 1979, 1980, 1982, Thomas Nelson, Inc., Publishers.

Examples cited in this book are composites of the authors' actual cases in their work at the Minirth-Meier Clinic in Dallas, Texas. Names and facts have been changed and rearranged to maintain confidentiality.

For general information about other Minirth-Meier Clinic branch offices, counselling services, educational resources and hospital programs, call toll-free 1-800-545-1819. National Headquarters: (214) 669-1733, or (800) 229-3000.

Library of Congress Cataloging-in-Publication Data

Warren, Paul, 1949–
    Things that go bump in the night/by Paul Warren, Frank Minirth.
        p.   cm.
    "A Janet Thoma book."
    ISBN 0-8407-7770-1
    1. Fear in children.   2. Fear in children—Case studies.   3. Fear—Religious aspects—Christianity.   4. Adjustment (Psychology) in children.
I. Minirth, Frank B.   II. Title.
BF723.F4W37   1993
155.4'1246—dc20   92-17106
                                                                              CIP

4 5 6 — 97 96 95 94 93

Contents

PART ONE

The Power of Fear

Understanding the Deep-seated Fears of Childhood

1

The Monster in My Closet Is Growling

Dear Troid,
This is weird, man. This is really weird. (I had to look up "weird"; it doesn't look right any way you spell it.) Writing letters to a cat telling what I think. I mean, I could just talk to you, Troid, you know? You listen. You don't say anything. But I don't think I want to hear some of this out loud. So I'll do like Dr. Warren suggested and write a letter to you. Besides, he said "First we're going to do a invatory of all the people who are important to you," and I said, "the dog and cat, too?" and he said "by all means. They're important." Then he said "write a letter to each one." So I'm starting with you because you seem like the easiest place to start.
First off, I hope you don't mind being called Troid instead of your whole name Mergatroid. They do that to me too. I'm James but they keep calling me Jim or Jimmy. I mean Mom and Dad and my teacher, Mrs. Hoy. The kids call me lots of other names, but I won't tell you all those. They aren't very nice.
I hope you like that porthole pet door Dad installed in the side of the house above the porch roof that lets you come into my room from outside. I think it would be so neat to be able to climb up the maple tree to the porch roof like you do. No thief is ever going to be able to climb like that Dad says, and even if he could, he couldn't squeeze through that little round hole. Only

you fit. Sometimes I imagine doing it like you do, and I wonder what it would feel like to be able to climb all around like that, but I'm really scared to climb. I hate climbing. But you're a cat, so you have to. Do you hate it too, down deep?

Mom told me you're exactly my age. 10. She says that's old for a cat and young for a people.

I spose I should tell you why I'm doing this. Mom took me to see Dr. Warren. He's a child si-kia-tris doctor. Mom thinks I'm afraid too much and she wants Dr. Warren to help me be braver. I don't know what making an invatory and writing letters is sposed to do, but here goes.

I'll write to you again tomorrow after I figure out what to say to Hector. What do you say to a dog? Never mind. I forgot cats don't talk to dogs.

Your friend,
James

Only a week before James wrote this letter to his cat, his mother, Elaine Tanner, had visited Dr. Warren's office at the Minirth-Meier Clinic. She had told his nurse, "I need to see the doctor about my son, James. I'm having trouble getting him to go to school."

Soon after that the nurse ushered Elaine Tanner and her children, James and Aubrey, into the doctor's office, and she sat down cautiously on the brand-new sofa.

"Nice colors." She ran her hand across the smooth fabric. "Plaid, but a very subdued plaid. How did you get the perfect color match in the wing chair? Special order?"

"Yes. In fact, it just arrived." Dr. Warren sat back in his own ample, overstuffed leather chair.

Mrs. Tanner nodded sagely. "Every time I redo the living room I find myself special-ordering pieces. I imagine you would have a terrible problem keeping your furniture looking clean and nice, with all the people who stream through here. I have a hard enough time just with guests on weekends."

Mrs. Tanner continued on for several minutes about the

rigors of keeping her house in decent order. Dr. Warren noticed that as she spoke, her son James squirmed, obviously uncomfortable.

Beside Mrs. Tanner sat her daughter Aubrey, just turned four. Through Dr. Warren's mind ran the constant thought, *My, but isn't this little girl personable!* It wasn't just the child's four-year-old innocence or the big blue eyes or the wavy, collar-length blonde hair. Little Aubrey projected cheer and charm as dazzlingly as any television game-show host.

"And so, Doctor," Mrs. Tanner continued, "I was hoping you could help Jimmy in these next few weeks. I realize it's not much time, but school is starting in less than two months."

"You say James had a problem at the beginning of last school year?"

"It was terrible. I didn't know what was happening until I read an article describing school phobia. That's James exactly, right on the button. He's really a rather quiet boy. Gets along fine with others. Makes pretty good grades. But his first day of school was a disaster!"

"Entering third grade then."

"Yes. He starts fourth this year. He turned into a monster. A monster! Kicking and screaming. Begging. Crying. I had to drag him to school, literally drag him. Yes," Mrs. Tanner bobbed her head, "school phobia. Definitely."

"Aubrey here doesn't go to school yet."

"Day-care. I work as a dental assistant weekdays."

"Does she express any fears about being separated from you?"

"It never came up. You see, the dentist I work for also has small children, so he uses a room in the clinic as a nursery. He has his mother-in-law come in and babysit the children—his, my Aubrey, and the receptionist's two. It's a wonderful arrangement. Aubrey is right there and I can visit her frequently, between patients."

"Does she display any other fears?"

"Nothing you wouldn't expect at her age."

"Can you elaborate?"

"Well, she's afraid of things under her bed, and monsters, and things in her closet. You know. That sort of thing."

"Every night?"

"Well, yes. But again, that's not unusual at this age. Jimmy here had them. And his father says he had them too."

"How do you deal with them?"

"With the monsters? There is no such thing. You know that."

"Apparently Aubrey isn't quite so certain. I'll rephrase. How do you deal with her concept of them?"

"Oh. Of course." Mrs. Tanner looked a bit embarrassed. "When she gets very upset, I mean, *very* upset, I check her closet and under her bed, and tell her there's nothing there." She glanced at little Aubrey. "Because there isn't, of course. You know. It's the sort of thing you do when a child thinks there's bogeymen and robbers in the closet."

"Every night."

"Yes. She's at that age."

"How long does it take?"

Mrs. Tanner frowned. "Well, uh, an hour—sometimes longer. The longest is sometimes about three hours before she falls asleep." She hastened on. "But it's Jimmy who concerns me. He's so timid. Not exactly shy. He does fine around most adults. But, well, he's a scaredy-cat. It's not quite natural, you know? You can see he's not puny or runty or anything."

And it was true. James looked like a normal little boy—average size, average weight, average blondish hair, average fair-complexioned face, average everything.

ONE SCARED KID

And then, not the least like James, there was Darryl, twelve years old. His fingers were tobacco stained, his hair was so moussed he probably had to shampoo with industrial solvent, his clothes bore all the designer labels in vogue this week, and his attitude made the Terminator look like a weenie. During his first session with Dr. Warren, he made it very clear that he was in charge of this show. "When I don't want to talk about something, I'll let you know." By the fourth visit he had dissolved into tears and wailing.

"Beneath that tough exterior and brash behavior," recounts Dr. Warren fervently, "there was one scared kid."

THE DANGERS FEARS POSE

Fears. Everyone has fears. So what's the problem?

"Fears," says the clinic's Dr. Minirth, "are survival mechanisms. They're the ordinary responses to unusual, and therefore potentially dangerous, stimuli. When they're normal they serve us well. When they get out of hand they can damage or destroy us. They can be crippling and self-fulfilling, and that is so unnecessary it's tragic."

Every child—from the toughie like Darryl to the baby not yet weaned—harbors deep, primal, arching fears. Dr. Minirth cites a survey of one thousand children ages two to fourteen in which 90 percent expressed an intense, irrational fear of some natural object. In another study, 43 percent of the surveyed children, who ranged from ages six to twelve, admitted to many fears and worries, some verbalized and some hidden.

How do we help children avoid such fears? Not by using logic, that's for sure. We're not fooling anyone when we check under the bed and in all the closets and say, "See, there are no monsters here."

A handful of fictional television characters have gained immortality in the American memory, and *Star Trek*'s half-human, half-Vulcan Mr. Spock may lead the pack. His enslavement to logic made him a charming and sometimes irascible foil to his *Enterprise* crew mates, who valued intuition and hunches above cold reason. More intriguing by far, though, were Spock's deep and painful inner conflicts. He struggled constantly to keep his human emotions at bay while letting his Vulcan logic shine through. In that struggle he touched a nerve in his television audience, for exactly that war frequently rages inside every adult.

But not kids. They blissfully proceed through life totally unburdened by reason and logic. And that is a fact we adults must keep constantly in mind when helping children deal with fears.

**Fears never spring from a base of logic.
And fears never, ever respond to logic.**

Patiently explaining to children why they should not be afraid doesn't do a thing toward allaying their concern. But it does have one effect: in the child's mind, it removes any differences between rational and irrational fears. The child sees no line between the two.

Like James, the boy introduced at the beginning of this chapter, seven-year-old Michael suffers school phobia. The minute he leaves the house, he feels overwhelmed by the terrifying thought that a robber might enter the house—his home—and hurt his mom or even kill her. Is this fear irrational, or just highly unlikely? Just what would Michael do about the situation if he were home? Nothing, despite that silly film, *Home Alone,* which depicts a small boy besting bumbling burglars. The point is, to a child it makes no difference whether a fear can be labeled rational or irrational. Fear is fear, untrammeled by reality.

Indeed, most children can never put their deepest fears into words, and only rarely can they recognize the true nature of their worries and fears. These silent, underlying concerns go light-years beyond the things we normally associate with fear, such as a bite from a dog, noises in a dark night, the possibility of flunking a test tomorrow, a monster or robber in the closet. Different fears take over as the child grows and changes, and each new fear must be addressed. Each is predictable for that particular stage of growth, and each is necessary for proper emotional development.

For our discussion of fear in children, we have divided the child's growth into four stages:

- The baby stage: newborn to twenty-four months
- The preschool stage: three to five years
- The grade-school stage: six to twelve years
- The adolescent stage: thirteen to eighteen years

Each of these stages is illustrated in the following case vignettes of our own and our friends' children, plus those in our clinical practice. You might want to think of an experience from your own childhood or your children's lives as you read through them.

The mother of eighteen-month-old twin boys felt they were old enough that she could return to work, so she arranged for a neighbor to keep them four hours each day. One boy turned on his babysitter, throwing such a fit that the windows vibrated. The other simply sat down in a corner and watched the world through huge, sad, doleful eyes. Both children in the baby stage were coping with two severe fears: fear of abandonment and fear of annihilation if they were separated from Mommy. The loud one was responding with what we call separation anxiety. His brother displayed inhibition. Both were equally frightened.

For more than six months, a three-year-old boy latched onto his mother so intensely that any time Daddy came near her the boy shoved him away and/or kicked him in the shins. Needless to say, Daddy got fed up with this nonsense in a hurry. This boy, in the preschool stage, was coping with his fear of adults' power, Daddy's power in particular, as he worked through what we call an Oedipal phase.

A nine-year-old girl preferred spending recess in the library rather than spending it on the playground. After her exasperated teacher booted the girl outside to play ("and stay outside until the bell rings!"), the child's mother petitioned first the superintendent and then the school board to win her child permission to stay inside. This girl in the grade-school stage was coping with her fear of injury by avoiding situations, such as play, in which injury might happen. This fear loomed strong because earlier fears had never been resolved.

A sixteen-year-old girl would probably have been more successful riding the family's all-terrain vehicle if she didn't keep running into things. As soon as she got her driver's license she upgraded to running into things with the family's Toyota. Down deep inside, this girl in the adolescent stage was coping with her fear of growing up.

You may know of cases similar to these in which behaviors are undergirded by simple, basic fears common to every child. As we continue, we'll take a second look at these concerns, along with others, and discuss how they are best uncovered and handled.

Ideally, the fears of each stage of growth are comfortably (although sometimes temporarily) resolved before those of the next stage arrive. If, for some reason, the basic fears are not allayed, they persist into subsequent stages of the child's growth, surfacing time and again in various disguises. Much too often, we at the Minirth-Meier Clinic can trace the problems of unhappy adults to unallayed fears of childhood.

Addressing the underlying fears every child feels, then, can be viewed as preventive medicine. By helping the child work through fears, you help him or her deal not just with fear but with many of life's other slings and arrows as well. Fail to resolve basic fears and the child faces life with a potentially crippling handicap.

Take care of the robber in the closet, or it will rob the joy from life later on.

Fear can steal many joys from both children and adults, such as the pleasures of creativity, the exhilaration of risk-taking (we're talking about the measured risks a vibrant adulthood requires, not stunts like jumping out of airplanes or driving at high speeds for no clear purpose). The fearful child dreams dreams, but nagging worries prevent the pursuit of them. The fears emerge in the adult as depression, procrastination, timidity, or bitterness, to name a few. Satisfaction with life and self evaporates, stolen by that robber in the closet.

FRIGHT, FEARS, AND ANXIETIES—DIFFERENT BREEDS OF CAT

Not every fear in children is the sort of fear we're talking about. There are subtle but important differences between true fears and frights, phobias, and anxieties. These differences don't mean a whole lot to the mother who is trying to peel a screaming, thrashing four-year-old off her kneecaps, but they *are* quite different, as you will see as we delve into them.

Fright Versus Fear

Paul and Vicki Warren were going out of town overnight, but that should not pose a problem. After all, their son Matthew was, at that time, about two and a half—not a baby anymore. The babysitter, a wise and charming older lady, arrived on schedule. Wise and charming she might be, but Matthew didn't know her. As Paul brought the luggage to the door, Matthew began wailing, terrified.

"You're all right. It's okay. This kind lady will take good care of you. You don't have to be frightened of Mrs. Beal. It's all right, Matthew. We'd certainly never leave you with someone who wasn't very nice. You and Mrs. Beal will get along great, Matthew. See? You have all your toys here and your warm bed. You're safe here. It's all right."

On and on it went. For half an hour Vicki and Paul addressed Matthew's fright. Finally they simply had to leave, their son's howls echoing in their ears like a hundred-decibel guilt machine.

An hour later, Dr. Warren, the child expert who would have assessed the problem in two minutes in a clinical setting, finally identified his own problem. He and Vicki had addressed Matthew's apparent fright about the babysitter. They completely missed his *real* fear: Mom and Dad were going away. As the suitcases had landed in the foyer, Matthew's basic fear of never seeing Mommy and Daddy again had kicked in. And his parents had not said one word to reassure him that "we'll be back."

Fright is an experience or physiological response to an event in progress at the moment, an immediate danger. Matthew was frightened of the babysitter and the situation she represented. Down deeper, he feared abandonment.

For a classic example of fright, picture a large dog, let's say a Newfoundland, approaching a four-year-old. The kid panics, terrified, and we nod sagely. Of course. The dog's mouth is big enough to hide a basketball, and its teeth resemble a garden rake. Naturally the child is afraid of being bitten.

Actually, though, underneath the fright lies the child's far more basic fear, that of being overpowered. Here's a dog in the same weight class as a Nissan Sentra. It need but knock the child over to confirm the fear. Even a little terrier, lively and apparently out of control, can trigger fright. The key phrase is "out of control," meaning beyond the child's control. We can reassure the child until we're blue in the face that this gentle old dog will never bite. But the terror persists, and the fright rages on.

By observing the child awhile in this situation, we could avoid premature conclusions. In this case we would see that the child was not afraid of the dog's biting but of its jumping and shoving. The visible fright misled us so that we misinterpreted the child's response. When we understand the real fear, we pick up the child or simply move in close, protecting him or her from being overwhelmed. As a result, the fright subsides.

What does the child fear? That is the *fright*. Why is the child afraid? That is the underlying *fear*.

Parents are great at dealing with children's frights. They are usually lousy at dealing with children's fears.

Anxiety

Anxiety is a feeling, or an affect, that is not specifically directed at a particular fright. In most cases, it's a generalized fear reaction in which neither you nor the child has any inkling of what's going on. The cause may be obscure, but the anxiety reaction itself is as clear as spring water. The child's twisted face and terror-filled eyes, the tears and howling all signal a major freak-out. Look for anxiety reactions especially in one- to two-year-olds who have no verbalization skills to help them either understand or localize the source of fright or fear.

Phobia

A phobia is an unrealistic, overblown fear of some object or experience. Actually, it is one of a child's basic fears that has been redirected onto other things. Take again our example of the Newfoundland versus the four-year-old. Let's assume this time that the child has a true phobia of dogs. From Great Danes to Chihuahuas, all dogs terrify the kid. The child has displaced a basic preschool-stage fear, that of the power of adults, onto a fear of dogs. His or her phobia can persist into adulthood, although it will likely shift to other objects. Not many adults have a phobia of dogs, but the phobia can transfer to a fear of crowds (agoraphobia), a fear of high places (acrophobia), a fear of enclosed places (claustrophobia). . . .

"Wait!" you cry. "Everyone's got phobias of some sort.

In fact, nearly anyone can suffer claustrophobia under certain circumstances."

That's true. Claustrophobia might come labeled as cabin fever, suffered by people who have been pent up indoors during a long northern winter. Or it might be island fever for those who have been limited by the confines of a small area such as an island. Daniel Boone carried cabin fever to extreme. He had territory fever. Crying, "Too crowded! Too crowded!" when settlers moved within half a mile or so of his cabin, he pushed ever westward to new frontiers. That's how he ended up in Missouri, a long, long way from southeastern Pennsylvania, where territory fever first struck.

We measure the severity of phobias by whether they impair function. How much, if at all, does this phobia limit the person's ability to maintain personal relationships, work efficiently, proceed normally through life? True phobias cripple function. When the child absolutely cannot go to school, cannot stand the sight of a dog, cannot leave the house, cannot go up in an elevator, that child— or adult—has a serious problem.

In a nutshell, a fear is something specific of which you are afraid. And you are aware of what you're afraid of.

An anxiety, on the other hand, is an obvious fear reaction. But with an anxiety, you are not really aware of just what it is you're afraid of or where the reaction is coming from. In reality, differences between fears and anxieties are not all that clear-cut. We find elements of each in both; one tends to grade into the other.

THE GOOD NEWS: FEAR HAS VALUE

"Fears in children," says Dr. Warren, "are necessary for growth. All children, for example, must go through the stage in which they fear the monster under the bed or the robber in the closet. With help, they resolve that fear and from it they grow another notch."

The scared kid has a good thing going for him. Basic,

underlying fears of childhood are the primary opportunities for growth. They are not threats to happiness or a reason to stop growing. They are temporarily unpleasant at times (more so for the parent than for the child) but ultimately they are very fruitful.

Fears are necessary for growth. Without them, a child cannot develop emotionally.

The child resolves fears through play and through experiences gained from relationships with others. Play and relationships. Children are creatures of play. But even more are they creatures of relationships. Material things mean very little to them compared with relationships.

In a stable, average family setting, children will do the necessary internal processing of fears on their own. Should their fear-processing mechanisms be blocked, short-circuited, or prevented, however, they will need outside help. Even when the processes are functioning normally, children can benefit immensely from the support of an adult helper, a journeymate in life.

THE PARENT AS JOURNEYMATE

For most parents, dealing with childhood fears is like being turned on a life-sized game board with nary a hint of the rules about how the game is played. Because small children rarely understand their own fears, the parents, ex-children, hardly ever recognize the fears from when they were growing up. Therefore they haven't a clue as to what's going on in their children's innermost sanctums. That's why Elaine Tanner, introduced earlier, had no idea that her daughter Aubrey also had deep, underlying fears as well James, the son with school phobia.

In her initial visit with Dr. Warren, the doctor suggested, "Mrs. Tanner, I'd like to see Aubrey also. She—"

"But she's not the problem. Jimmy is."

Dr. Warren sat back and laced his hands across his middle. "Let's say your dog has puppies and—"

"That's not funny, Doctor. That happened. Hector isn't a Hector. She's a Hectorette."

Dr. Warren has long since learned when to keep smiles to himself. "Let's say one of the puppies shows signs of worms. Do you treat that one or do you treat them all?"

"All of them. But that's not the same thing."

"Not the same thing exactly, of course. But the general idea holds true; if one puppy gets worms, it can infect the others simply by being very close to them all the time—proximity. Similarly, if there is a problem in a close-knit family, it will cause reverberations in the other members because of sheer proximity; they're all together. In fact, the other members may be able to offer insight into the primary patient's problems, sometimes without knowing it."

"Well . . ." Mrs. Tanner looked at Aubrey a moment. "Do you think it will help Jimmy?"

"I think it will."

"Well, I suppose . . ."

"I suspect, from what James and I have been doing with inventories and letters, and from what you've said today, that some fears are as yet unresolved in both children. And because families are units rather than aggregates, you may be called upon to reexamine some fears and misgivings in your own life. Your children need journeymates, and—"

"What's that?"

"A journeymate is a person who understands a child's fears and problems and walks beside the child as the child resolves them, guiding if needed. The journeymate, therefore, must be older, wiser, and more mature than the child. The journeymate does not resolve the problem for the child. The child must do that. A journeymate cannot spare the child grief or struggle, but he or she can share it."

"But Doctor, there are some things a child simply should not have to face."

"I could not agree more. On the other hand, there are some things a child must do for himself, or he cannot grow properly—he or she, of course. I can't assure you success in this venture, but I can assure you that whatever effort you make will pay great dividends for your whole family."

As parents and journeymates to children, we must address any fear, rational or irrational, and because its rationality doesn't matter to the child, it should be immaterial to us, as well. Therefore:

> **We must address the fear from the child's perspective, not ours.**
> **We must allow the child to be afraid and empathize. We want to talk to him or her and hear about the scared feelings.**
> **Moreover, we must balance the child's fears with facts and invest ourselves in the process.**

This book will explore the ways you can help children address the fears that invariably grip them. Some parts may be difficult to read if they stir old dragons in your own memory. We urge you to persist to the end and to make the information found here a part of your own life. In many ways, children cannot handle the fears of life by themselves.

We'll walk with you through the four stages of childhood, identifying the fears associated with each stage. We'll explore the ways you can allay a child's natural, God-given fears. We'll discuss how you can use those fears as they should be used, to help the child grow into a happy, healthy adult who can make a positive mark in the world. And when something big has gone awry, we'll talk about repairing the damage of unresolved fears from the past.

Paul told Timothy, "For God has not given us a spirit of fear [some translators use timidity], but of power and of love and of a sound mind" (2 Tim. 1:7). We will talk about practical steps that will assuage the "spirit of fear" so the true Spirit can shine through.

And we'll take a look at how, for better or worse, the child's deepest concerns are affected by the rest of the family: parents and siblings, as well as the cousin staring off into space with a finger jammed up one nostril who just put a live frog down your back. The goofy uncle and the straitlaced aunt, the doting and not-so-doting grandparents, all these relatives loom large in a child's life. It pays to be able to see exactly how they play a role so that you can help enhance their good effects and minimize their bad ones.

And through it all, we'll not lose sight of the fact that many parents are rearing their children without a mate— or with a mate who is not the child's biological parent. The job is more than doubled when the parent is single or the family is blended. But there *are* ways to cope, and there are some things that you simply cannot do yourself. We'll explore them all.

BABY PICTURES

The elaborate process of experiencing basic fears, vanquishing them, and moving on—ideally all with the help of a journeymate—begins very nearly at birth. What concerns could a baby possibly have? When you think about it, plenty. The newborn isn't even dried off yet and already it owes the hospital more than four thousand dollars!

But that small concern does not interest us here. Instead, we'll start in the next chapter to build a picture of how, deep down inside, an infant begins its lifelong process of dealing with the world.

PART TWO

Infant and Toddler

The Bottle and Banky Set

2
Rock-a-Bye Baby

THE FEARS OF INFANCY

Dear Troid,

I asked Dr. Warren what I should write in my letters and he said anything I want. So I think I'll explain to you what happened last night. Since you're a cat you probly don't understand.

Mom and Dad were going to go out to dinner and see a movie without the kids for once, is what they said. So they got Mrs. Dottmeyer to babysit. You know Mrs. Dottmeyer. She's the old lady next door with gray hair who has Willard. I saw part of a movie once about a rat named Willard, or maybe it was the kid who owned the rat, but anyway, it made me think of Willard because he's a rat too. A real jerk. A people rat. But that don't have anything to do with Mrs. Dottmeyer.

Anyway, she came over about six. You know that. You watched her. And why do you always hide upstairs when she comes over, anyway? She's not going to hurt you. Aubrey started yelling and acting up. Then I started crying but I don't know why. Maybe cause Aubrey was. Then Dad got mad and Mom took an aspirin. Mom says she'd expected me to do that when I was little but she didn't expect me to do it now, and Aubrey she expects to do that because Aubrey really did it when she was little. Anyway, Aubrey screams like that because she's scared, Mom says, and Dr. Warren agrees.

I'm sorry it scared you so much you wouldn't come out from under my bed until midnight just about. So I thought I'd better explain it to you because cats don't scream and carry on like that when they're scared. You just hide.

I wish I could just hide.

Your friend,
James

In the incident James described vividly (the babysitter's arrival), both James and Aubrey exhibited fear reactions common to their ages. For that matter, so did Troid. James's and Aubrey's fears did not pop up suddenly. They were rooted deeply in the past, clear into infancy. Even adults' fears can be traced to their experiences as babies. Richard Kell, an adult in our counsel, is a case in point.

MANSIONS OF THE MIND

Richard Kell's wife got tired of his getting home so late every night. When he took a part-time job on top of his fifty-hour-a-week regular employment, she really hit the roof.

"We don't need the money that bad!" she raged. "Homeless people who owe the Internal Revenue Service ten thousand dollars don't need the money *that* bad!"

Fights between the Kells grew more frequent. The intensity escalated. Neighbors referred to the sessions as "Kellfire and brimstone." Eventually Richard sought professional help.

"I'm a rational man," Richard told his counselor, "not overly emotional, not easily frightened. But last Saturday we got in one of our fights and Doris said, 'I'm not going to keep living like this. Life is too short to spend it this way.' And then she started talking about maybe a divorce would be best for both of us.

"I panicked. I just plain freaked out. I can't begin to express how panicky it made me. And I can't figure out why. I'm not that kind of person."

Finding the roots of Richard's problem took some digging. To make a long example short, we discovered that deep down inside, he believed that if he lost his wife, he would literally lose himself, the thing we call the "meself" when we describe it as a primal fear of very young children. He would no longer be Richard Kell. He would be annihilated.

To the rational mind, including Richard's, that's nonsense. But the human mind is not always rational. It lives in a mansion of many rooms, and only one of them is the cheery, sunlit room of reason. Certainly the mind dwells there on occasion. But it also explores other rooms: conscious memories, memories beyond the conscious, messages from the past, experiences, fears, and primal fears, to name a few. It stalks the dark corridors and the shadow-filled cellars. All the rooms, bright and dark, contribute to the decisions the mind makes, even when it falsely believes those decisions came out of reason alone.

THE FIRST FEAR—ABANDONMENT AND ANNIHILATION

Children rarely bother with the reason room. Babies don't even have one. In Richard's case, his panic arose not from reason or even fear, but from one of the biggest rooms in a baby's mansion, the *first* fear. Because that room had not been closed off and boarded up early in his life, his thoughts were free to return to it, deep in the far recesses of the mansion of his mind.

We believe the first fear is not just of being abandoned, but also of losing one's personal identity—one's "meself"—by being abandoned.

Echoes of the Past—When the Mind Goes Back to That First Fear

Drop a newborn (No, not really. Just hold the infant with both hands and deliberately lower your hands suddenly; a couple of inches is plenty.) and the infant responds with a cut-and-dried set of actions. The baby flings its hands out and pops its mouth open. This startle reflex, called the Moro reflex, is both natural and healthy. Doctors examining newborns look for it as a sign that all is well.

To protect themselves from a huge, hostile world, even very young babies will attempt to get away from the scary situation when they are frightened. They might also cry or hold their breath.

As they advance into childhood, many transient fears and anxieties may surface. That's okay; it's normal to be worried. Other fears, not always tagged with an easily seen sign, are just as natural to the tiny one. They are just as much a part of natural health, and their resolution will pave the way to happiness later.

The infant depends utterly upon others for everything—love and affection, food and drink, warmth and protection. In a very practical way, the child would cease to exist if he or she were abandoned.

How does one board up a room that basic?

At Minirth-Meier, we never treat infants, of course. But we often find the infant's room still open and accessible in older people who are our patients, people such as Richard Kell. In his case we saw that it was necessary for him to understand two things:

First, there probably was not going to be a divorce. He and Doris both wanted to work things out. They both valued their marriage and were mutually committed to making it work, and work well.

More importantly, though, he had to become comfortable with the fact that even if there was a divorce, he could not lose his personhood. He would continue to be who he is regardless of external circumstances. To most people, whose first fears were allayed in infancy, it seems stupid to believe you could cease to exist if your spouse departed either voluntarily or involuntarily. Indeed, the notion sounded stupid to Richard too. His reasoning mind accepted the truth, but his unconscious thoughts stayed away from the room of reason and prowled instead that dark room from the most distant past.

Richard's parents divorced when he was three months old, and in an unusual chain of events, the father gained custody. A series of nannies and then a stepmother cared for Richard. They nurtured him well. He was loved and protected by them all. But love from others simply was not the same as the love and attention he had never received from his natural mother.

We convinced his nonreasoning mind (at least partially) of the solid nature of his personhood by repeatedly bombarding it with new messages, the facts: He had not lost his mind. He was not going nuts. His *self* was not in danger. We also reached deep accord by sympathizing and empathizing. We understood, and we said so. We knew the fear that fired his panic reaction was both real and legitimate. We helped his reasoning mind convince his nonreasoning mind that the panic was actually an echo from the past.

We see a variety of problems that arise in children and adults when that first fear is not resolved in the beginning. Inconsistency in relationships is one such problem. The love-hate relationship, such as Richard and Doris's, is another. Inability to make solid emotional attachments occurs frequently in these people too. They distance themselves from everyone because they never learned to trust or depend.

Even though he depended upon his wife for his identity, Richard Kell kept his distance from her. His real spouse, the identity in which he invested the most of himself, was his work. We urged him to cut back his work hours so he could make more time for Doris. She, in turn, had to be worthy of Richard's frail, wobbly beginnings of trust by encouraging their mutual intimacy.

Richard had to work long and hard to cope with the

problems his unresolved first fear still generated. Fortunately for most of us, this resolution comes naturally to infants whose parents provide *object constancy*.

Object Constancy

"Oh, Aubrey would howl when I left the room!" exclaimed Elaine Tanner. "Jimmy wasn't nearly that bad when he was very little."

"Can you describe his reaction when, for example, you left him alone in a nursery?" Dr. Warren asked.

"Well, let's see. Not much reaction, really. For instance, I'd leave him at the church nursery. He'd stop whatever he was doing and get this sad, sad look on his face. But he didn't throw a fit the way Aubrey does. She just goes wild—loud and screaming. I gave up trying to leave her there. I'd either work in the nursery myself or take her with me into services."

While Elaine Tanner described this less-than-elegant reaction, charming little Aubrey, like a Shirley Temple impersonator, sat smiling sweetly.

Elaine was describing two of the very common reactions that indicate an infant, pre-toddler, or toddler is afraid. And, of course, there are technical words for them both. *Separation anxiety* was Aubrey's way out. She let it all fly. James displayed *inhibition*. In the presence of other adults, and particularly if Mom was not immediately at hand, he quit whatever he was doing—stopped playing, stopped exploring—and withdrew with a frightened look on his face. We begin to see these two reactions in children as young as five to nine months old. They are very evident by toddlerhood.

Far and away the best approach to handling the fear of losing Mommy, a fear that is present in every tiny child, is object constancy. This means that the object of the child's need and affection—Mommy and/or Daddy—is constant about returning. And that requires an abandonment experience. There can be no return if no one has left.

**The great lesson to be learned at this age is
that loss does not mean abandonment. From
that lesson will derive lesson number two:
loss does not mean the end of existence.**

Picture how a mommy inflicts an immediate tangible loss—an abandonment experience—whenever she disappears from her baby boy's sight. It happens when she leaves the room, tucks him into his crib at night, even, at first, when he turns his head away. Recall how you play peekaboo with a baby; cover his eyes and he goes away. *"Wherrrrre's baby? Therrrrre's baby! Peekaboo! (Giggle, giggle, giggle)"* From baby's viewpoint, what you see is what you've got, and what you don't see isn't there. Mommy returns every time.

Daddy goes to work. Daddy returns. Mommy goes to work. Mommy returns. Mommy and Daddy go out for the evening or to an overnight engagement. Mommy and Daddy return. Repetition drives the crucial lesson home.

Little Meghan, seventeen months old, never got that lesson. Her daddy went to work, true, but her mommy stayed home. Meghan was never left with a babysitter. Meghan breast-fed, you see, and it was easier to just take her along everywhere. She had no nursery experience, no prolonged absence by a parent. Isn't *that* object constancy, when the object—a parent—is constantly present?

Not really. What Meghan experienced was not true object constancy. It was *object permanence*. The object was there all the time. Meghan never had to experience the fear that Mommy might not return because Mommy never left. No fear equals no experience to learn from. Therefore, object permanence, in which there is no temporary loss, simply does not do the job. And Meghan was a very, very fearful little girl. Any unusual situation, any stranger at the door, any animal wandering into the yard could drive her to a terrified frenzy.

Meghan illustrated the foundational message of this book:

Fear is a child's opportunity to learn, and therefore is necessary to growth. In order to develop fully, children must resolve their deepest fears by meeting them and working them through.

Meghan was never given the opportunity to experience the basic fear of abandonment and then to have that fear allayed. She needed to have the experience that the object is not there and then the object comes back, first triggering and then allaying her natural fear of abandonment. *Is Mommy here? Yes, no. Yes, no. Will she come back? Yes!*

We coached her mother (who was as fearful as Meghan about the necessary "cure") on ways to provide mini-abandonments: away for ten minutes, away for twenty minutes, away for an hour. On every occasion, Mommy assured Meghan she would return soon. On every occasion she returned soon but not necessarily when Meghan wanted her back.

It took awhile to turn Meghan around, but Mommy got with the program right away. She left a sitter with Meghan when she did the grocery shopping and reveled in cruising the aisles without a child hanging out of the cart grabbing everything in sight. She and her husband went out to dinner one evening for the first time since Meghan's birth. It was very difficult for both parents—yet they loved it. Meghan's excessive fearfulness abated in a matter of months.

Meghan's parents reassured her constantly as she learned her lessons, and we suggest you do the same for the small child in your care, particularly the fearful child.

"Meghan, we're leaving for a few hours. We will be back."

"We will be back."

"We will be back."

Over and over again.

A small child like Meghan cannot respond verbally and does not fully comprehend Mommy and Daddy's verbal message. Through immediate experience the message becomes reality, and each time Mommy and Daddy do, indeed, come back, another board nails itself across the door of the first fear room.

What if the child must go to bed before Mommy and Daddy return? "I'm a little mystical about that," says Dr. Warren. "You don't have to wake the child, but do go in. You probably will anyway, to check. A gentle pat on the back with a whispered 'I'm home' can't hurt a bit."

There is profound symbolism in this gesture for Mommy and Daddy, as well as the baby. The act of announcing the return puts flesh on the commitment of the parent to the child. *I'm not going to leave you. I'm back. You're safe.* The parent responds as much as the child does to that physical expression of commitment and return, affirming the parent-child relationship at its deepest level.

Object constancy is best learned, therefore, through healthy parent-child relationships and actual experience. And object constancy is the only solid way to alleviate the first fear of life.

Great. But what if one parent leaves—for good?

One and One, the Hard Way—Single Parenting

Let us assume for a bit that you are a young couple bent on divorce, and you have an eighteen-month-old child. You simply cannot make it work out. It should never have happened in the first place. But here it is. Now you've got to make the best of it. What *is* the best of it?

In such cases we ask both spouses to make absolutely certain, for the sake of the child, that the separation occurs in as orderly and predictable a way as possible. The surgical cut must be clean and smooth. The details of the separation must be worked out ahead of time, and one of those details is: where will the new single parent get support?

If it all goes smoothly and all the preparations are in place, the divorce will still bring terrible pain to the child.

But, to the further detriment of the child, it almost never goes smoothly. The single parent's supports are never in place ahead of time, the future is never planned, and the child's life almost never stabilizes promptly on the new course.

Very often when a family breaks up, the single mom moves in with her parents. Our experience tells us that should almost never happen. When Mom and child move in with Mom's parents (or when Dad takes his child and moves in with his parents), Mom becomes the little girl again (or Dad becomes the little boy). That is always destructive—for all three generations.

We were talking about this very thing at a backyard barbecue not long ago. Dave, one of our friends, laughed and said, "Hey, I hear you. My parents are in their late seventies. I went back to Pennsylvania to visit them recently. One night while I was there, I went out to see my brother, who lives in the next county. We met at a restaurant halfway between his place and my folks'. I'll be hanged if Mom didn't say, 'Now don't stay out too late.' And she was still awake listening for me when I got home, about 1 A.M. 'Don't stay out too late.'" Dave wagged his head sadly. "I'm fifty-two years old!"

When the adult child moves back home, the parent-child relationship automatically kicks back in. If the adult child and the grandchild are hurting—and persons in the throes of divorce hurt terribly—the nurturing-parent instinct kicks in too.

What the newly single mother (or father) needs is a support system waiting for her or him apart from the immediate family, one that is set up and in place before the separation begins. The system must be comprised not only of other women (or other men) in the same situation, who are almost certainly floundering also, but also people in other, stable circumstances.

Frankly, that's what the local church should be doing. Within an active church are other adults who can offer practical help and emotional support for both parent and child. An active church can provide a stable, multi-age group of friends and even substitute parents and siblings. But churches also find this hard to do.

It's also not only appropriate but necessary for single moms or dads to get a day off from parenting once a week, perhaps through a mother's-day-out program. It's good for the child—object constancy—and it's also good for the single parent, for obvious reasons.

"What should I have said to my two-year-old?" Fern Roberts, a divorced mother of two, asked, looking exasperated. Her son Michael, now nine years old, was entering our counsel to ease his school phobia and some other problems.

Fern reflected back on the events surrounding her divorce. "We tried to keep the ugly truth from the children as long as possible, of course. They were so young. I shouldn't have had two babies so quickly; I see that now. Michael was two and Gail was six months. But what do you say?"

Dr. Warren asked, "What *did* you say?"

"To the baby, nothing. I told Michael his daddy was away on a long trip."

"Let me speculate: It didn't wash."

Fern grimaced. "Obviously. It didn't wash. Michael was all right while we were staying in the motel. But then I moved my part of the furniture from the house into an apartment and Michael just came unglued."

It is tempting to tell a one- to two-year-old child anything in this situation, assuming that children this age will buy it. They do. At first. But eventually the truth will come out, not just verbally but in a hundred subtle ways. Tiny children have wonderful intuition about situations. They are very sensitive to the feelings of others, particularly of their parents.

We recommend you tell even the youngest child the truth. You must keep it very simple: "Daddy isn't going to live with us anymore." As the child grows, that basic statement will have to be restated in more complex terms. But don't try to fool a kid.

Be prepared for the next certain fear the child will entertain. It goes like this: *Daddy left. Will Mommy leave next?* That's when the natural fear of abandonment will go hog-wild. Again, treat it as we treat all fears—indeed, as we treated Richard Kell's irrational fear. First empathize, and second, counter fear with facts.

"I know you're afraid. It's all right to be terribly afraid. I will never leave you. It's safe. I won't go."

Fern continued, "I had such a terrible time. For the first year I couldn't find decent day-care, and I absolutely had to go to work."

"How many sitters did the children have that first year?"

"Actually, only two. The first one lasted two months. She just didn't work out. Then I left the kids with my mom awhile and some friends awhile, but they weren't sitters, actually. They were just stopgap measures. The second sitter, then, turned out great. They're still with her."

"All those people were stopgap to you. But look at them from the children's point of view. None was Daddy or Mommy; all of them were strangers, or nearly so."

Fern considered that for a few minutes. "I see what you're saying. I should have had a day-time sitter already set up so they would go directly there, right?"

Right.

As the Child Sees It

Fern's situation reflects another difficulty for small children that we see frequently, the special dilemmas posed when babies come close together.

Pretend for the moment you are a child of fifteen months, without real verbalization skills yet, but you're starting to get the hang of words. Without a clue, Mommy disappears. Your greatest fear has just been realized. You may not even survive. A succession of smiley faces bounce you from crib to crib for a week or so (and when you're younger than two, every day is forever) and then Mommy reappears.

What's this? She has another baby! You're not the baby anymore! You're not getting half of Mommy's time anymore. Mommy may have returned, but Sweetie, you've been dumped.

That scenario happens all too frequently in some subcultures. When Mommy is going into the hospital to have child number two (in the previous scenario we added the possibility that complications keep Mommy away for more than a day or two), there is no way to prepare the small child who is about to be abandoned. A child younger than two simply doesn't have the verbalization skills. During Mommy's absence, the child feels an intense sense of loss and abandonment. And as he or she gets passed around to other caregivers, the stress multiplies. If the length of separation exceeds several weeks, Mommy comes home a stranger. Not only that, she has another baby. The fear of abandonment has not been allayed, but reinforced.

If this situation or a similar one occurs in a small child's life, be aware that you must be understanding, and you must pursue lessons in object constancy with particular vigor. Board up that room that has been left gaping open.

To Think About . . .

Let's assume you care, at least part-time, for a child aged zero to two. It may be your own child or a grandchild in your regular care. You may work at a day-care center or nursery. Whatever. We'll frame these exercises as if you are the parent of a baby. Adjust them as necessary to your specific situation.

1. These are the routine instances when I can or must be away from the baby (work, appointments, simply leaving the room . . .):

---

2. These are non-routine instances when I leave the child:

_____

_____

_____

3. These are instances when I wish I could leave my child for awhile:

_____

_____

_____

4. Here are three things I can do to reassure the child before I leave (such as talking about returning, leaving a personal possession with the child):

a. _____

b. _____

c. _____

5. Here are three things I can do or say upon my return (such as reminding the child of my promise, praising the child):

a. _____

b. _____

c. _____

6. The most successful occasion when I left the child and returned was:

_____

_____

_____

7. This is why I think that occasion worked:

_____

_____

_____

_____

8. This (these) occasion(s) was an unmitigated disaster, either because the child refused to calm down or something else went wrong:

_____

_____

_____

9. The above incident(s) could have gone more smoothly if I had:

_____

_____

_____

We overheard two acquaintances talking as they entered the church sanctuary prior to a worship service one Sunday. One young mother looked as if she had been fighting grizzly bears. "My little girl goes into the church nursery screaming and clinging to me every time! I feel terrible leaving her there."

"Terrible!" the second young mother exclaimed. "But Mrs. Petrie is so good with the children. It's bright and airy. The only problem I can see is that now my three-year-old thinks the church experience centers on chocolate-chip cookies."

The first woman nodded. "Easy for you to say. Your Jeff marches right in. No clouds, no rain."

"There's a lot of magnetism in chocolate-chip cookies."

"But my Becky is immune to them. Should I do it? Should I keep leaving her there? Am I a bad mother hurting her like this?" (At the clinic we get this question almost constantly.)

The second woman offered wise advice. "A little rain makes flowers bloom. Becky is learning important lessons."

"Such as?"

"Such as, that you'll come get her afterward and that the separation is temporary. I guess you could sum it up by saying she's learning to trust you even when you're not with her."

Parents often come to us laden with guilt. "I have to put my child in day-care and I feel awful about it." The parent's tone of voice clearly indicates it would be less cruel to toss the kid into a shark tank. There are positive aspects to day-care beyond the obvious financial necessities. Day-care can be therapeutic for the preschooler who has spent every waking moment with Mom. This is particularly true if the mother and child have become very dependent upon each other.

The three-year-old child of friends of ours was a scared, timid little boy. Then Dad's work hours were cut back and rescheduled. Mom had to go to work part-time. She placed the boy in a small center that was staffed by the same lady every day. The child's fears literally evaporated.

There is a caveat here, however. The day-care should be provided and constantly sustained by the same person from day to day. Institutional day-care, no. Personal day-care, yes.

THE SHAPE OF THINGS TO COME

A generation ago, behaviorists assumed that, because a child is too uncoordinated to work productively between the ages of two and four or five, he or she simply vegetates during these years. They thought children spend this time in growing physically, learning to walk across a room without falling over, idly playing, and developing and honing the necessary skills to be a truly exasperating little squirt.

We know now that theory could not be further from the truth (except maybe the little-squirt part). Children experience, face, and conquer predictable new fears at this age. They learn the first lessons about their own sexual identity. They come to grips in the most primary way with their personhood. And you, the parent, play a key role you may not even be aware of. Let's look at that next.

3
Fears of the Toddler and Early Preschooler

Hi, Troid,

Well, that was a show you could put on TV, wasn't it? I'm not sure you saw it all. You took off in one of your fits of the crazies about the time it was going on.

I'm talking about when Aubrey tried to shove Mom off the sofa. Dad was sitting there watching TV when Mom came in from doing the dishes. She sat down close beside him. I mean real close beside him. Aubrey started fussing and trying to squeeze between them and when Mom pushed her away and told her to stop acting like that, old Aubrey yelled louder. And then here you came zooming out of the hall and onto the wing chair and then you bounced up onto the back of the sofa and then you took off back down the hall. You were gone, so you didn't see Mom twist around to give you a swat to get you off the furniture (you know you're not supposed to be up on the furniture except the recliner) and Aubrey pulled on Mom's skirt and almost dumped her on the floor. Then Dad got real mad and swatted Aubrey on the backside and that's when the atomic mushroom cloud went up.

For once it wasn't me getting yelled at.

Don't pay attention to Hector. Mom says she's in heat. That's why she acts that way, and she'll get over it.

Willard was a rat again. He shoved me off my

skateboard. I'm not going to ride my skateboard anymore.

Your friend,
James

Elaine Tanner related her version of the incident during the next counseling session. "She's been this way for months. Doctor, does it mean she's . . . well, not quite normal?" Elaine Tanner looked extremely worried. "She was never such a daddy's girl before."

"Very normal. In fact, necessary."

Elaine didn't seem to hear. She continued on, preoccupied. "Roger says it's just since we've been coming to you, and for some reason you've changed our family relationship. Well, I, uh, don't think that's quite it. I say Aubrey loves me just as much as ever because when we're at work, she insists as much as ever that I visit her frequently between patients. I just don't know."

"I trust," Dr. Warren suggested, "that when James was Aubrey's age, more or less, he attached ferociously to you, just as she is attaching to her daddy."

Elaine stared at him for a long, long moment. "I'm not sure I want to talk about that."

"As you wish. You are never under coercion here. Neither is James, for that matter." Dr. Warren waited. Silence is a powerful spur to conversation.

"Well, uh . . . thinking twice, I suppose perhaps I should. You're right. And ferocious is a good word for it. James glued himself to me. Just glued himself. He wouldn't let me leave him for a moment. He would shove Roger away from me. He tried to do whatever I was doing. Even ironing and things like that."

"At what age? Do you remember?"

"Not long after his third birthday. Roger was furious, let me tell you. He said it was unhealthy for James to be that way because he'd grow up to be a mama's boy. James would act like that and Roger would punish him, but it didn't do any good. In fact, even today, Roger says James is so fearful because he's a mama's boy. He says if I'd been firmer with him when he was three he'd be braver now. Is Roger right, Doctor?"

Dr. Warren sat back and mulled his answer a moment. "I can see that Roger would be very concerned. There are several forces at work here and they're disturbing to parents. By age three or four boys and girls both are getting more sophisticated in their understanding of life. Their basic fears likewise become more sophisticated. At the same time, they are developing their sexual identity, their maleness and femaleness."

"That's exactly what Roger is worried about!"

"It's a lot of growth for a child to accomplish in a brief time. But there's much more: the beginnings of conscience, too, and discipline. And it's all tied together. Let me explain what's happening a step at a time. We'll start with the basic fear."

CAN I LOSE MOMMY AND DADDY'S APPROVAL?

In *All I Really Need to Know I Learned in Kindergarten*, author Robert Fulghum attributes life's crucial lessons to the first five years, and rightly so. A lot of growth and sophistication happens in the first years. Even the basic fear of abandonment becomes more sophisticated.

By age three or so, a child's fear of losing Mommy and Daddy shifts and expands to include the fear of losing Mommy and Daddy's approval.

Will they love me when I mess up? How do I know when I'm messing up? (Remember that a child starts out from zero with regard to right and wrong.)

Next door to the Tanners live the Dottmeyers—and James Tanner's nemesis, Willard Hutchison. Eleven years old and entering fifth grade, Willard has been a walking

Death Star his whole life. He isn't the biggest kid in fifth grade, but that doesn't stop him from being the bully of grades one clear through six. Rules were not made for Willard; they were made for other people. Willard cuts a wide swathe. His teachers agree that he will be instrumental in bringing world peace someday; all the nations will rise up together in defense against a common enemy: Willard Hutchison.

Willard's mother left his father before Willard was two. She came home to live with her parents, the Dottmeyers, bringing Willard along. Eventually she met a wise and handsome man named Blaine. "Me or the kid," said the wise Blaine after one taste of Willard, "but not both." She chose Blaine and left Willard with Mom and Dad. Now she visits Willard every two weeks or so, if she and Blaine aren't going somewhere else.

Willard's grandmother feels ever so sorry for poor little Willard, who was given such a raw deal in life. He needs a little pampering, a little slack, and she provides it. Does Willard need a computer in order to shine at school? She buys him a three-thousand-dollar model with a 40K hard drive. Willard filled the whole hard drive with games he never plays. Does he need new socks? Grandma buys him a complete wardrobe. Did Willard play a harmless little practical joke that backfired? Don't be hard on him just because you had to rebuild your whole engine when he put that stuff in your gas tank; you're only young once. Besides, he didn't understand the consequences.

Willard's grandfather has less than passing interest in the brat. He wants to get his daughter straightened around so that she can take Willard back and accept a little responsibility. Granddad doesn't pamper Willard; he pretty much ignores him.

Willard is understandably confused and hurt. After all, he was abandoned. But there is much more in his life to make him the way he is. About age two, when a child begins what we call individuation—becoming his or her own person—true discipline starts. The first discipline is strictly external. Mom and Dad (or, in Willard's case,

Grandma and Granddad) set limits, and provide consequences when those limits are breached.

You don't flush the cat down the toilet. You don't tear pages out of books. You don't wander into the street. You don't stick beans in your ears. When you do, an appropriate form of lightning strikes.

Ideally, as children experience consequences from outside themselves, they begin to internalize those experiences. *Whoa! If I avoid doing this, I avoid the consequences. If I refrain from this impulse, Mommy and Daddy won't act disapprovingly.*

And I make another important observation: *Even when they do act disapprovingly, they continue to love me. They don't get rid of me.*

Powerful, powerful messages, those!

By the age of two and a half to three, and on into four, conscience begins to grow from nothing to something, from externally controlled behavior to internally controlled behavior. Moral and behavioral standards emerge. The child begins the lifelong process of shaping and refining those standards.

Discipline takes on an important added dimension. Sure, it builds conscience. But another thing, a beautiful thing, happens too. Discipline also becomes a way to dispel that fear children have that somehow they can lose Mommy and Daddy's love by displeasing them. The child has crossed a definite line. Consequences have occurred, and Mom and Dad still love the child. Unconditionally. They keep the child, no matter what. The child gets payback, certainly, but the payback is not the loss of the parents or the parents' unconditional love for him or her. The child crossed the line inadvertently or deliberately, and survived. Another dark and dangerous room gets boarded up.

Willard has never been disciplined. Somewhere in the dark, inner corridors of his mind lurks the fear that there is a line he can cross and thereby lose everything. He's sure it's there, but he can't find it. Ever more frantically, Willard is seeking that line. He crosses one line after another, lunging from outrage to outrage, trying to find it. Still the nagging fear remains that there's something out there he can do that will cost him the people he loves. The severity of his transgressions escalates as he gets older, stronger, and more fearful deep inside. He attempts wilder and wilder things, trying to find the line. Willard is a bully. One tough guy. He also is one terrified kid.

"Of course," you say. "He's spoiled. Spare the rod and spoil the child."

That's only partially correct. Willard may be spoiled, but the situation is more complex than it first appears.

THE SPOILED CHILD

Lack of consistent discipline goes beyond spoiling. Apart from the fact that the child's basic, primal fear goes unresolved, his or her conscience also takes on a skewed twist. We call it *entitlement*. The child comes to believe, and believe very strongly, that rules are for others. Danger? Others may be subject to danger, but not this child. Behavior? Others are required to toe the mark, but for this child it's optional. He or she is entitled to all things, to everyone's love and respect, to the fulfillment of all desires. Should the child not receive all to which he or she is entitled, it's someone else's fault. Should the child receive unpleasant consequences of any actions, it is because of others' blunders.

Willard is certain that he's better and smarter than all those other dweebs. They also recognize and respect his superiority—or else.

Caution: When we talk about appropriate consequences, that means discipline based on parents' standards, not parents' emotions. Parents who react with anger and rage to what a child has done deliver a damaging message. The child perceives it as, *I am worthless. I'm an object upon which to vent rage. See how my parent rages? I caused that.* Such messages do nothing to help ease the basic fear or shape the conscience.

There is another side of entitlement called *exemption*.

This is the attitude that rules are for everyone else; this child stands above authority. He or she is exempt, past rebellion and into defiance. The exempt child doesn't care what anyone thinks or what standards of behavior have been laid out. We will discuss exemption at greater length later on. But for now, be aware that it is one possible end of the road called entitlement.

The very young haven't been entitled long enough to have shifted over into exemption. Certainly not all entitled children eventually come to consider themselves exempt from law and obedience. Few do. But entitlement is always the precursor. We see frequent cases where entitled children were literally created by fearful parents who didn't want their little ones to feel rejected, disadvantaged, or brought to grief. Just as often we find parents who fear making a scene, so to speak; or they fear they will damage their little ones by denying them anything or forcefully disciplining them. Very often, the fearful parent begins the process of entrenching entitlement in their children right at this age, in the preschool years.

The seeds of entitlement, exemption, and a sense of invulnerability exist in all kids. Now is no time to let these traits sprout. Overindulgence can be reversed. But the longer the parents wait, the harder it is. In our practice we observe that if overindulgent parents see the light when the child is at this age and impose a fair and loving discipline, they stand a good chance of turning the situation around. Some storms will surely rage, and remnants will persist. But now is the time.

WHY A SLOG OF SLIME IS LIKE AN AIRPLANE DISASTER: TRANSFERRING FEARS TO OTHER OBJECTS

What better way is there to relax than to loll on the wide, warm beaches of Padre Island? With each gentle wash of the surf, fingernail-sized coquina clams pop out of the sand and burrow back in. Seaweed sloshes, the gulls cry, and the mind wanders free. Elsa and Dave were doing just that, sprawling on towels and watching their daughter Becky, two and a half, play and laugh and eat sand along the water's edge.

Becky suddenly froze, transfixed. Terrified, she let out a long and constant howl that would have warned ships' captains away from shoals. What in heaven's name could have frightened her that badly? Elsa scooped her up while Dave checked the sand carefully. A pinchy crab? Something more sinister? Eventually they figured it out. Becky had been attacked by a glob of seaweed.

As Becky was growing, her basic fears centered less and less on being abandoned. That room of first fears was pretty well boarded up by positive experiences. Her awareness and attentions were starting to turn outward, toward the huge world around her. And her young mind, not yet grasping what is benign and what is not, feared things that, to adults, are illogical things. She had no trouble assigning frightening attributes to things that an older person would know are not scary.

Becky's imagination was more active than an adult's because it was untrammeled by any extensive knowledge of reality. And before you smugly rejoice that you're grown up now and can sort the benign from the dangerous, know this: we find that adults still do the same thing, but with a different perspective. Adults fear things that, in and of themselves, are not particularly fearful; but still we fear them.

Some years ago, in a comedy-drama television series depicting life at a police station, someone was interrogating a doting old fellow who was certain Martians were bombarding him with harmful rays. The detective made a skull cap of aluminum foil to solve the old man's problem so they could get on with the questioning. The comedy side of that scene was the fact that all of us know people who fear illogically. And all of us, deep down, fear illogical things, ourselves.

For example, how many people intensely fear flying? Maybe they fly in spite of their misgivings. But they don't put their full weight in the seat. Sure, they know airline safety far surpasses highway safety, but that does not allay their fears. The airy room of reason stands vacant and neglected.

The same thing happens, without the fear, when hopeful people buy lottery tickets. They probably know they are more likely to be struck by lightning than to win some state lotteries. Still, millions of people toss statistics—and logic—out the window and stand patiently in line waiting to buy tickets anyway.

Dispelling the Slog of Slime

"How did you dispel Becky's fear of seaweed?" we asked Dave later.

He shrugged. "Picked it up and threw it into the surf. Then we sat down with her and played pile-up-the-sand for awhile and she was off and running again. Do you know how boring pile-up-the-sand is?"

"No. What is it?"

"You just sit there and pile up the sand. How come her attention span is measured in nanoseconds when it's something important and it's interminable for something like pile-up-the-sand?"

Dave and Elsa handled it well. If their response had been a cavalier, "Oh, that's nothing. You don't have to be afraid of that," Becky's fear would have persisted. The fear was not based on logic. So logic would not quell it.

Rather, Dave and Elsa's response was relational: *It's okay. Mommy and Daddy are here with you. We'll help you. We'll protect you. It's all right to be little, to be afraid. You're safe.* They didn't even have to say it out loud. They picked Becky up. They sat down with her. They played with her awhile. Those actions spoke louder than words.

Relationship is everything.

Consider the case of a four-year-old boy we'll call John. He was so sure those giant bugs were crawling around under his bed when he wasn't looking. Verbal reassurances weren't making a dent in his fear. Fortunately, at this age, imagination can do anything. Absolutely anything. And a dramatized or staged cure for something need not appeal to logic the way it would to us so-called rational adults.

Working together, the boy and his father commandeered from the kitchen one of those pump bottles with a trigger, the kind you use to spray window cleaner. They filled it with a secret potion designed to kill giant bugs and spritzed under the bed. End of bug problem.

But transferring fears to objects in the big, wide world is only part of the small child's changes. There's also that problem Aubrey and James presented to Elaine and Roger by shoving one parent away in favor of the other.

WHAT IS THIS OEDIPAL THING?

Nearing age four and a half, Aubrey Tanner was coming into it on the late side; James, at barely three, was at the early end. Some people call it the Oedipal complex. The term comes from an ancient legend expressed in a number of both classic and modern plays. A king named Oedipus, through a strange and torturous chain of events, ended up inadvertently killing his own father and marrying his mother.

Like nearly all legends, this one springs from our innermost fears and desires, things almost never expressed consciously, things that seem "sick" if they do manage to rise to conscious level. A young man falls in sexual love with his mother? No, no!

What Is Actually Happening

The Oedipal twist in the small child's mind is not actually sexual. It is far more basic than that. We think we've worked out what goes on, unspoken and unexpressed of course, in the child's mind. Let's use Aubrey as an example (incidentally, in girls it's Electra, not Oedipus). It works this way:

Aubrey becomes aware that Mommy and Daddy are

fundamentally different. External roles are a part of it, but it goes deeper than who cooks and who cleans the toilet. She probably is not aware of the primary physical difference between male and female. Intuitively, though, Aubrey discerns that Mommy is woman and Daddy is man.

To say Aubrey "falls in love" with her daddy (and James with his mommy) is not accurate and does not do justice to the depth of the truths about males and females that the child is grasping now. This is not a sexual phenomenon but a phenomenon of attachment. Aubrey attaches fiercely and jealously to her father just as James did with his mother. Aubrey wants to marry her daddy. James wanted to marry his mommy. At this age, the child neither understands nor cares about the physical implications of marriage. This is soul bonding, not body bonding.

Now Aubrey intuits that Mommy and Daddy are united to each other. Their bond is stronger than the bond between mother and child or between father and child. They love Aubrey, certainly. But they are mated to each other.

And somewhere in here, a subtle but crucial shift takes place. James no longer wants to marry Mommy. He wants to grow up and marry someone *like* Mommy. Aubrey will decide she wants to marry a man like Daddy someday. It's a tiny but, oh, so significant difference. For if the child cannot marry the parent, the child is free to be a kid. Without the responsibility that union with an adult would require, the child can get on with his or her proper and appropriate business. Growing up.

Recall the scenario we mentioned in Chapter 1 in which a three-year-old boy defended Mommy by kicking Daddy in the shins. Now that you see what was going on there, can you think of other situations you've seen that reflect this phenomenon? How?

_____

_____

_____

What Can Go Wrong

Dr. Warren loves to draw golden triangles for his counselees. The triangles look like the one in Figure 1. Mommy and Daddy and each child in the family are linked by the bonds of familial love, which represent the sides of the triangle. Ideally, the thickest line, the strongest bond, lies across the top, between Mommy and Daddy.

GOLDEN TRIANGLE

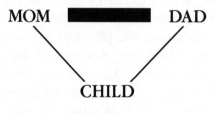

Figure 1

But what if that bond is shaky because the marriage has hit a rough spot? Or what if it is broken because the marriage has ended in divorce? When either of these situations occurs, the bond between parent and child takes on an inappropriate thickness, as shown in Figure 2.

DIVORCE

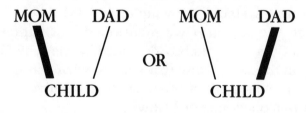

Figure 2

To illustrate, let's pretend Elaine divorced Roger and took Aubrey with her. Almost without exception in such situations, the parent-child bond thickens and takes on new significance. It is no longer mate-mate, but parent-child. "It's you and me against the world, kid. We only have each other." Parent and child depend on each other, not just situationally (sharing responsibilities, one picking up the slack the other leaves), but emotionally.

In an emotional sense, the child has married the parent. The message for Aubrey has become, *You are no longer free to be a little girl and grow up and marry a man like Daddy. You are married to Mommy and you and Mommy depend on each other. She needs you; you cannot leave her. You cannot be your own person.*

This phenomenon transcends gender. Boys and girls can "marry" either Mommy or Daddy, however the custody falls.

Divorce is not the only situation that generates problems. If the marriage bond is weak (see Figure 3) one parent may turn to the child for emotional support and solace the other spouse cannot or will not provide. Again, this can happen within or between genders.

IMPAIRED MARRIAGE

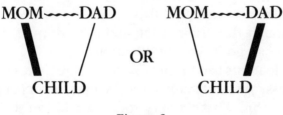

Figure 3

Let's pretend Elaine and Roger are emotionally distant. Elaine hungers for an emotional union, a bond. How does Aubrey respond to Mommy's need? Does she, in effect, say, "Sorry, Mom, but I have to be a kid and grow up. I can't meet your emotional needs"? Hardly. Even if little Aubrey grasped the situation, which never happens, she would have no choice. The child will meet that adult's unmet need or die developmentally trying.

Making the Best of Oedipus Rex

The single parent of a small preschooler, then, is in a serious double bind. The child needs role identification and the single parent has a 50 percent chance of being the right gender to fulfill it. Moreover, there's that inappropriate emotional bond to worry about.

Here is where the parent absolutely needs an outside source of support. Assume for the moment the parent is a mother. Her child needs a solid male model, whether the child is a boy or a girl. Unfortunately, particularly in today's social climate, married men avoid any sort of close relationship with a divorced woman and her children. For one thing, the man's wife feels jealousy toward a potentially predatory female who is impinging on her spouse's time and energy. It doesn't matter that this is not really the case. The jealousy surfaces; she can't help it.

Also, men may worry (perhaps unconsciously) about untrue allegations. *If I get too close to this woman and her child, will that be wrongly interpreted? Am I opening myself up to potential gossip and defamation, maybe even a lawsuit?* Rumors can destroy a reputation even faster than facts can. And there is always a possibility that even though the original intentions were pure, the relationship can go in wrong directions.

Grandparents can fill the role to a degree, provided they do not assume, under any circumstance, the role of parent to the parent. That's a very tough act to pull off. Or an aunt or uncle may be able to model the appropriate gender role. These bonds are not the same as a strong marriage bond, but they can help fill the gap. Choose carefully, whomever you seek.

Also, we urge the single parent to monitor the parent-child relationship very closely. Throughout your life, not just during this vulnerable early-childhood period, guard against any emotional attachment that goes beyond parent-child.

If you are a single parent, use these statements to help yourself think about an appropriate relationship with your child. Adjust and modify them to relate to yourself:

_____ I go to the child for advice. ("Which tie looks best with this shirt?")

_____ The child takes on a partnership role around the house. ("Will you help me balance the checkbook?")

_____ The kids take care of themselves in ways they wouldn't have to if I were still married. (The children make breakfast, pack their own lunches, let themselves in the house alone after school, do their laundry and possibly yours too . . .)

_____ Whether the child understands or not, I find I can unload my problems and feelings a little. ("You wouldn't believe what my boss said to me today!")

Any one of these statements is a big red flag. Each indicates that the relationship is going beyond where it ought to go. Children need chores. They need structure. They need emotional attachment to you. But if that attachment is something you would normally feel for a spouse, if the chores are things the child would not have to do if a spouse were in the picture, if you find yourself treating the child as a confidante, burdening the kid with adult loads, by all means back off. Reconsider. Adjust. Give back the kid's childhood and find your own emotional support elsewhere.

"So what do I do about Aubrey?" Elaine asked. "And Roger? He thinks it's cute. But he certainly didn't think it was cute when James was going through this stage. Men." She sighed.

"Be patient." Dr. Warren tapped his sketch of the golden triangle. "Right here, where Mom and Dad are deeply and securely invested in each other, that family is a safe place for a child to be. The process will resolve itself. Aubrey intuits that she can be comfortable with her own sexuality, her own gender role."

"But what about James?"

"It's the same for him. But Aubrey and James both require one more thing: role identification with the parent of the same sex." Dr. Warren sat back. "That's psychobabble for, 'dads, play with your boys; moms, play with your girls.'"

Elaine's face fell. "Oh no! Not more Candyland!"

FAREWELL TO OEDIPUS

Children do not fear seaweed forever. As time moves on, their fears take on different targets that teach them different things. And yet, all intertwine. They come to terms, more or less, with who they are sexually. The gender role phenomenon and the fears accompanying it overlap and melt into the next major manifestation of fears, a fear of the power that is in adults. For a time, too, children fear and distrust their own sexuality in a strange, symbolic way.

The parent can help the child immensely in resolving all these perplexing fears and changes. We'll look at that in the next part of this book.

The Deep-seated Fears of Childhood

INFANT AND TODDLER
THE BOTTLE AND BANKY SET

- *I fear being abandoned.*

- *If I am abandoned, I fear I will lose my meself.*

- *I fear I can lose Mommy and Daddy's love and approval.*

- *The Oedipal phenomenon*

PART THREE

Late Preschooler

The Sandbox Set

4

The Cat That Went Bump in the Night

THE FEAR OF POWER PEOPLE

Dear Troid,

I don't think you remember this, because you weren't even a full-size cat yet. But you used to scare the willies out of me. There was this one night I was getting my clothes out for school the next morning, I think I was in kindergarten then, and you got in the closet and I didn't know it. I slid the closet door shut and went to bed. That's when you decided you wanted out, you jerk. You started bumping and scratching and I flipped my wig, man! Don't you ever do that again. Except it's not as scary now. It doesn't even sound as scary when I write about it. But it seemed really scary then.

Willard was being Willard yesterday. He shoved me down the steps of the schoolbus. Said I wasn't getting off fast enough. The bus driver kicked him off the bus for three days but I don't think it'll do any good. His grandma will just drive him to school. She likes to do that anyway, I think. At least the bus ride will be nicer for three days.

Dad and I got into a marathon Monopoly game Friday night. It lasted til almost 3. That's the latest I ever stayed up, but then you know that because you're up all night and you know who's up and who isn't. He won, but it took a big piece of luck. He landed on my Virginia Avenue 4 times and Illinois Avenue twice but I hit his Boardwalk 3 times in a row. 3 times in a row!

*How often does that happen? That was the greatest
game! I never knew Dad is that good at Monopoly. This
going to Dr. Warren isn't such a bad deal after all.*

Your friend,
James

In his letter to the cat, James touched on several
facts he certainly did not consciously know about. One is
that, for awhile, something hiding in the shadows is a
vivid fear. Another is that the fear abates—assuming it is
comfortably resolved. Should it not be resolved, as you
know by now, it will surface later in unpredictable ways.

POWER PEOPLE

Children age two or three usually do not fear monsters.
Monsters are a product of imagination based on some life
experience. Their fears attach more to inanimate objects.
The three- or four-year-old graduates to animate objects
such as barking dogs and big bad wolves (some of us hang
on to that one, thanks to myth and fable). Then those
fears shift to objects with more human attributes. The
progression from inanimate to human over this period of
years reflects the child's growing awareness of the surrounding world and of the child's own human-ness.

I'm Afraid of the Power of Big People

This age group, four or five, faces a new fear. (You can
see why it is so important to allay the old ones; what a
heavy load builds up if these naturally evolving fears pile
on top of each other unresolved!) This one is the power of
adults—the possibility of being overwhelmed. Adults,
parents included, become a massive, sinister presence.

Sinister? Not on the surface, perhaps. Who can be
afraid of dear Aunt Gertie, who's three feet high lying
down and waddles around in cotton print housedresses,
fuzzy slippers, and an apron? She's no more sinister than
cocoa with marshmallows. But children's underlying fear,

generalized to encompass all big people, lurks down there somewhere. Should sweet Aunt Gertie suddenly turn into a snapping, snarling, frowning witch, that fear would pop into the open instantly. And to become fearsome, Aunt Gertie doesn't have to lift a finger or threaten anyone. The mere potential is sufficient, you see.

An adult watching such a personality transformation in Gertie would gape in disbelief, but the child would believe instantly, and cower.

Note that this is a God-given fear. It comes to all children just as does eye color. And its purpose is growth. As the child deals with that fear his or her understanding of adults and of power grows and matures too. God represents and possesses the ultimate power, All Power, so these early lessons form an especially important foundation for the theology and faith to come many years later.

But children don't fear parents that way, do they? Dr. Warren relates one of his own family's experiences: "I don't know exactly what we were doing out in the garage. Cleaning it up maybe. Matt, three or four at the time, was helping. We were doing it together. That was the theory. Whatever Matt's job was, he wasn't doing it well at all. And frankly, I was getting pretty impatient. Then Matt burst out crying and my profession caught up to me. I knew what it was. But he verbalized it for me anyway: 'Daddy, you're so big and strong, and I'm afraid of what you might do.'"

> **The child of three, four, or five innately fears not just adults but even more the adults' powerful potential to hurt, to overwhelm. And those adults include parents.**

"I'm a pretty overwhelming guy," Dr. Warren admits, "particularly to a small child." He is quite tall and quite wide and stands very straight. He towers without trying. But little old Aunt Gertie can trigger the same fears he can. To a child, every adult is ten feet tall.

Enter the Bogeyman

Gloria's mother is weird. Goofy. She was weird even when Gloria was very small, and now that Gloria is twelve, her greatest embarrassment in life is Mom. Sometimes she packs some funny little surprise toy in Gloria's lunch box. One day when Gloria came home from school, Mom had covered up all the furniture with bedsheets and they ate cookies and milk sitting on stools at the ironing board. (Men came in the next morning and painted the ceilings.) Mom might show up in her shorts after school at the playing field and play softball right along with the kids, or maybe she would referee. Gloria could die!

The weirdest thing that Mom ever did by far almost ruined Gloria forever—according to Gloria, at least. Gloria, then age six, had to dress in costume for a school play. Now that was one big, big advantage of having a weird mother; your costumes, whatever the occasion, were always brilliant successes. One element of this particular costume was a long, stringy black wig. Gloria was the hit of the play. But on the last night, after the play, after Gloria had taken her bath and was headed to bed, she walked into her room and . . . and . . . started shrieking.

Mom had put that familiar, totally harmless wig on Gloria's totally harmless giant brown teddy bear. The bear sat in the corner where he always sat, but he looked so . . . so . . .

Gloria couldn't stop screaming. Mom assured her it was just a joke, but the memory of that teddy bear haunted her for years. Years!

Gloria and other young children cannot see fear. It's an abstract thing, a construction of the mind. Abstractions and the discussion of them are an adult province. The child must give the abstraction a palpable form somehow in order to deal with it. Thus is born first the menacing slog of slime, then the animate fearsome thing both real and imagined—dogs or monsters. Ultimately the fear object takes on human form, what we call the bogeyman. In other words, as the child grows, the innate fear of adults' potential to harm comes closer, by steps and stages, to what it actually is.

When Gloria's mom playfully slipped the stupid wig on the stuffed bear, the bear took on a sinister and unfamiliar near-human form. Seeing it triggered the transfer of Gloria's inner fear of the bogeyman to the wig-wearing teddy bear, which became, to Gloria, as real as a nasty-looking human out to do her great harm.

Other ways primal fear might surface, particularly for a preschooler, are as fears of large objects, animals, dark places, unfamiliar environments, bad people, supernatural creatures, sleeping alone . . . high places . . .

Gloria and her mother learned the hard way that children do not deal with the abstracts of this world until they are perhaps seven or older. That is to say, a person in a mask or a teddy bear in a wig can be fearsome, even when the child knows who is wearing the mask or the wig. Later, the child learns that the abstract is who it really is; the concrete is that hideous face on the surface.

By about twelve, Gloria would be thinking completely in abstracts. She would instantly know if the third Santa Claus she saw downtown really is Saint Nick or just a substitute. Fears follow this same concrete-to-abstract pattern.

An important purpose of myths and legends—the fairy tales of our own youth—is to bring the primal fears to light, to give unexpressed terrors an overt expression. The primal fear of grown-ups forms the basis of some of the oldest stories. For example, in ancient Ireland's city of Ulster the cycle of tales included the folk hero Cuchulainn, whose son grows up and seeks out his father—and Cuchulainn slays him. In the early German culture the hero was Hildebrand and in Persia it was Rustem.

Later, Gloria's fear of her parents might also take a new twist. At age three to five she fears what her parents might do—their potential for harm. When she reaches ten or twelve she may be afraid of what they might think—their attitudes.

By age four, the child's fear of the power of his or her

parents has become primary, particularly of the opposite-sex parent. After all, the parents represent Every Adult. Little girls especially harbor a sophisticated and complex version of this basic fear. It's not just the possibility of being hurt but of being overpowered. Girls sense that some adults—the males—have more power and do more things because they're, well, uh, luckier. The child risks not just damage but inundation. When father plays with daughter, and this includes playing with dolls and other "girlish" things, the little girl absorbs an important message: the male need not be overpowering.

Parents in this stage can make a giant contribution to the child's growth, simply by playing.

POWER PLAY

Ralph is a state park ranger. All day long he patrols beaches, finds lost kids, checks the restrooms, stands around in the sun telling tourists how to reach the main highway, keeps an eye out for underage drinking, directs people to the water fountains, chitchats with the lifeguards, and writes an occasional ticket. When he gets home around six, he feels totally drained.

And his four-year-old Marcie wants to play.

He changes his clothes while, in her room, she puts on her white uniform, the plain little dress her mom made out of a worn-out bedsheet, a zipper, and an hour's sewing. He pops open a can of his favorite beverage and lies down on the bed in her room. She becomes his nurse, bandaging "sore" fingers, hands, arms, feet, and legs with torn bedsheet strips. She takes his temperature a zillion times and listens to his heart with a stethoscope that really works. Barely.

Ralph answers her medical questions and responds to her incessant babble with half an ear. He may doze off. He smiles a lot. And Marcie is very, very happy.

Ralph would probably be amazed to realize that he is performing powerful play therapy on his little girl. (And note that neither of them needed an eighty-dollar toy. That worn-out bedsheet sufficed beautifully.) What he can do with this simple play can only be done through play and only by him.

Play is the medium by which children process the many, many lessons they must learn, and learn quickly, about life. This age span, from three up to grade school, is a crucial time for parents to be playing with kids. There are several reasons why.

Play is an incredible discharge of energy in many dimensions. Children this age are full of physical energy. (And heaven knows what an understatement that is. Marcie's mouth opens when she awakens and she doesn't cease talking until she falls asleep.) They also vibrate with an emotional energy and a high curiosity factor; they're living life full-throttle, trying to make sense of their world.

To that end, they are constantly using play to enact and thereby assimilate real-life situations. Marcie in her white uniform is just as happy being a waitress and serving Ralph an imaginary dinner in an imaginary restaurant. Sometimes she's a beautician or barber who does his hair. Rich man, poor man, beggar man, or thief, she's processing life. But there's much more involved as well.

Play is also the way children process their inner fears and conflicts, including that innate fear of the power of adults. They cannot work out their fears intellectually. Verbal processing certainly doesn't wash; their verbal expression is not yet deep enough or extensive enough to handle the job. They don't have a broad range of knowledge and observation upon which to draw. So they dramatize their conflicts, then bring them under control—enact them, vanquish them. Play is very hard work.

Think about Marcie being a doctor or whatever. Now think about her daddy, one of those powerful adults she most fears, getting down there with her. Picture the immense symbolic significance of that. He has brought himself down to her level, literally and symbolically. He has entered her play world and she is not threatened. Most important, he has joined her in her work as she resolves the questions and conflicts of life.

He has become her journeymate.

He is not doing the work for her. She's managing her own processing. He takes part simply by being there. The fact that he joins her brings Marcie a very strong subliminal message. Marcie sees that *the person I fear most has joined my work and he is not fearsome. He will not hurt me. He is on my side.*

What a practical lesson Ralph is giving Marcie: *I love you. You are safe with me. I am with you as you go your way.*

Roger Tanner conveyed just that same message when he engaged James in a marathon Monopoly game. Dr. Warren had advocated that Roger spend time at play with his children. But what about Aubrey? She can't count money yet or take on the intellectual skills Monopoly and such games require. If Roger were to play with four-year-old Aubrey, what games and activities might he choose?

"A perennial favorite is Candyland," Dr. Warren suggests. "Another is tic-tac-toe; all you need is a pencil and the back of an envelope. Or use a deck of cards and try Concentration, if you don't mind losing. Children this age are phenomenal at games of Concentration. Remember that it's not the game so much as the playing."

GETTING TO KNOW YOU

Ralph's play with Marcie serves another vital function— if he can keep himself from falling asleep.

> **The parent who simply listens to the child will learn a great deal of value about the child. Play is by far the single best way to know your child and to communicate.**

Most of preschooler Marcie's play is focused on dealing with conflicts (real or perceived), though not always directly. Sooner or later, however, she will probably act out her conflicts and fears. Only by portraying them, giving them voice and substance, can she see them well enough to grapple with them. Ralph can help in two ways as she does that.

If Ralph can take an active mental as well as physical part, he will hear what conflicts she's trying to sort out. He will learn what makes her tick. Also, by listening he may see opportunities to guide Marcie's understanding.

Through the medium of play a child can experience the wisdom of adults when preaching would never connect.

For example, let's listen in on a conversation between Ralph and Marcie as she assumes a waitress role in her white-bedsheet uniform.

MARCIE: Pretend you come in the restaurant and ask for dinner, and I give you dinner, and it's all lima beans, and you don't like lima beans, and you get mad and yell, and then I bring you a piece of chocolate cake, and you kiss me right here on my nose. Okay?

RALPH: Okay. But let me get this straight. I'm the one who doesn't like lima beans?

MARCIE: Uh-huh. They're yucky.

RALPH: I thought you were the one in this family who doesn't like lima beans.

MARCIE: Pretend, huh?

RALPH: Right. Okay, here I come into the restaurant and I've had a lousy day, all right? Everything has been going wrong before I got here. And I don't want anyone crossing me, all right? Because grown-ups are sometimes like that. Here I sit down (Ralph scowls and perhaps snarls).

Pause for a moment and look at all Marcie has told Ralph. Lima beans, which she hates with a passion, loom large in her life. But the bigger issue in this play episode is an angry adult out of control. With an offering of something desirable to the adult—in this instance, chocolate cake—she assuages the adult's anger. She thereby defuses the situation, reducing the possibility that the adult will hurt or overwhelm her. The adult responds with a gesture of affection. By setting up this scenario, she is asking herself, *Is this how to deal with menacing adults in real life?* Then she experiments with a possible answer: *bribe the brute.*

Look, too, at what Ralph has told Marcie. Marcie projects her opinion of lima beans onto Ralph and he acknowledges it. In this way he says (without actually saying it), *it's okay to dislike things.* As he enters the restaurant he explains why he is being obstreperous, giving her the message that adults' behavior reflects something going on in their lives that has nothing at all to do with the child/waitress. He is angry, perhaps even belligerent, but the child is not the reason (this is an especially important lesson because children, being egocentric, instantly assume that they have somehow caused all the faults and problems in the world).

Ralph could tell that to Marcie—use a nonfiction explanatory, if you will—and would probably get nowhere. Kids don't absorb verbal lessons well. By dramatizing his message, by putting it into the play context she herself created, he successfully shows her something important and useful about adults.

The play continues:

MARCIE: Hello. I'm your waitress today. Can I get you dinner?

RALPH (STILL BELLIGERENT): Yes. Bring me dinner. And it better be a good dinner, with lots of steak and potatoes, hear?

MARCIE (EXITS TO THE STOVE, PREPARES A PLACE, SERVES IT): All we have is lima beans and potatoes. Is that okay?

Note that at the last moment she hedged her bet and added potatoes to the beans-only menu. The idea of a totally angry adult, even in her controlled-play context, was too frightening to consider.

RALPH: This is terrible! I don't like these things. I want something else. What else do you have?

MARCIE (HASTILY PREPARES A DISH): How about chocolate

cake? It has lots of icing and Mommy made it today. The cook made it today.

RALPH: Oh, hey (nibble nibble). This isn't bad. I like lots of icing. You sure are a good waitress. (He kisses her on the forehead.)

MARCIE (IMPATIENTLY): You're supposed to kiss me on the nose.

RALPH: Okay. I'll kiss you on the nose too. (He does so.) You're a good waitress!

The praise he bestowed went far beyond the usual build-the-kid's-self-esteem kind you've often heard about. At a nonverbal level, he expressed to her that he enjoyed the situation. That experience—a powerful adult actually enjoying the game with her—did much to allay her innate fear.

What about when you are a teacher, a day-care worker, or a nurse and you play with kids all day? Dr. Warren has exactly that problem. "That's one of the toughest challenges of my job," he says. "When I get home, I'm washed out from playing with kids. I've been playing Candyland or playing in the sandbox all day with kids my son's age, and I've just had it. For awhile I got into a rut of not playing with Matt, and he was right at this age we're talking about. I had to really discipline myself to get back into it. Play is the purest form of therapy. It's my most important tool for helping children."

Dr. Warren observed a definite correlation between the amount of time he played with Matt and Matt's comfort with himself. Matt was less reticent, more open about talking over feelings, less fearful of new situations, more ready to go to bed at night—in short, less afraid of life and of grown-ups, his father in particular.

The small child in your care, whether or not you are the parent, will benefit too profoundly to neglect this tool. Activities that may seem so boring and redundant to you—drawing, stacking blocks, pretending—are, oh, so meaningful to the child.

And again we say:

Play is the purest form of therapy.

Playing with a child is not a one-and-done thing. "There. That fear's been resolved tidily. I've done my duty. Back to watching football on TV." Fears, concerns, and conflicts are always a part of the child, just as they are constantly a part of adults. As the children grow, the fears change shape, change focus, change scope, and as these changes occur they must be resolved anew.

Also, play is the best way for a parent to keep a finger on the nature of a child's changing fears and perhaps offer a little help. Dr. Warren's son would literally act out fearful conflicts. By remaining observant, Dr. Warren could sometimes cautiously intervene, staying always in the play context. "Oh, here! You're hurt. Let me take your soldier off the field in my ambulance. Vroom, vroom."

Kids never say, "I have some things to work out; will you play with me?" But that's what they need.

The basic fear we have been discussing does not show itself in its own honest form. It shifts shape, presenting itself as things that seem like nothing to do with power or adults. For the child age four or five, that generalized fear of power transforms itself from what it actually is into the monster in the closet. It's that skulking robber, or a slobbering monster lurking in the shadows, or a green hand waiting to grab any ankle unlucky enough to get close to the bed's dust ruffle.

How do you expunge a monster with no physical form?

DISENFRANCHISING THE BOGEYMAN

Elaine Tanner sat down on the new plaid sofa and rubbed her hands together. "You said last time that we'd start dealing with Aubrey's night fears. I'm ready, believe me."

"You had a tiring session last night." Dr. Warren pulled his chair near the sofa.

"It was terrible! I tried absolutely everything. She went to bed at eight-fifteen and that was a struggle in itself. Screaming all the way. We looked in all the drawers, in the closet, under the bed, behind her desk . . . Dr. Warren, there's not enough space behind her desk for a spider to hide, let alone a monster. And still she screamed and howled. I lay down with her finally about ten o'clock but she wouldn't get to sleep until nearly midnight."

"Every time you tried to leave the room she started up again."

Elaine sighed. "I'm so glad you said that. Obviously it's not the first time you've heard this sort of thing. Doctor, what am I going to do?"

We will explore Elaine's problem in detail in the next chapter. Then we'll look at some general guidelines that can help, not just children this age, but children any age.

5
Facing Fears in the Daily Grind
PRACTICAL GUIDELINES FOR PROBLEM-SOLVING

Dear Troid,

I've got a couple of things to write about today. One thing is, Dr. Warren made me admit today that sometimes I really don't like Aubrey. I always sort of knew it, you know, but I never really admitted it before. I hate the way she steals Mom every night. Sometimes I want to snuggle with Mom, but Aubrey is always there. Or read—just sit and read with Mom, you know? Then Mom says "bed time" and hops up and in she goes with Aubrey. Every night.

I'd stage a fear show myself, the way Aubrey does, but I'm afraid to. Isn't that stupid, Troid? I'm afraid to be afraid.

The other thing is Willard found out yesterday that Mom makes peanut-butter cookies. I guess his grandma only makes choclit chip cookies and he's getting tired of them, but I don't see how anyone could get tired of a grandma's choclit chip cookies. Anyway, he says I have to bring him some of Mom's peanut-butter cookies every day or he'll punch my lights out. He said don't tell Mom anything, just bring them. OK so I didn't tell Mom. I told Dad. Dad said that's nuts. Just tell him you couldn't make Mom make cookies even if you wanted to, and that's the end of that. I think Dad called the school too. But what he said to me was that I should just use common sense sometimes. I don't think he realizes Willard isn't common.

And I don't think Willard realizes Mom uses a box mix.

Your friend,
James

James had a specific problem that needed a specific solution. Helpful as it is to know theory about fear, the practice is what makes the difference in James's life and in any other child's.

TACKLING FEARS IN PRACTICAL, DAY-TO-DAY LIFE

Figuring out the theory of why a child is scared to death of the dust bunnies under the bed is an important part of the solution, but it is not, in itself, the answer to the problem. The harried parent, such as Elaine, has to be able to apply the knowledge in a practical way. Some techniques work well, others do not.

What Doesn't Work

To the pre-kindergartner, the bogeyman, the noises outside the window at night, the ghosties, the ghoulies, and the three-leggedy beasties loom large. Unfortunately, grown people tend to address these things in ways that reinforce the fears. There are several ways Elaine and other parents with this problem should *not* approach these scary creatures.

"I'll carry this for you."   Looking for monsters, Elaine riffled through all the drawers and looked through all the spaces, even when there were no spaces. By so doing she was saying, in effect, *I'll carry this for you. I'll work it out for you. First we'll see where the monsters are—if there are any. You'd like to check the drawers, but you're so scared. I'll walk through it for you.*

Aubrey still believed in those monsters, and not a thing Mommy did altered that belief. Simply not finding them didn't mean they weren't there. Then Mommy went to sleep with Aubrey in the child's bed. And when Mommy lay down, she said nonverbally, *Since I have to stay here to prevent them from getting you, they must exist after all.*

Remember that children think symbolically. They are not bound by reason and logic as grown-ups pretend to be. So children are very good at intuiting unspoken and secondary meanings, even though they cannot put such intuition into words.

"Mommy is scared too." Stop and think. What covert message does that message send? What overt message, for that matter? The last thing you want to convey to a small child is that the imagined danger threatens the parents as well.

The other pole is equally disastrous:

"There's nothing to be afraid of. Now go to sleep." With that cavalier statement the parent dismisses as wrong or insignificant the child's very real fear. The parent is addressing the fright, not the fear. And the child knows it.

Elaine tried that, over and over. Roger always resorted to it. All they did was build a wall between themselves and Aubrey. They didn't hear her unspoken fear. They didn't really understand. They were not there for her. Because they refused to get involved with the danger, whatever it might be, she had to face it alone, and it's too scary to face such fears alone.

Roger, and at times Elaine, didn't address the fear; they boxed it up. They willed it to disappear and falsely assumed that willing it so makes it so. Budget analysts and congressmen too often try that approach on national monetary crises. But willing it to disappear doesn't make it go away in any other line of endeavor, either, from politics to theology.

Boxing up fears instead of dealing with them does more than just rob the child of growth. It robs the child of joy in life, now and later.

What Works

In his office, Dr. Warren said, "Elaine, we've been talking about how little children relate to other persons and the world."

"You mean their interests are all in personal relationships."

"Right."

Elaine leaned forward in her seat, speaking rapidly and enthusiastically. "After you said that, I tried something. Aubrey loves to watch TV. And frankly, when I'm terribly busy, I use it as a babysitter. Good programs, of course, 'Sesame Street' and things like that. And she just gobbles it up. So when she was in the middle of her TV show and really wrapped up in it, I said, 'Aubrey, let's read a book together.' She hopped up and came running over. I said, 'You have to turn off the TV if we're going to read a book,' and she ran right back and turned it off! I was amazed. She watches her shows religiously."

"If Roger or you were asked to turn off your favorite program, you'd have to think twice."

"That's it! That's it exactly." Elaine's head bobbed vigorously.

"Knowing what you know now, that children value personal relationships most of all, how would you approach the monster in the closet?"

Elaine sat back again frowning. "Lie down in her bed with her. But I've been doing that and it doesn't work. Doctor, I certainly don't want her to stay up with us."

Dr. Warren nodded in agreement. "What I would recommend is the same thing I always recommend. Be a journeymate."

Picture digging up the garden for spring planting. The soil has lain fallow all winter. It's cold and wet, so the work is hard. You could dig up the soil with your bare hands, gouging your fingers in as deep as possible, raising and turning the loosening dirt. It would take a long time and the job would not be done well. At least a part of your garden would not respond at all to that sort of perfunctory plowing. Ah, but should you use a garden spade, the job is done—and done well—in less than an hour. You've tilled the soil down nearly a foot. The beds will drain well; the plants will resist drought because their roots will grow deep.

A journeymate is the spade with which your child spades his or her garden. The spade does not dig; the child does. The spade is a tool. Oh, the child might be able to do it alone, but only with the tool can he really do it well.

If you are the child's parent, you are that tool.

Empathy first, then facts. This is empathy: "I know you're scared. So was I when I was this age. I'll walk you to bed. I might sit beside you awhile, talk to you, maybe read you a story. Then it's sleep time."

This is what the child hears: *Your fear is real. Valid. And survivable. I understand. I'll walk through it with you, but I won't walk through it for you.*

And this is the salient fact: Mommy and Daddy are nearby. Therefore you are safe.

While this discussion has focused on Elaine's specific problem with Aubrey, this system works for other expressions of fear as well. Sometimes the symbolic gesture, such as Elaine's checking closets and drawers, actually works.

Let's take a totally ridiculous example. Let's say a child secretly fears that the shoelaces on his Sunday shoes might come up and strangle him. Since he's not particularly sanguine about the fact that it's impossible, one fact he can relate to is, there must be something you can do to keep shoelaces from doing that.

You might tie them in a double knot, and talk about how hard it is for such knots to come undone and produce loose ends. If the child is small, you can figuratively chew out the shoelaces. "Now you guys stay put. I'm going to tie you so you can't do that again!"

Don't forget, then, the third step, being a journeymate. "Mom and Dad are close by. We'll walk through this with you. The shoelaces don't have a chance."

Once you allay a fear, do you mention it again? Might talking about it, or dwelling on it, not get it started anew?

Keep in mind that most fears don't go away totally. They just slip into the background. They may wither or they may emerge in some other context. Seldom are issues resolved permanently. You resolve it for now. Then you re-resolve it later because kids are in a continual process of growing up and looking at new things from new directions. Things resolved at this level, ages three or four, have to be examined again when the child is seven or eight and possibly dealt with anew.

So, no. We don't dwell on fears past. But neither do we refuse to mention them. They were, and are, a significant part of life, not to be assiduously ignored. "Do you remember when you were terrified of scary things under your bed?" will eventually be met with, "No, I don't."

This resolution through facts-plus-empathy is all well and good for both child and adult—until 3 A.M. when the child leaps bolt upright, shrieking and crying. Now what?

NIGHT TERRORS AND NIGHTMARES

You are running through city streets and no one is paying attention to you. You must escape. You are in a hayloft now. You did not climb the vertical ladder and crawl up through the square hole in the loft floor, and yet it's perfectly logical that you're there. As you watch that hole in the floor, a lioness emerges. She is looking all around. Here is another. A third sticks its head up. You awaken.

You had them as a kid. You may still get one occasionally. Nightmares and night terrors attack this pre-kindergarten age with a vengeance. Nearly every child experiences nightmares. Night terrors are much less common. Let's look at the differences.

Night Terrors

Late, late in the night your child seems to awaken in a panic. The kid is absolutely frightened to death, screaming deliriously. You try to awaken the child to alertness or any form of responsiveness at all, but nothing works. The eyes are wide open; the mouth and vocal cords are certainly functional. But you can't get through. Eventually, the poor little dear goes back to sleep. The next morning, the child can't remember a thing.

While night terrors are an absolutely horrible experience for the parents, the kids apparently have no conscious memory of them. We have come to believe that night terrors have a physiological source, not a psychological basis. Probably they are more a physiological sleep disturbance, an electrical phenomenon. They tend to go away by the time the child reaches age six or so. Most children who have night terrors don't experience them for very long. If night terrors persist, the situation merits medical observation.

Nightmares

Again, your little one bolts upright, screaming. The child has been awakened by a bad dream. Crying, babbling, and upset, the child is wake-able. At least for a brief time, the child can either remember specific details of the dream or simply that it was a scary experience. Rather than being physiological phenomena, nightmares, we think, may have a lot to do with the handling of conflict. The mind is wandering through deep dark rooms determining what needs to be addressed in those recesses. Nightmares are intense dreams in which the child dissipates psychic energy and works through conflicts. Usually, unless they persist, they are not signs of serious problems.

. . . with an important exception. We have found that in

the most frequent cases where nightmares persist, especially in teens and particularly in girls, some sort of abuse may be part of that child's life. This is not, of course, to say that every instance of persistent nightmares points unerringly to abuse. Not so. But we certainly consider it a big red flag.

Handling Nightmares and Night Terrors

Your child begins screaming in the night. Surely the little thing is being attacked by something at least leopard size or larger. You run in. You turn on the light. What next?

What you do is determined by what you have when the light comes on. For night terrors, from which the child cannot be awakened, you are the safety net. That's all. Hold the little one, prevent the child from falling or being hurt, and ride out the episode. We doubt that children in the throes of night terrors are aware they are being held and comforted. This is not to say that you ought not do it. This is to remind you to expect no response.

Nightmares are quite a different breed of cat. The child becomes at least partially aware. Thus the presence of Mom or Dad becomes most important. Equally important, the parent must comfort with empathy.

"But, Doctor," Elaine Tanner protested, "that's what I do, comfort her. I don't mean just when she goes to bed but when she wakes up at 3 A.M. in a sweat, screaming."

"Do you take her into bed with you?"

"Roger hates it. She's constantly moving. She's an eggbeater."

"By so doing, Elaine, you are saying in effect, 'You poor little thing, come sleep with us, because you'll never get over that horrible, horrible experience by yourself.'"

"Walking through it for her again, right?"

Dr. Warren smiled. "You've learned your lesson well."

"Let me guess some more. Ignoring her won't do it either; that's the opposite approach."

"Exactly right, not harsh inattention. The best course is

an approach down the middle between the extremes: 'I know it's pretty scary. I'll hold you a few minutes until you feel better. I'm here; you can rest safely.' "

"And then you leave."

She grimaced. "You make it sound easy."

"It's not, for either of you."

Elaine sat back in the lovely plaid sofa looking weary. "Amen and amen."

PRACTICAL JOURNEYMATESHIP

Not every problem is just like Elaine's problem with Aubrey, and sometimes the way to a solution goes down different paths. "Common sense," insists Dr. Minirth, "it's just common sense. Horse sense, some call it. Usually, it's all most people have to do. Think about the problem. Listen to your child. Apply common sense." We have been discussing the underlying causes of fears, but parents want relief for the surface symptoms also. Here are some steps along that particular road.

Control the Environment

Specific fears may reflect a disruption in the child's environment. Remember that children are practically powerless to alter or control the world around them. If something is happening in the child's world that you can control, then fix it. Here are some ways. As you look them over, think about specific circumstances of children you know. How would you adapt each of these suggestions to that specific instance?

Alter the situation. Julie, a girl of five with persistent nightmares, lived with two siblings and three step-siblings. Her mother learned that her stepbrothers were sexually molesting her. Mom could not change what had happened, but she could control its possibility of happening again. She instantly removed the boys, sending them to live at their other parent's home. Had that not been possible, she would have made certain she or another trusted adult protected Julie at all times, particularly during times, such as night, when Julie was most vulnerable. As a first step in Julie's recovery, the nightmares eased.

When Willard tried to shake down James for cookies, Roger called the school.

In neither of these cases did the child have any power to change the way things were going. The adult, the journeymate, had to step in. Should a problem crop up for a child you know, how could you adjust the circumstances? What control, what power do you have? And what *can't* you control?

Talk. Just talking about fears is an excellent catharsis for grown-ups and kids alike. To be most effective, talk is best structured by the child. "With one boy I worked with," Dr. Minirth relates, "we'd go to the zoo. Or just go down and throw rocks in the creek—do kid things. And while we did kid things, he talked."

Think of a child you know. Now think about some things you could do or places you could go that would be appropriate to that particular child, to grease the skids of conversation, so to speak.

Sleep. Sometimes kids just need more rest. In our practice we all too often see children who need seven to nine hours of rest each night but they're only getting five or six. They are allowed to stay up late, or they are required by circumstances (Mom and Dad have to get to work, for example) to awaken early.

Aubrey wasn't getting enough sleep. Neither was Elaine, for that matter. By the time they completed the nightly ritual of seeking out the monsters and mollifying the child, Aubrey didn't actually fall asleep until well past ten. On the days Elaine worked she had to rise at five-thirty to be at work by seven to prepare for the day. And Aubrey had to be up and out also.

It's amazing how just plain rest helps so many problems.

Use music. "Music hath charms to soothe the savage beast." It does pretty well on kids too.

"Right," Elaine snorted. "Have you listened to music lately? Rap. Rock. Those frantic videos. Soothing? In a pig's eye!"

"You do have to be selective," we respond to this kind of complaint.

There is indeed music that is relaxing, positive, uplifting. Consider the Gaithers singing, "You are the only one of your kind." It's a great esteem builder, countering the fears generated by kids' self-image (which is usually pretty negative). Explore the vast world of the classics. "The Carnival of the Animals" by Camille Saint-Saëns is a delightful place to start. Try some Brahms, some Tchaikovsky, some Dvořák. Good music doesn't have to be slow and stodgy to be restful. Ask your library about videos of ballets such as *The Nutcracker* or *Coppélia*. Try music instead of TV as background for kids' homework time, for bedtime and pre-bed, and for meals.

Use recreation. Dr. Minirth tells of a child whose mother described her simply as "crazy." Mom was ready to institutionalize little Becky, who, at age six was so disruptive her first-grade teacher declared her not quite ready for prime time and sent her home. Dr. Minirth probed Becky's home life and learned about this schedule:

4:30 A.M.—Family up and out of bed

5 to 5:30—Family devotions

6 to 6:15—Make bed, clean up room

6:15 to 6:45—Breakfast and pack lunches

6:45—Catch bus (actually a van) for the one-hour ride to a private school

4:10 P.M.—Arrive home from school

4:30 P.M.—Dance lessons (ballet on Tuesdays, tap on

Thursdays) or Brownies (Wednesdays) or fitness class (Fridays—because school does not offer adequate physical-education program)

5:45—Dinner
6:30—Quiet time
7:00—Bedtime preparation
7:30—In bed

And that was just Becky's schedule! Dad and Mom had equally demanding down-to-the-minute routines that extended from one end of their eighteen-hour day to the other.

"It was literally driving Becky nuts," says Dr. Minirth. "That would drive me crazy too! Children develop serious fears when rigid, overscheduled, overfilled environments keep them constantly occupied. There's no room for loafing and imagination."

Unfortunately, loafing was anathema for Becky's parents. Only when they entered counseling and began to work on their own obsessions did Becky show any improvement at all. Becky needed recreation and free time. She didn't just crave it. She *needed* it.

How does your child's schedule look? Study it down to the minute the way Becky's was written down.

Laugh. Lighten up!

"There is nothing funny about it," Elaine fumed. "James knew my floors were waxed when he harnessed Hector to the coffee table."

"He, uh, harnessed . . . explain, please."

"Well, he claims he was just showing Aubrey how Eskimos hitch up dogsleds. Hector gouged scuff marks all over three rooms trying to get away. Fortunately, the twine broke before the table did."

The scene would surely make anyone laugh—except the floor waxer. Roger made the mistake of laughing about it when he came home that night. He was re-waxing until nearly 1 A.M.

Humor, in general, goes a long way toward easing a

child's fears and frustrations, just as it does adults'. The saying that "we laugh most at what we fear most" has more than a kernel of truth to it. Promote laughter; see the funny side when the opportunity arises.

Find some funny things to do. Rent a video and watch it together—enjoy a mutual chance to yuk it up a little.

Take a vacation. Sometimes a change of pace will break a child's habitual responses and enable healing. The vacation needn't be a trip to Disney World every time something goes wrong. Getting away for the afternoon, or overnight, may be enough. Several mini-vacations usually work better with children than one long, grueling trek. Break out of the rut; step out of the humdrum, at least momentarily.

Name three or four places within fifty miles of you that would offer a nice one- or two-day getaway, kids and all.

Exercise. Kids especially need active, physical ways to simply blow off steam. In essence you are rechanneling the child's energy from dwelling upon fear to doing something physical and energetic. We find that good exercise improves both physical and emotional well-being. The physiological value of good exercise cannot be underestimated.

Have a medical workup. At the clinic we usually begin here, with a medical workup, particularly if the child has not had frequent physical checkups. "It would be a shame," Dr. Minirth points out, "to treat a kid for fear and then find out he had a mitral-valve prolapse."

Medical problems can produce symptoms that resemble fear. Besides mitral-valve prolapse and some other heart conditions, we look for certain tumors, temporal-lobe seizures, psychomotor seizures, hyperthyroidism, and attention deficit syndrome (the latest thinking suggests a dopamine imbalance may have something to do with this). All can produce fear symptoms not usually associated with physical problems.

"We had a young girl several years ago," Dr. Minirth continues, "whom we thought might have multiple personalities. When our neurologist got a brain-wave print, we could see she was having seizures. Once the seizures were controlled, the other problems disappeared."

The medicines a child takes can sometimes produce anxiety and fear symptoms too. Children vary profoundly in their reactions to essentially similar doses. Asthma medicines, for example, may have this kind of affect.

Use medical approaches only when appropriate. "Can't you give him a pill?" wails the frazzled mother.

"The rule is," we always respond, "when in doubt, don't use medicines." Then we add, "and some drugs useful for adults we never use on kids."

Occasionally, a child is so locked into an obsession, a fear, a state of mind, that normal feelings and mechanisms cannot reach the surface. In some such cases, medicines can break the grip of the psychological problem long enough for other forms of therapy to turn the child around. For instance, we might use small doses of an antihistamine to help a child get enough sleep to recover.

In all cases, medicine is not a cure. It is a means, a temporary device, to break a cycle or problem so a cure can commence.

We can do more, however, than just control the environment. We also use what might be called mental approaches to help the child process and allay the basic fears.

Reality Therapy

Reality therapy is a little bit like adjusting the environment. It is simply a matter of thinking up a course of action, and trying it out awhile. It works this way:

Decide what, realistically, is causing this surface fear. Brainstorm: What are five or ten things we could do to overcome this fear this week? They might be totally different things or an increasing progression of the same thing. In the Tanners' case, for example, Elaine and Roger came up with all sorts of answers for Aubrey's bedtime problems, some of them absurd. They could slip the kid a sedative (absurd end of the spectrum) or lock her in a closet (also absurd). They could try reading her a specific story each and every night. Because children take great comfort in routine and ritual, they could set up an elaborate ritual at bedtime with the final step being that of going to sleep: after bath and toothbrushing, we walk up and down the stairs twice, do five toe-touches and five deep knee-bends, turn around three times, hop into bed, pull the covers up then down then up, say good night, high five, then go to sleep.

Monitor the symptoms at the start and at the end of your grand experiment. How are you doing? Is it worth continuing? Be sure to give the experiment enough of a try.

The husband of one of our clients called this the experiment-in-terror option. It's particularly good for controlling surface symptoms—the problem behavior you can see.

"For three nights I tried reading her a story, tucking her in, and leaving," Elaine moaned. "She screamed louder than ever. It just didn't work."

Seven nights might have. Children are creatures of habit. When you devise a plan, stay with it long enough to change the child's habitual way of approaching the fear. Also, keep in mind you're probably trying to change the child's intentions. Aubrey didn't want to be alone. Screaming solved her problem.

"With the action-plan approach, common sense prevails," says Dr. Minirth. "Don't get fancy or creative. Just look at the problem squarely, keeping in mind the goal is to overcome what produced the fear."

Cognitive Approach

If one way to reach children is through the story—call that way fiction—then this is the nonfiction approach.

The word *cognitive* refers to thought processes. Basically, you'll try to change the way the child thinks. In this case, you're going to try to alter the way the child thinks about a fear or its symptoms. The older the child, the better your chance of success here. Plain old preaching doesn't work on kids any better than it works on adults. Instead, this approach is an attempt to get kids to use balance and common sense.

"Most fearful kids I see have the underlying belief, *I must be perfect,*" Dr. Minirth explains. "Parents introduce that without meaning to. You might say it's the theme of the family."

Dr. Warren concurs. "Usually the parents have not mastered the concept that it's okay to be imperfect. They don't realize that nobody can be perfect. We're called to be mature in Christ. That's not perfection in everything we do."

There is also a hunger in every child to earn everyone's love and approval. Everyone. All the teachers, the school administration, the parents, the friends, even total strangers who stop to ask directions to the interstate. Because of this hunger, children are great little pessimists. They love to focus on the negative. Technically, we call that *selective abstraction.*

Further, because children are born egocentric, they tend to personalize everything, to place themselves as the focus of their surroundings. Everyone is watching. Everyone is paying attention to what the child is saying or doing. Everyone is eagerly waiting for the kid to slip up.

Children also tend to magnify their own ups and downs. When some little thing goes wrong, it's the end of the world (quite a few adults have trouble riding the bumps, too, incidentally). Every bad break is a crisis.

In contrast with their gift for magnification and hyperbole, children minimize the good things. "The teacher said I did real well but she was just saying that."

Dr. Warren was discussing the cognitive approach with Elaine. "A child may earn a 95 percent grade, but she focuses on that 5 percent wrong. Or how about the child who gets all A's and one B? Does he celebrate the A's? No. He mourns the B."

"James does that very thing! He can work himself into a real snit over a grade that's lower than he expected. What do I do?"

"The cognitive approach—where we try to change the way a child thinks about something—works best when you yourself assume the attitude you want to promote in the child and then just keep hammering it home. You want to model for children the belief that you want them to adopt."

"But what do I say?"

Dr. Warren sat back in his chair. "Let's practice some responses. James comes home with four A's and one B on his report card. How about, 'Hey, I'm glad to see you aren't perfect. Neither was I'?"

Dr. Warren continued, "Or how about if James says, 'I don't dare stand up in Sunday school and recite my memory verse. They'll all be staring at me'?"

Elaine mulled that a moment. "That's not fair. We have already been discussing how strongly I'm bound by appearances, about pleasing people. I can't help it. It's the way I am."

"Apply common sense. Stand back as if you were a third party and analyze the situation."

"I suppose, logically, the other kids in Sunday school would be thinking about their own turn to stand up and wouldn't care much whether I lived or died."

"An excellent answer! I assume you'd rephrase it somewhat for James."

The game was afoot now. Elaine said eagerly, "I could ask him if he paid close attention to the other children's answers. I bet he'd say, 'Well, no, not really.' And I'd say, 'Well they're not paying any better attention to yours.'"

"How about this situation: James comes in from school and says, 'We had a substitute teacher today, and she said I have the clearest handwriting of anyone in the class. But she didn't really mean it.' How might you respond?"

"Why would she say that if she didn't mean it?" Elaine asked in all seriousness. Then, laughing, she caught herself. "Of course. Why *would* the teacher say something she didn't mean?"

Playing devil's advocate, Dr. Warren gave James's expected reply: "Just to be nice."

"Why does she want to be nice to a little kid she doesn't even know—especially enough that she'd lie?"

"Because she's a nice lady."

Running with the game, Elaine persisted. "You learned that the nicest people are those who speak the truth. Jesus calls Satan the father of lies. Is she evil?"

"No, she's good. But she's just trying to make me feel good."

"By praising ugly handwriting? You'd see through that lie in a minute."

"It's not ugly. It's pretty good handwriting."

Elaine sat back smiling broadly. "And I think so, too, Honey."

Behavioral Approach

The behavioral approach is an attempt to literally alter behavior patterns. These methods are used by professionals more than any other treatment for both light and severe problems.

Desensitization. "We had a child who was utterly terrified of airplanes," Dr. Minirth recalled. "Call him Randy. His parents were especially worried because Randy's grandmother was in extremely poor health and they were afraid they'd have to fly to New England fairly soon.

"So Randy and I talked about it awhile. I didn't try to talk him out of his fear or belittle it. It was real. It was *really* real. He'd break into a cold sweat when an airplane flew over Dallas at twenty thousand feet.

"Then we went for a drive out past a small local airport. We talked about the planes on the ground; all of them were single-engine craft, light planes. A couple of weeks later we took a drive out past Dallas-Fort Worth

International Airport. After awhile we could not only drive by as airplanes were landing and taking off, we could walk in the terminal. He was slowly desensitizing, you see.

"When the grandmother died and he had to fly, Randy's parents took a night flight so that he couldn't see much. You're never outside, and at night it's usually hard to see the exterior of the plane unless you put your face right up to the windows of the terminal. Randy was still very frightened, but he could handle it.

"Now that doesn't mean the cause of his fear was cured. It wasn't. His obsessive fear of airplanes was a surface symptom of a deeper problem. Unless we dug out that deeper problem, his fear would surface again in some other way. But there was the immediate symptom and a time limit on overcoming it. The practical matter was getting Randy to fly in an airplane without freaking. You have the real, underlying fear and the symptom. Sometimes, as in this case, it's the symptoms you have to deal with first."

Positive reinforcement. You've heard many times about reinforcing and approving the good behavior you desire in the child. That's all part of the behavioral approach.

Extinction. This, in a certain way, is the opposite of positive reinforcement. Obviously you want to be careful not to reinforce a fear. By refusing to give the fear symptom undue attention, you are promoting its extinction, its cessation.

Elaine was indirectly reinforcing Aubrey's fear of going to bed by giving too much attention to it. Elaine had to deal with it, of course, but she overplayed it. The symptom was never going to fade—that is, go extinct—as long as it was being fed by all that coveted attention.

Relaxation techniques. Using music or quiet times to unwind are behavioral methods called relaxation techniques. Usually, the parent needs them more than the child. If the parent can relax, the child will find it easier to relax also.

Modeling. This technique already has been described several times, including in the preceding sentence. By learning to relax, the parent helps the child relax. This is a very good behavioral approach because it accomplishes two goals at once. By preparing the way for the child, the parents must first master the behavior themselves. Both generations win.

Assertiveness training. This is the only good way to help a child who is out in the world unprotected. Assertiveness training helps shy children take up for themselves. Primal fears made James much more timid than a child his age and size should be. Those fears had to be addressed, but assertiveness training would help relieve the surface symptom. James needed help, not just with the depths of his problems, but with getting across the schoolyard in one piece.

Although parents can talk to a child about personal worth and dignity, assertiveness training itself is best done by a professional. A school counselor or psychologist can help.

Symptom reporting. There are many variations on this technique that you, as a parent or supporting adult, might want to use with a child in your care. Ask the fearful child to list all the felt symptoms in great detail. Frequently. Eventually, he or she tires of it and the symptoms taper off. Warning: It requires nerves of iron and eternal patience.

Flooding. This is not a technique we use on children. Essentially, flooding is throwing a child who fears water into the deep end of the pool. Children need trust and nurturing, and flooding provides neither. We mention it here only as a warning.

Insight Approach

Throughout this book we've been talking about this method off and on. Let us briefly outline and summarize it here as a technique for altering behavior.

"We start by explaining that true anxiety exists on three levels," Dr. Minirth said. "There is anxiety about being anxious. People who have experienced an anxiety attack are scared to death of another one.

"Second, they're anxious about their world, about what's going on in their lives right now. The commonest cause of fear and anxiety in children today, bar none, is that the parents will separate. Think about it. The children's whole world is destroyed. Why shouldn't they be anxious?

"And third is the deep-seated anxiety from way back. You have to go to the heart to understand this deepest level."

With this understanding of anxiety, you can use some of the techniques professional counselors use. Let us pretend you are out on your bike, riding with James. He confides, "I don't dare go out on the playground when Willard's playing soccer. He'll bodycheck me and I'm not even in the game."

One technique is to *reflect,* restating in your own words what the child just said. In response to James's stated fear, you might say,

_____

_____

Then you might briefly describe the essence of what emotions James probably felt.

_____

_____

Another technique is to *repeat verbatim* James's statement, or at least its key words.

_____

_____

You might do a little *interpretation*. "I guess I'd be a little bit worried." Or:

_____

_____

You might try a little *confrontation*, but be very cautious, especially with kids. "A few minutes ago, James, you told me you're not really anxious about going out at recess, but I see that you're nervous. Your fingers are twitching." Remember: to use confrontation with children you must be very gentle.

Self-disclosure. Sharing your own feelings about the situation is always good. "In that situation I would feel . . ." or "if somebody hit me, it would make me fearful," or:

_____

_____

Ask a question to help James articulate his own feelings. "What do you feel?" or:

_____

_____

You may not be trained in these methods, as the pros are. But by applying common sense (there's that phrase again), you can use these same techniques on a nonprofessional level.

Group Approach

People hear "group therapy" and think about formal, facilitated therapy sessions. But on a nonprofessional basis, you use this approach all the time in school, Sunday school, camp, and retreats. It influences a child's thoughts whenever there is more than one child in the family.

When you are all in a group, you can say things the child would never listen to if a single person were saying it to him or her in private. Group interactions alter denial and provide feedback.

When adults are talking one-on-one, denial kicks in almost automatically: "You look worried." "I am *not* worried! Just tired." Children are less sophisticated with their denial, and the younger the child, the more unsophisticated and less articulate the defenses: "You look worried, Tommy." (The three-year-old clouds up.) "Waaaaaaaah."

In a group, tell the adult, "You look worried." The adult replies, "I'm just tired," and a chorus of other voices chime in "Oh, suuuure," attacking the denial. A child's denial, naturally, is even easier to attack and break through because it's less case-hardened.

Feedback helps children many ways in a group situation. It provides support, insight, and vicarious learning. For example, here are random nuggets of feedback we have heard in informal group sessions at a kids' camp:

"Let me tell you what I did when my parents were fighting."

"So when that bunch of guys headed right for me, I didn't know what to do."

"I'm really scared to go over to my uncle's house. What if he hasn't changed from the last time? Did I ever tell you about the last time?"

"Hey, I finally figured out how to spit a mile. We were at the Grand Canyon last year on our vacation, and we were standing on the rim . . . yuk, yuk, yuk. . . ."

Such sharing, some jocular and some serious, does much to help a child understand and deal with fears. The child sees that *other kids feel the same things I do, and they cope all right.*

Comprehensive Approach

Here's where common sense *really* kicks in. Put all the above approaches together, thus treating the entire person as we do in the clinic—spirit, soul, and body.

As good as cognitive and other approaches are, the core of a child, and an adult as well, is his or her emotions. You must get below the thinking process, using emotion to reach the heart and soul. Emotions rule the world.

A proven way to do that, particularly for children, is with the story. Children are storytellers, as are all persons. Those stories are powerful devices for dealing with fear. That's what we'll look at next.

6
Tell
Me a
Story

Dear Troid,

We had fun today with Dr. Warren. All we did was sit around and tell stories. He said draw pictures as you tell it if you want, but I didn't want. You'll be happy to hear I told a story about a cat. It was a real, true, scaredy-cat who was afraid of everything. And then it ate some special food that made its claws grow real long, and its teeth grow real sharp. Suddenly it wasn't afraid anymore and all the other animals were afraid of it. You would of loved it, Troid.

Then Dr. Warren told a story about a cat too. A lion. A lion couldn't get the thorn out of its paw and couldn't even walk the paw hurt so bad. A mouse came along and the lion was going to eat it. The lion was too hurt to hunt, you see. And the mouse said, don't and I'll get the thorn out. So the mouse did, and the lion's paw healed up, and later the lion wouldn't catch mice, so the mouse's friends and family were all safe.

Dad says you aren't worth diddly at catching mice because you're too fat and lazy. I like to think some mouse took a thorn out of your foot once. But then, you are kind of fat.

I think next time I'm going to tell a story about a kid who can play softball. I messed up at softball in school today. I was in the outfield and the ball only came toward me once the whole time, and I missed it. I can't catch balls and you can't catch mice. You don't really try. Neither do I.

Your friend,
James

James was learning the power of the story. The cat in his story was a surrogate for himself and his dream of gaining boldness and power. His proposed story about a softball player was founded in his own ineptness at the game. Stories are an important tool for shaping children and helping them resolve their fears. Counselors use them all the time.

THE POWER OF THE STORY

"Stories. I love 'em." Dr. Warren sat back in his chair. "A small child doesn't think in adult terms—in nonfiction, if you will. You can preach to a kid until you're blue in the face and never make a dent. I can explain to a child what is happening in his or her life, but it doesn't do much good. The way I reach a child, especially a child less than, say, nine or ten, is through stories. I tell stories."

The Story As Model and Teaching Tool

Dr. Warren smiles. "My favorite story is Daniel. Think about it. The lion's den. The furnace. There is so much to learn in that story. It models the very highest personal standards and, of course, it entertains, as well."

When Daniel and his three friends, princes of Israel, were enslaved and dragged off to Babylon, their city lay devastated. Their God had promised He would be there for them. Now all was lost. In Babylon, the king chose a group of special cases. Slaves with a future, some would say. Daniel and his friends were among them. Daniel received a new identity as Belteshazzar; his friends became Shadrach, Meshach, and Abed-Nego. They even had quarters in the imperial palace itself, and new foods—royal foods, including excellent wines.

"We talk about the intense fears children face, sometimes alone," Dr. Warren pointed out. "Think about the fears that hounded Daniel and his friends: fear of the unknown, of hostile and very powerful people, of being abandoned by God Himself. This story speaks to a fearful child because Daniel experienced exactly the same feelings.

"What would most people do?" Dr. Warren asked. "Probably take it and run. But Daniel and his friends stood firm and resisted the easy way to wealth and luxury. They talked the chief eunuch out of giving them rich foods and good wine and stuck to water and vegetables. They walked into a roaring furnace rather than betray their Lord. All these are splendid examples of facing fears bravely. The child learns intuitively from the example. An essay won't do it, and certainly not a doctrinal statement. But a story will. A very powerful, very rich story."

Who tells these stories?

THE POWER OF THE LAP

Elaine Tanner wrinkled her nose. "You mean, all you do is tell stories?"

Dr. Warren nodded. "For the most part. And I ask children to tell stories to me. It's a window I use to see inside them."

"But children's stories are babble. You should hear what Aubrey comes up with sometimes."

"Did you ever tell your parents stories when you were little?"

"I don't remember."

"What do you remember?"

Elaine pursed her lips and pondered a few moments. "I remember my mother reading to me occasionally. Never my father. And I remember Mother taking me to the library to get my first library card."

Dr. Warren nodded. "It's amazing when I talk to adults about their memories of early childhood. So many adults have fond memories of Mom or Dad reading a story every night at this age. They don't remember gifts received, but they remember that. And it's amazing how many young parents today fail to do it. They don't have time. It's a lost art."

"Roger and I both work long hours. We don't have time to sit and read."

"Except at bedtime."

"Well, yes. But the idea is to get Aubrey to go to sleep, not tell her a story. The children watch videos—you know, good ones." She frowned warily. "You don't object to videos, do you?"

"Not at all. But I object when they become the only source of stories."

For two reasons, much of the value of the story is lost when television, videos, and films are the storytellers. One, imagination is seriously curtailed. When the audio and visual images are all laid out, the child's imagination has nothing to do. It is the child's imagination, through internal fantasy, that must work out problems and conundrums. If the imagination is not in play, learning and processing are not happening.

Secondly, there is no personal contact between the storyteller and the listener. Television, films, and videos are not bad. They serve a purpose. They can step into a gap, but gap-stepping is not the same as gap-filling. They cannot replace the unique experience of a child sitting on the grown-up's lap, literally nested in the embrace of a caring adult (besides, think about what that does to allay the primal fear of being overpowered), hearing a story with eyes, ears, and imagination.

It is absolutely crucial that parents read to their young children regularly. Nothing can take its place.

There is no substitute for those two elements: personal contact and the play of imagination. Whether the child is creating the scene or imagining what it is like as you read, the imagination must do its work of processing life. And in children, nothing happens outside relationships.

Stories also provide a primary learning tool.

THE POWER OF THE LESSON

Look at the lives of Daniel and his friends from the opposite viewpoint. What gave them the strength to resist the easy way out? Again, it is the story.

"Over and over in Deuteronomy and elsewhere, God commanded the people of Israel to tell the stories of their history to their children," said Dr. Warren. "This was their primary means of transmitting history, through oral tradition. God instructed the Israelites to leave remembrances around the land to trigger memories and the retelling of stories. For example, study the story of the memorial stones in Joshua 3–4 and the clear commandment in Joshua 4:2–7.

God knew the Israelites' children would someday ask their parents, "What do these stones mean?" Then their elders would tell them the story. Daniel and his friends grew up hearing such stories. That's how they learned culture, history, and ethics.

What it comes down to is this: Daniel could say, "No matter what this guy Ashpenaz says, I'm not going to compromise what I was taught as I sat in the laps of my forefathers."

THE STORY AS THERAPY

A friend of ours asked her small daughter, "Is it all right to kill animals for food?"

"Sure," the child replied.

Together they watched the film *Harry and the Hendersons.* In that movie, the Henderson family (literally) runs into a bigfoot, a Sasquatch. They name him Harry and end up taking him home. They come to love him and try to protect him from the evils of uncaring men.

Afterward, our friend asked the girl again, "Is it all right to kill animals for food?"

Wide-eyed, the child answered, "Oh no!"

"Do you realize," our friend told her daughter, "that watching that one movie completely changed the way you think about something important? A life-and-death matter. And you couldn't tell it was doing that. That is how powerfully movies can affect you. You must always be careful of what movies and books are teaching."

You will recall that kids, especially the young ones aged three to five or six, do much of their processing about the world through fantasy, not fact. They figure out right and wrong, good and evil, what is important and what is not, by exploring options through imagination and fantasy. Then they internalize all that processing; it goes from their eyes and ears directly to their hearts without a lot of conscious, cognitive brain work going on at all.

There is a reason for that.

The Built-in Story

When God revealed Himself through the written Word, He did not mean it just for His chosen people, the Jews. He meant it for all men, as He eventually dispersed the Jews and sent the Christians out beyond all the coastlands. This sending out is referred to by theologians as the Great Commission. And with what did God equip the commissioners?

Written stories.

Think for a moment about the scope of His plan. He declared His intent to reach every person in every culture on every continent in every political unit in every decade of every century of post-Moses history. Impossible! Yet see how well He did it!

He did it by programming the story into mankind just as He included hair color, eye color, skin tone, and other physical attributes. Men and women can intuitively understand stories they have never heard before. Adults, in their infinite wisdom, feel they have grown beyond the story into the realm of reason. But children are still back in the innate story, because reason is not yet important in their lives. The younger the child, the more powerfully the story speaks. That is why counselors can use stories so effectively to convey a message.

The primal story almost always addresses some primal fear of childhood. It gives voice and shape to the fear, bringing it to the surface so the child can discern it, resolve it, and process it. Every culture has its primal stories.

We refer to these basic tales as archetypal. One example might be drawn from the encouraging words of Psalm 118:22: "The stone which the builders rejected / Has become the chief cornerstone." This idea from the ancient psalmist is used in the archetypal story of *Cinderella,* which depicts an unwanted creature, rejected and jeered, who emerges as beautiful and desirable. It is the dream of the small child who almost invariably doubts his or her own desirability. The *Cinderella* archetypal story has given powerful underlying meanings to several hit movies recently that would otherwise be dismissed as fluff. Hans Christian Andersen built his beloved story *The Ugly Duckling* on the framework of *Cinderella.*

Another archetypal story has the Good-Triumphs-over-Evil theme; it is retold over and over and is the ultimate theme of the book of Revelation. A variation, *Beauty and the Beast,* always speaks powerfully as true love triumphs over gross ugliness. Again, it reflects the fear of childhood that "I am not lovable. I'm ugly." Another archetype, Young Man on the Cusp of Manhood Comes of Age, speaks powerfully to the same fear. The prodigal son is one such story. His father loves him despite his ugly lapse into sin and foolishness. The child can blow it, as did the prodigal, and still be loved. What a powerful message!

Archetypal stories are populated by identifiable archetypal characters. These characters provide something the imagination, programmed in advance, can grasp and see as it processes the surrounding world. Some archetypal characters include the Reluctant Hero, the Ardent Hero, the Villain, the Siren, the Mentor, the Sidekick, the Malevolent Trickster, the Sky Father, the Earth Mother. When these characters play out the primal stories, everyone can recognize them. Everyone—especially children—can then participate vicariously in the characters' solutions to fears and dilemmas.

Are we suggesting then that the Bible is myth and fiction? By no means! We are explaining that the primal story is built into us so that every person, even a child, can intuitively grasp what God is saying about Himself. We believe in an inerrant Scripture that is the foundation for not only faith but mental health as well. But whether we accept Scripture as accurate is beside the point. The story is the medium God uses to teach and shape us.

Missionaries who have worked in so-called primitive cultures will attest to the power of Bible stories to instruct and explain. The Sky Father (God) united with the Earth Mother (Mary) to produce the ultimate Hero who would triumph over death itself. Jesus at Gethsemane is the Reluctant Hero. Overturning the moneychangers' tables, He is the Ardent Hero. Characters often shift roles. Satan, the ultimate villain, also appears as the Malevolent Trickster, such as in Genesis 3 and the first scenes of Job. A Navajo who grew up on tales of the trickster coyote, and the old Norseman who heard the stories about the evil and mischievous character Loki, will both see through Satan's wiles in a moment.

Children, particularly young ones, use symbolism in quite sophisticated ways. You recall that a three-year-old can displace a fear of powerful adults onto an inanimate slog of slime. That is symbolic: the slog takes the place of the actual fear object. Stories are powerful in part because children are comfortable feeling and using that same kind of symbolism. Told stories are more potent for that reason than are videos or television, which show too much.

As an example of this symbolism, dragons serve an important role in childhood. They personify danger and their demise clearly shows the child that those primal fears lurking deep within can be conquered. They personify evil, and when vanquished put hope in the mind of the child who then can see good overcoming bad. The dragons and the stories in which they appear give visible dress to invisible concepts. None of this processing in children is conscious. None is rational in the adult sense. But it goes on, all the same.

Fairy tales, fables, and true stories appeal to the child on the most primal level. Bible stories are especially instructive because they bear directly the print of the Master's hand. Applied diligently, they can shape a child's life. And ours. Adults, some denominations in particular, dwell on the New Testament Epistles, feeling that is where the real instruction lies. But to the child, and to adults more than they will admit, the deepest instruction lies in the Hebrew scriptures, as Jacob wrestles with his angel and Jonah wrestles with his fears.

To teach and reach a child, you tell a story.

But that does not help physical skills. There was still James's dilemma. He was a total ninny at softball. He suffered that grade-school disaster of being jeered at by the jocks. He had another problem, you'll remember, which his mother labeled "school phobia." Next we'll discuss how we dealt with James's problems at a practical level. And we'll explore how dealing with childhood fears shapes a child's conscience.

The Deep-seated Fears of Childhood

INFANT AND TODDLER
(THE BOTTLE AND BANKY SET)

- *I fear being abandoned.*

- *If I am abandoned, I fear I will lose my meself.*

- *I fear I can lose Mommy and Daddy's love and approval.*

- *The Oedipal phenomenon*

LATE PRESCHOOLER
(THE SANDBOX SET)

- *I am afraid of the power to hurt that big people possess.*

- *Nightmares and Night Terrors*

PART FOUR

Grade-schoolers

The Skateboard Set

7
Avoiding Entitlement

Dear Troid,
The neatest thing happened yesterday. Dad helped me
learn how to do wheelies on the skateboard. I never
ride my skateboard much, you know, and when I do
sometimes Willard is out there to mess me up. It's not
usually worth it. But yesterday we must of spent an
hour. That's nice but it's not the neatest thing though.
The neatest thing was what Dad said. He said he was
scared a lot when he was my age. You know what,
Troid? I think maybe he understands some.
You don't. I don't expect you to. I don't know why
they call scaredy-cats scaredy-cats because you aren't
scared much at all. You just climb up on something
high and sort of stare down your nose at the world.
I wish I could do that. But knowing Dad feels that
way is almost as good.
I'd write more but I don't have time. Dad and I are
going out to practice batting. See you.

Your friend,
James

James was progressing much farther down the
road toward confidence than he guessed. The realization
that a journeymate, an adult, understands does much to
allay fears. And allaying fear leads to self-confidence.
James's father, Roger, was growing too.

THE ROOTS OF ENTITLEMENT

Roger Tanner explained his incipient male-pattern bald-
ness by claiming that "grass doesn't grow on a busy

street." Elaine said that was because the grass couldn't get up through the cement. Roger's hips were a bit wide and his shoulders a bit narrow. With his horn-rimmed glasses and the plastic protector in his breast pocket he looked like an accountant, Mr. Average Guy. Actually he was one of the most sought-after general practitioners in Collin County . . . in fact, one of the few general practitioners in Collin County. People from Fort Worth and beyond trampled each other in the streets to be the patient of Dr. Roger Tanner.

Dr. Warren engaged Roger alone in conversation. They talked about their practices and told a few war stories. Then Dr. Warren got down to business. "Your wife mentioned something about income tax."

"That was unfortunate. I don't mean to sound hostile; I'm certainly not. I want to help Jimmy, but that's not a matter for discussion in this office."

"It seems to me that being in serious arrears with the IRS could have a severe impact on your family life."

"My family life and professional life are separate. That's professional."

"As I talk to your wife and son, I detect bitterness on Elaine's part that you invest so much of your time in your practice."

"She doesn't understand how demanding our profession is. You do, of course."

Dr. Warren nodded. "Your job is to support the family. Your wife's job is child rearing."

"Exactly."

"Your son and I have been playing games."

Roger smiled. "I would imagine that's an occupational hazard of your profession."

"Well put. I've gotten to be an expert in Tinkertoys. Yet, during those games James has revealed, without actually saying so, that he harbors some crippling fears. He has been resisting school very strongly."

"That's an understatement."

"He fears participation in active sports. He fears adults,

bigger children, animals other than Hector and Mergatroid. In fact, I believe he feels uncomfortable around
Hector. Hector nips, I understand."

"Hector's short on patience. We're hoping that spaying
her will calm her down."

"Do any of these fears feel familiar from your own
childhood, Roger?"

Roger Tanner froze. His face tightened. His foot, dan-
gling from his crossed leg, twitched.

"From what I see in James," said Dr. Warren gently, "I
would guess that your own childhood was plagued by
fears. And incidentally, your wife's too."

The silence hung heavy, begging to be broken.

Minutes later Roger cleared his throat. "When I think
about my son, it frightens me. I see myself in him. I see
him going through the kind of childhood I went through.
And I don't know what to do. There isn't anything that
can be done. He is like he is and that's that. I believe that's
what frightens me most—that I can't help him."

"If you could help him, you would do so."

"Of course. Seeing him with the same kind of childhood I had . . ." Roger's voice trailed off.

"I trust you are sincere in that. Because you can help
James immensely, if you are willing to do so."

"I'm willing."

When There Is No Journeymate

In his youth, Roger Tanner had no one to buffer him
and walk beside him as he resolved his fears. Thus they
went unresolved. Several things are happening in his life
now, in adulthood. He is a model of overachievement: Mr.
Nice. Marcus Welby. He works harder and harder. Hyper-
responsible toward his patients is another way to describe
it.

He is also a model of irresponsibility. It's not that he's
trying to escape taxes or cheat Uncle Sam. It's just that he
procrastinates. He doesn't file in a timely manner. He fails
to assemble the records his accountant needs. In fact, his

records are so botched up he doesn't even try anymore to put them right. Elaine wouldn't have learned about his tax problems at all, had she not stumbled upon letters from his accountant and the IRS.

And Roger is getting more and more extreme, polarizing himself in the area of hyper-responsibility and hyper-irresponsibility. We believe this is a form of self-punishment. The fears of childhood have cloaked themselves in new dress and reemerged from the forgotten rooms of his past. As his parents and family elevate him more and more toward sainthood, he secretly fears more and more that he's a hoax. One of these days all his friends and family will realize he's really not all that good. Then the world will come crashing down. So he has to work even harder lest he be found out and punished.

How about You?

Could some of your child's fears be a reflection of your own? Think back to when you were a tyke. What fearful things happened that you still remember? What terrors plagued you?

For example, Dr. Warren remembers:

_____ Being bitten by a dog

_____ Being scratched by a cat

_____ Being kicked or stepped on by a horse

Write your fearful experiences here:

I remember an animal, a _____, perpetrating this outrage on my person: _____

Falling is always scary. I remember falling:

_____ From some height

_____ From a vehicle, especially a moving vehicle

_____ Off a horse or pony

_____ Down some stairs

I remember the following incident when I was left behind, either voluntarily or involuntarily. (For instance, you might remember how bad it felt when your parents went on business trips and left you at home):

_____

_____

_____

I still remember these incidents of my childhood that frightened me very badly:

1. _____

_____

2. _____

_____

3. _____

_____

Looking back, I can see that these incidents could contribute to some of my specific fears of childhood:

_____ A fear of being abandoned

_____ A fear of losing Mom and Dad's approval

_____ A fear of the opposite sex or my own sexuality

_____ A fear of adults and adult power, their potential to hurt

_____ A fear of failure (*Can I succeed? Do I have value?*)

_____ A fear of facing the world on my own

Now that you've taken a look at the fears in your own background, however unsettling that look might be, reflect on this question: *How might these fears and uncertainties be influencing the children close to me?*

What, for instance, did Roger's fears have to do with James?

We believe that James, at ten, and Aubrey, at four, will follow their father. If he deals with the issues that are causing his problems, they will deal with theirs. If he fails to face his own fears, outside counsel such as that of the Minirth-Meier Clinic will be of severely limited value to his children.

On the surface, the fears and issues of father and child

seem unrelated. But deep inside they are the same; only their expression has shifted.

Roger's early fearfulness is reflected in James's fearfulness. But fearful parents do not always raise children who appear fearful on the surface. That fearfulness might also erupt as entitlement and exemption.

TO CATCH THE CONSCIENCE OF THE KING: LESSONS OF CAUSE AND EFFECT

Next door to the Tanners, Willard and his grandparents represent another path that unresolved fears may forge.

Fearful parents (or surrogates such as grandparents) may raise an entitled child.

Entitled, you recall, is a five-dollar word for a fifty-cent concept: spoiled rotten. The spoiled child is king and all the world exists for him or her. Nobody wants spoiled kids around; they're destructive, disruptive, and annoying. Teachers dislike them. They require special attention, robbing the teacher's time and energy. Parents quickly get tired of spoiled children's demands and then start to feel trapped and frustrated. The worse it gets, the worse it gets, spiraling down, down, down.

But annoyance and frustration are the least of an entitled child's woes (try telling parents that, when they're on the front line of the spoiled child's demands). Entitlement may prevent the child from developing a conscience. And that is a far more serious woe.

The development of conscience begins in infancy and grows by age-dependent stages, paralleling the other forms of growth. As the child's independence and awareness of the outside world increase, so, ideally, will his or her conscience.

In essence, a two-year-old has no conscience. All discipline, all sense of what is right and wrong, all value judgments are imposed from outside. If Mommy and Daddy say it, it is so. We refer to that state as "no internalized conscience." Right and wrong are external concepts.

Friends of ours very nearly lost their two-year-old in the kind of swimming-pool accident that emergency professionals report all too often. "I turned my back for only a moment," the mother wailed. "I had to answer the phone. It was a short call, less than two minutes. When I turned around, she had fallen into the pool." And then, perplexed, the distraught mother added, "She knows better than to get near the pool. We've told her a hundred times . . ."

I've told her a hundred times. External control. Conscience, the definition of right and wrong, imposed from outside. The child lived, and today she is bright-eyed and normal, but tragedy lurked very near.

Many, many parents, we find, overindulge their one- to-three-year-old because, after all, the little dear is too young to know right from wrong. That is true. The little one is. But day by day the child, like a blank slate, is being written upon. Below the verbal level, the little dear is blotting up right and wrong from the rules and disciplines the parents display.

Cause and effect need to exert their lesson. The child performs an inappropriate action. The child is punished. *Aha!* The little bell comes on. *That's wrong. This is right.* The child internalizes the feelings we recognize as conscience because he or she gets punished, although *punish* is a poor word here. A better word is *consequences.* Consequences are not always a scolding or a spanking or even a trip down to the police station. Consequences may just be an unpleasant result or a feeling of shame. By allowing inappropriate actions and by shielding children from the consequences of their actions, the parents can gravely undercut the learning process. Kids never develop a conscience spontaneously.

As children grow, they internalize right and wrong, first in black and white and then, as maturity approaches, in shades of gray. What used to be imposed from the outside now comes from the inside, at least when it is expedient to do so. Older children will still lie (heaven knows adults do, too!), but they know it's wrong. They might steal, particularly if they feel they won't get caught, but their consciences will tell them, inside themselves, the same thing their parents and the law tell them from the outside.

They have internalized the moral controls that guide them.

Some children have more difficulty internalizing conscience than do others. In those cases, parents have to be more dedicated in discipline and example. A very small percentage of kids are genetically incapable of easily internalizing conscience.

James's parents, though battling fears themselves, exercise reasonable control over Aubrey and James. They are instilling in both children a strong sense of conscience. The children's unresolved fears take the form of other fearfulness.

Not so Willard, the walking Death Star. His grandparents are fearful people, both of them. And they pity him (*poor child, so disadvantaged by inadequate parents*). So they protect the poor child from the bumps of life. That is, they protect Willard from the consequences of his own actions. As a direct result, Willard possesses the conscience of a boa constrictor. Just ask James.

When it comes to entitlement, incidentally, boys are no worse than girls but it shows up more in them. Boys get physical in their teen years. Their moms may feel intimidated, and rightly so. Here's a guy with no conscience who comes on like a commando raider. Mom backs away. Girls will feel just as entitled, but they do not behave so physically, nor are they as big. Girls act out their entitlement in other ways. All entitled kids are masters of manipulation, but girls particularly so.

How does one catch the conscience of the king? How do we turn entitlement around and instill in spoiled children an internal sense of right and wrong? In the clinic we come up against this constantly.

We believe that the earlier you start, the better your potential success. We mentioned this previously in the discussion of preschoolers. Today is not too soon.

Willard's grandmother would be the first to cry out, "Oh, no! We've been giving Willard his way for too long. We couldn't crack down now if we wanted to. Why, even in small ways, if we try to tighten up, he absolutely has a fit. No. It's too late."

It's never going to get any "less late." We already pointed out that parents attempting to tighten discipline and structure in a preschooler can expect storms. Children in the early school years will generate much bigger storms. Still, the prognosis for healthy change is bright, although remnants of problems from overindulgence will linger.

When children are young, the stakes are pretty low. That is, the consequences of their youthful indiscretion have not escalated to alcohol, drugs, or promiscuity. Thus, the earlier the better for parents to take a stand and draw appropriate lines. Children who would grow and nurture a sound conscience must have parents or surrogates who let them get hurt while it doesn't hurt too much, to help them internalize controls.

Fortunately, and particularly with very small children, you have children's innermost natures working in your favor. You can turn their fear to your advantage. Remember Willard's fear that there was something he could do to lose what he held most dear. He was seeking the lines and not finding them. Every time he crossed a line, it wasn't there anymore. As much as Willard would howl and carry on if his life were suddenly more structured—that is, if the lines were thickly and clearly and closely drawn—his innermost being would know he needs those lines. He would fight them desperately, he would cross them deliberately, but he would know they were there. And he would learn that crossing them would not forfeit the love he craves. That fear would abate, and as it faded, Willard could take a giant step forward toward responsibility.

Parents who wait until early adolescence, when separation of parent and child begins naturally and the fears have shifted, will find change of any sort very difficult. The parents' influence is diminishing drastically and their children are naturally and correctly turning more and more to people outside the family. Already entitled, the kids will turn to other kids and adults who can reinforce the rebellion, the sense of invulnerability. Almost always, parents have to depend on some other residential situation to turn the child around. If the entitled child reaches adolescence, parents absolutely need outside help.

One form of outside help is therapy, of course. Another is detention, or alternative residence. There are times when the only way to help child and parent together is to separate them, to get the child out of the home. Alternative residence is not a cure-all. It brings its own problems. Residence personnel are often understaffed and therefore forced by necessity into power struggles. This makes it an unfortunate us-versus-them situation. Often children in these situations are considered management problems rather than people in need of help to grow. We find sometimes that residence kids, too, have been abused, neglected, and mismanaged by the system, as well as by their families.

Therapists and workers also often find themselves in a frustrating, nonproductive trap. Several of us in the clinic work or have worked with children in detention. Entitled kids can be absolute monsters, but just as often they are absolutely charming. They look so salvageable, so attractive. The workers get their rescue fantasies up in full gear. The more they invest of themselves, the more they discover that they actually mean nothing to the child. They are a means to the child's end—to get his or her own way. In their desire to help, the workers sometimes forget the cardinal fact: manipulation is ingrained and well honed in the entitled child. So is absence of conscience.

Exemption

The other side of entitlement is exemption. As we mentioned before, these kids (and adults!) are past rebellion.

They're defiant. "I'll do what I please. I am exempt from your silly rules. Rules are for lesser mortals."

The exempt child possesses absolutely no conscience. When outsiders try to impose rules upon him, they deserve whatever he wants to do to oppose them. In his own eyes he is smarter. He is stronger, at least in some way. He is above everyone else. Not every exempt child will turn into a serial killer or rapist, of course. But as you look at the actions and statements of those extreme lawbreakers, you can see exemption in every one of them.

Girls, of course, slip from entitlement into exemption just as much as boys do. It is the exempt girl who is positive she cannot become pregnant, no matter how much she fools around. Others may need a high-school diploma. She does not. If she takes to the streets, as some do, things will go her way. Just watch. The forces of destiny move others, but not her. She does not need God.

One example of a child who's headed for exemption is James's black hole, Willard. Willard's entitlement is a pain in the patoot to everyone around him, but is their temporary discomfort reason enough to try to change Willard's ways? Absolutely. Having parents or surrogates who are too fearful to take a stand puts Willard—and every such child—at enormous risk for self-destructive behavior.

> **Chasten your son while there is hope, / And do not set your heart on his destruction.**
> **(Prov. 19:18)**

Tied with this whole issue of indulgence and entitlement comes an issue that looms very large in the heart of every child: what is fair and what is unfair.

It Ain't Fair!

Little Aubrey was pouting, and that was highly uncharacteristic of the Sunshine Princess. "It's not fair! Jimmy is allowed to do lots of things and I'm not!" It was the only negative note Dr. Warren had ever heard from the child (of course, he wasn't the one who had to get her to bed at night).

James griped, "They let Aubrey get away with murder. I was never allowed to do that stuff. It isn't fair!"

Fair and unfair. It's the watchword of kids this age because of the black-and-white nature of their world. They're into justice, big time.

This is the time when children must learn the ugly truth about justice and fair play:

Life is not fair. But it should be just—which it is not always, either.

Fairness is not the issue, actually. Trust is. Kids must learn that, and this is the age to learn it.

James described what fair means. "Fair means you don't take one kid to the doctor because the other one doesn't have to go, so you're treating the one kid unfairly. But if you take the other kid to the doctor when he doesn't have to go, that's unfair too. Fair is, parents can't stay up any later than little kids. That's treating everybody all alike. That's what fair is."

Unfairness can stick in the craw for a lifetime. Elaine recalled, "I crocheted a doily in home economics in the eighth grade. My teacher looked at it and said it was nice, but that it didn't represent enough work to earn highest marks. Aprons and slippers were earning A's, but she gave me a B-minus. Do you realize how much time crochet requires? I spent four hours just on one round alone!"

Eighth grade. Twenty years ago. And the unfairness still burned bright in Elaine's memory.

James's notions of fairness aren't at all what Elaine and Roger have in mind, of course. Adults generally don't see fairness in the same light kids do. They see fairness, instead, as what is appropriate for each family member— not a case of even-steven for all concerned, but appropriate.

Mom and Dad set the tone of the family, obviously, according to what they believe to be the best interests of each member. Implied in their power and control is, *Trust me. I know it doesn't seem fair to you, but we're saying with our actions, trust us to do the best for you.*

Elaine sniffed. "The kids don't buy it. I tell Aubrey to go to bed and instantly she's whining, 'But Jimmy, grouse grouse grouse.' We tell Jimmy to go to bed and there he starts saying, 'But you get to stay up. Dad gets two pieces of pie and I can only have one.' It doesn't matter that he doesn't have enough appetite to handle two."

"He will."

"Oh, I know. I dread when he gets to be twelve and really gets hungry. But you see what we're up against."

" 'Up against' is a good phrase for it," Dr. Warren agreed. "All kids complain about what they perceive as unfair. Don't get distracted by that. Your message, both explicit and implicit, is, *Trust me. Trust us. It will come out best.* You're not out for fair as the children define fair. You're out for *just.*"

Fearful parents may also raise children who express their fears as extreme shyness and avoidance.

The Shy and the Mighty—The Timid, Fearful Child

"I didn't really notice how shy Jimmy is," Roger mused, "until Elaine mentioned it. He doesn't get along well with kids his own age and he doesn't seem to want to be around adults."

"Do you feel his shyness is cause for concern?" Dr. Warren asked.

"You've heard the term 'painfully shy.' *Painfully* is the key word there. That's what I was. I suspect he is too. Yes, I'm concerned."

"Have you ever told him that? Ever voiced your concerns?"

Roger's face went blank. Apparently it would never in a million years have occurred to him to discuss the matter with James.

There are, of course, degrees of shyness, and James

would probably rank at the low end of the seriousness scale. Degree of shyness may simply be a genetically determined temperament characteristic. Some children are gregarious and fit into any crowd scene instantly. Others would rather be off by themselves, doing one-person sorts of things in familiar circumstances, avoiding contact or relationships with others. Then there are the shy children like James, mildly reluctant to enter new social situations. By temperament they don't adapt to change or to social situations quickly. But they can adapt well, given a little more time than most folks. These children, like James, can benefit immensely from a journeymate. In our practice we differentiate these children who are shy by natural temperament from the children who are victims of excessive fears.

Because school is the major reality of children's lives, school is where the shyness shows most clearly. We identify two problems common to children suffering the burden of fear: school avoidance and school phobia.

School avoidance and school phobia.   "School phobia," Elaine said, bobbing her head. "I read about it in a magazine article. That's James's problem, all right, and it says you can only solve it with therapy."

Dr. Warren nodded. "And what did the article say about school avoidance?"

"You mean, as something different from school phobia?"

"Yes, a separate situation from school phobia."

"Nothing. It only talked about phobia."

"Let's discuss school avoidance."

In the comic strip "Calvin & Hobbes," Calvin zeros in on his school building through the sights of a fighter plane. He lets the guns and rockets rip, leaving nothing but a smoldering crater where once stood bricks and blackboards. His plane swoops into the sky, the deed done, as he cackles gleefully. In the final panel, he is walking onto the school grounds with a heavy sigh, nothing at all having changed.

Calvin takes his fantasies to the extreme, which is one of the charms of the comic strip. Calvin doesn't just want to avoid school, he wants to pulverize it.

School avoidance is extremely common. Nearly every child experiences it in some mild form. Parents may be able to detect it in the early grades or when the child must change schools or location.

School avoidance is characterized by a reluctance to attend, a fear of facing the new situation, of separating from Mom and Dad. In this case, the child's primary fear is of the new situation.

School avoidance: I'm afraid I can't be successful in this new situation.

Contrast that fear with

School phobia: I'm afraid to leave Mom and Dad.

School avoidance, then, is a fear of what's out there, while school phobia is a paralyzing fear of leaving home. Actually, there's some of each problem in the other. Both may be dismissed as "excessive shyness." Both are the manifestations of unresolved fears, but school phobia is the much more significant problem.

Easing the problem. "My wimpy little boy turned into a mighty monster! From Mickey Mouse to Mighty Mouse," Elaine said, wagging her head at the memory. "He kicked and screamed. It scared me. I was afraid he'd have a stroke or something, his face got so purple. He absolutely did not want to go to school!"

"First day?"

"A little on the first day. But the big blowup—I mean the really big one—happened when he was supposed to go back after Christmas vacation. The school is crowded and they were moving some of the classes out to the portables. You know, rooms sort of like mobile homes."

"And his was one of the classes."

"I tried to reason with him. I said things like, 'It's the same teacher and same students. It's just in a different place, is all.' And then I got stern. I told him to calm down and quit acting like that. Nothing worked."

"How would you do it were that to happen tomorrow?"

"That's what I'm asking you."

"What do we recommend for other fears?"

"Address the fear, not the fright. Reasoning with him and telling him to quit acting up is addressing the fright, true?"

"True."

"Balance fear with facts. I did that when I told him his school would be the same, just in the outside room."

"And?"

"You mean about the empathy. And the journeymate."

Dr. Warren nodded. "How would you phrase the idea of empathetic journeymate in words?"

And Elaine caught on. " 'I know it's scary for you. I'll walk with you on your first day.' " She sat back, beaming. "For the first time I feel hopeful about James and his school problem."

School phobia presents a far more difficult problem. On the surface it seems so specific about going to school. The child focuses on school (in psychological parlance, we would say the "presenting complaint" is school). In our practice we see some startling reactions. Children get sick at school, get hurt, react violently to what ought to be harmless, gentle situations. We see a lot of fear, panic, and temper outbursts, and somatic, or physical, complaints are very common. It takes a lot of digging to learn for certain that the real dynamic is separation from home.

In Chapter 2 we mentioned Fern Roberts, whose son Michael is genuinely school phobic. Fern divorced when her children were small; Michael was two years old and Gail was six months. Fern and her children illustrate a situation we find almost always in cases of true school phobia. When we see a child who is afraid to separate from Mom (or Dad, for that matter), we are looking at a mom who is afraid for her child to separate. Either there is a bad marriage or the parent is imposing major unfinished business on the child, or both. Unfinished business may be the parents' unconscious desire to keep the child young and dependent, or an unhealthy wish for the child to remain close, a surrogate partner. In any case, the unspoken message to the child is, *Don't leave me. I need you here.*

Fern had no idea she was projecting that message; she was not aware of it herself. We had to work with her first, before Michael's problem began to abate.

The intensity of a school phobia constantly amazes us. Docile, compliant kids may start swearing, screaming, and kicking. Michael Roberts, for example, was a pseudo-mature model of deportment. Every response Michael made was accompanied by a polite honorific: "Yes, sir." "No, ma'am." "Thank you, sir." He was just so suave and in control—until it came to school. Then he flat out refused. The battle of Iwo Jima was a picnic compared with Michael versus school.

When Fern tried to physically carry him from the house to the schoolbus, his flailing arms and kicking feet took out a picture window. As she dragged him down the sidewalk he took out an azalea bush. The other bus riders gaped in vicarious ecstasy. She hauled him up the bus steps and he took out the bus driver; the guy ended up with nine stitches.

In counseling, school-phobic children have told us:

"I really worry about something serious happening at home while I'm gone. Maybe a burglar will break in, or my mom will have a car wreck."

"All the time I'm in school, I'm afraid something will happen to Mom. I can't help it."

Michael said, "If I'm here in school there's nobody to take care of things at home."

Children making these statements are absolutely serious. It never occurs to them that a grade-schooler can't do much about any of that, should it happen. We find that these claims often are manifestations not of fear but of displaced anger at Mom for clinging so painfully. A grade-schooler would never dream of hating Mom or being down-deep angry, so the child projects the anger onto burglars and car wrecks.

Treatment for school phobia requires a therapist because the issues causing it are so complex. The parents cannot simply say, "Today you go to school." The parents, as well as the children, need help.

In such cases, the children cannot simply fold their hands and wait until we've satisfactorily addressed the parents' problems. They must go to school. So we develop a behavioral plan, setting step-by-step goals. Usually the first goal is for the child to stay there all day (occasionally half a day). Mom takes the child to school. A person at school comes out to the car to meet the child. The child may not end up in class. Class attendance is not the specific goal. Staying at school is. The child may go to the nurse's office or the counselor's office. The child does not call home. Mom does not call the child. Obviously, the child's school is as deeply involved in the project as is the therapist.

That goal accomplished, a new one is set up: class attendance. Once that goal is met, class participation, in stages, becomes the goal. And all the while the child is being reintroduced to school with his phobia reduced to manageable size, we work on the root problems, the linkage between child and parent.

Sometimes a child's anxiety is so overwhelming we must use medication to break the cycle. Hospitalization may be necessary. The issue here, you see, is enmeshment and separation, not school itself. We have seen kids miss a year of school as we tried to get their lives and their parents' sorted out.

Dealing Dad In

Willard the Scourge did not suffer excessively from school avoidance. In fact, he considered school as simply one more place to wreak havoc. He loved intimidating the likes of his neighbor, James. On the surface, he was the predator.

Poor old James was the prey.

Roger sat back in the plaid sofa, his mouth pressed into a thin, tight little line. "So you think that I can make a positive change just by becoming more involved with Jimmy. I don't think you realize what a mama's boy he is. Something goes wrong—he scuffs his knee or whatever—he runs to Elaine. Not me."

"Just as my Matthew runs to his mother. Yes," Dr. Warren said, "a woman naturally emerges as a nurturer. This might sound sexist or stereotypical. I don't mean it that way. I'm talking about the way children relate to adults. Men, fathers, are enablers. Again that can be misconstrued. Persons working with codependency issues talk about enabling in a negative sense. I mean a very positive sense. Fathers help their children do things—enable them to do new things."

"Mothers enable, too, in that sense."

"Absolutely. Mothers do so more than fathers. They teach children to master buttons, shoelaces, bicycles, tableware, a thousand things. Mothers civilize them. Housebreak them, if you will. I'm not talking about the way things actually are. I'm describing the way children *think* parents are—the children's perceptions of adults, particularly parents."

"So I should help Jimmy learn to do things?"

"For starters. He fears physical activity because he fears getting hurt. Rather, that's the presenting fear, the surface fear. Deep down inside, he still hasn't resolved that primal fear of adult power. By helping him do physical things—play ball, ride a bike, ride his skateboard, climb trees—you do two things. You become a journeymate with him, providing him with someone to walk beside him as he masters his fears, and you also allay that fear of adults left over from his earlier childhood. You, the most significant adult male in his life, are getting down on his level, relating to him at his level. He also needs his parents' approval, and by encouraging him you give him that as well."

"What do kids do who don't have a father? I'm thinking of a neighbor kid, Michael. His mother is divorced. No father."

"That, ideally, is where the church would step in, providing significant opposite-sex adults for children of single parents."

"Sort of a Big Brother thing."

"A role model, an enabler in the positive sense, a companion and journeymate. In the best-case scenario, the mother would have such help in place before the separation. That never happens. The next best is to find a man, perhaps with children the same age, who can partially fill the need."

Roger thought about that a moment. "This wouldn't be a boyfriend situation or romance. We're talking practical fathering, right?"

"That's right. An arrangement made for the child's welfare—the husband of a trusted friend, another father at school, whatever."

"Hmmm. You said 'for starters.' What else?"

"Talk to him. What was it like when you were a kid? Was life perfect, or did you—"

"Perfect?" Roger blew a raspberry. Then he sat quietly, thinking for a moment. "I get you. Let him know he's not alone in his fears."

"Exactly. We all have them. We all survive them. It's important for him to know that. And you are the one to talk about it with him because, as his father, you are the man he looks up to most."

"Which is what you meant when you said only I can help him."

Dr. Warren nodded. "It will cost the one commodity you have the least of: your time. But it will pay infinite dividends."

"I have patients who need me."

"And a son who needs you, also."

For a minute or two, Roger studied infinity beyond the office wall. He took a deep breath and let it out slowly. "One more thing. Have you any idea where I can find a video on how to play softball?"

BEYOND SCHOOL

Although school looms largest in a child's life, it is not 100 percent of a child's existence. Fears and concerns evidence themselves in ways that are not directly school related. Also, in these early years the child has to do a lot of learning and growing that is not (or should not be) connected to school. Let's look at some of those ways and lessons before going on to the next stage of the child's growth.

8
What Do You Think of Me?

Dear Troid,

Well, what did you think of that? You saw it all. I know you did, because you were up on the porch roof. I saw you there. I'm talking about when I was coming home from school and Craig and those guys were leaning out of Craig's mom's car windows yelling. I could of crawled in a hole.

Gretchen didn't have to say, "You couldn't hit a fly ball with a can of bug spray." She thinks she's so special because she's the only girl on the softball team. And Bruce calling me a weenie. But Craig was the worst, hanging out the car window like that, telling the whole world I'm a chicken. I'm not a chicken, Troid. I just don't want to play softball, is all, and just because I wasn't going with them to softball practice doesn't mean I'm a weenie either. I make good grades and those dweebs don't even notice.

Those guys are jerks anyway. All of them. Even Gretchen.

Especially Gretchen.

Your friend,
James

I'M AFRAID I'LL FAIL COMPETITIVELY

"There is this wonderful toy company in California," Elaine Tanner bubbled, "that only makes noncompetitive games. The players combine their efforts to prevent some terrible thing from happening."

"Such as?" Dr. Warren asked.

Elaine shifted on the new plaid sofa and crossed her legs. "Oh, there's one where everyone works together to save the whales. And one where you try to keep a bulldozer from reaching a beaver dam. They're cooperative games instead of competitive. I never let Jimmy play those cutthroat games."

"Why not?"

Elaine frowned, as if everyone understood the answer to that without asking. "Why, because if someone wins, that means someone has to lose. And little children are so sensitive and tender. They should never have to feel like they're losers."

"You are absolutely right, I believe," said Dr. Warren, "and also absolutely misguided. Let me explain why. Children, particularly those in early grade school, are extremely sensitive about losing. So true! It hurts, and they hate to do it. Loss can stay with them for a lifetime. But . . ."

Elaine was misguided in another important respect, he explained. Children must and will engage in some kind of competition among themselves. All the carefully structured cooperative games in the world will not quell their innate need to compete, to excel, to win.

Then what about the losers? Elaine is right about that too. Losing really hurts. Winning and losing are, in early grade school, intricately intertwined with the resolution of newly emergent fears.

We encourage parents to use play therapy, structure, and discipline to help a child deal with the prickly fear of losing.

The New Face of Play

About the time they start kindergarten, or perhaps first grade, children begin to identify not with the potential victim of harm but with the aggressor. Not with the Smurfs, but with the Terminator. They are learning about boundaries: Here is where I stop and that's where you begin; now how do I deal with that?

But the learning is not a cognitive thing. Again, the children of ages five, six, and seven learn hands-on, physically, by doing and experimenting and observing. By experience. Through imagination. These are still the door to growing up inside.

These experiences and observations that teach so much about personhood are based on rivalry and competition. "If I am better than you at Nintendo, that makes me different. I am me, and I can hop Mario over chopping jaws like nobody's business. But you can ride a bike without any hands and I cannot. You are you."

Separateness and similarity define personhood. Rivalry and competition identify what is separate and what is similar.

Play becomes broader now, more worldly, more detailed. A year or two ago, a doll could be anything. A corn cob, a bit of rag. Now action figures and Barbie dolls—lifelike play objects—take over. Toys no longer symbolize whatever it is the child is working on at the moment. They have to look like what they are. As they enter school, kids get into serious bike riding and skateboarding—action stuff. This reflects, in part, the fact that they are less tied to home and also that they're getting into more adult interests. And mobility is one of them.

Is this unique to our generation? Memoirs of Northwest coastal Indians four generations ago contain this item, which we paraphrase: "We were constantly scolding the children for being so lazy. When they went up to visit friends at the other end of the village [which was lined out along the seashore so that all the longhouses fronted on the water], they would shove off in the (large) canoe and paddle there. It couldn't be more than [a couple hundred yards] but they were too lazy to walk." The mystique, of course, was not to avoid walking but to use the adults' mature means of transport.

Children this age start getting into model building and other realistic representations of the adult world. *Ranger Rick* gives way to *Off-Road* magazine. Real life.

And, to Elaine's dismay, competitive games.

"I really like Monopoly!" James crowed. "I'll play with Craig's older sister and sometimes I win. Dad and I played one night. It was great. And Rook. Ever play Rook, Dr. Warren?"

Elaine looked crestfallen. "You see, Doctor? No matter how hard I try . . ."

"Like all children this age, James needs healthy competition. It's not just a preference. This is a genuine need for children. If you don't provide it, they make it. They know instinctively, no matter how they abhor losing, that you can't have success without some failure. But there are several balances that only you can provide."

The Role of Structure

"What balance?" Elaine looked dubious, with a sort of now-what-am-I-expected-to-do? expression.

"A balance between free time and structure, for one. Parents must provide an appropriate amount of structure with just enough free time."

"Easy to say. How do you know what's appropriate and how much is enough?"

"Excellent question! A good monitoring point is, How fearful is this child?"

Every child needs a well-defined program of what to do, balanced with an appropriate amount of free time to pursue his or her own interests.

> **Structure is knowing what you have to do, how much time you have to do it, and most of all, what happens if you get it done or fail to get it done.**

As we work with large numbers of children in this early-grade-school age range, we see the effects of every circumstance from over-structure to non-structure.

Over-structure is when every item of the child's day is organized. There is no room for imagination, no room for the random play children use to work through problems. Were Elaine to schedule every minute of James's nonschool time with lessons, organized play activities, and sports, his time would be over-structured. Were she to watch over his shoulder constantly as he went about his play and chores, he would be over-structured, or over-supervised.

When under-structured, given too much free time, a child becomes fearful and unhappy. He or she may act genuinely fearful. That's a key to look for. He may mask his fear by acting out. He may appear overly angry or active. Given a few more years, he may well turn to substance abuse to mask and dull the fear.

Latchkey kids lack structure in their lives. They get home before the working parent(s) and have all that loose time. Parents say, "She's supposed to be doing her homework," or, "He's supposed to get the laundry done." Rare is the child, though, who is mature enough, or pseudo-mature enough, to self-start. Lack of self-discipline is not a shortcoming of children. They are not mentally capable of structuring their own time. They need more miles, more maturity, before they can develop those skills.

"You don't understand," a confused father told us. "We try to impose structure of some sort and the kids instantly get all cranky. They hate structure! Making them do chores is hopeless."

Our reply to this is always yes and no. Children in the early school years are pretty law and order, black and white. They like structure and predictability, even when they complain about it. Children need chores around the house, not just because they feel they are part of the family, important as that is, but also it is a way to taste success in the eyes of their parents. Sure, they argue about it and grouse and try to foist the assigned task off onto an unsuspecting sibling (it never works; there is no such thing as a sibling who doesn't suspect). But it's a great feel-good experience to be successful at feeding the dog, taking out the trash, or whatever.

At this age, competition itself requires an adult's guidance and structure. As an example, we tell the story of

Fort Argument. It starts in the town of Toot Forks, Arkansas, a village so small it's not on any maps. Nothing more than a cluster of a few families, it rarely sends more than five or six kids to the consolidated county school in any one year. And those kids, left to their own devices, have built the world's greatest fort.

In the hoot-owl woods behind the village near the abandoned railroad tracks, they dug back into a steep bank. They raided a pile of railroad ties for the timbers to shore up the dirt walls and to lay ceiling beams. They covered it with black plastic tarp and so much leaves and duff you can't see it. So long as they were industriously occupied in its construction, the kids got along great.

They furnished it with plastic milk jugs of water and earthen benches. They stockpiled smooth, round stones from the creek—ammunition for slingshots. When they had cut up an inner tube and made the slingshots, they were armed and dangerous and ready.

Then Fort Argument fell apart—not the fort itself, but its personnel. The kids argued over who was in command. That settled, they argued over who died when in battle. They argued over who possessed the fort. They argued over every little thing any of them brought up. The fort wasn't fun to play in anymore and it stood abandoned for several years until a new generation of kids discovered it and renovated it . . . and after the renovation, fell to arguing.

Kids can get a game of softball together. But if that game is unsupervised and unstructured, they end up fighting. As much as they might argue against an umpire, they can't umpire themselves. They don't have the maturity yet.

Television, videos, and games such as Nintendo are themselves highly structured. With the TV and videos you sit and watch, period. With the games, you follow precise and unforgiving rules of play. But the *use* of these structured items is almost always unstructured, and therefore almost always subject to abuse. Never underestimate structure.

And Then There's Discipline

Discipline makes structure work. But it serves another important purpose. Discipline dispels that nagging fear in a small child's mind that somehow there is something one can do to lose the parents, or at least the parents' love. James's nemesis Willard, that dark cloud living next door, suffers from that very fear, you will recall. It does not automatically resolve itself. It lingers from age to age as the child grows. Willard rejects any thought of discipline. On the surface he would fight it bitterly were it imposed.

Down inside he would embrace it with open arms.

There is yet another use for discipline, the quelling of the curious fear that is just beginning to grow in these children. This nascent fear whispers in their ears that they can never finish growing up. Instead of galloping purposefully through life, they will end up stumbling in confused circles, stuck in some phase. Discipline helps dispel that fear by keeping them going straight and true, defining the road, the boundaries.

In summary, kids this age are very much into structure and what is right and wrong. If they can't see the limits and the way ahead, it's scary. They fit comfortably into structured boundaries.

Complaining the whole way.

THE SWEET SMELL OF SUCCESS

Put the kids' innate competitive spirit together with a well-balanced mix between structure and free time and you've got a perfect recipe for success. That all sounds great, but how, specifically, do parents go about that? And exactly what constitutes success, particularly in the eyes of children?

As they venture out of the house and away from Mommy to live a whole new life in a different world for part of the day, children also begin their lifelong lessons about the importance of success and achievement. They will define and redefine success and achievement until the day they die. At ten, James is doing just that. Aubrey, at four, soon will.

A new fear, unfelt before, emerges:

I'm afraid I won't succeed in life.

With its companion:

I'm afraid I have little or no value.

In other words, *What is success?*

The Fear of Losing the Power-Wielders' Approval

With these new concerns comes a subtle shift of power. Preschoolers feared the power of adults (parents in particular) to hurt and overwhelm. Now, as they enter school age, they fear losing the approval of the power-wielders.

With the shift comes a big, big kink in the plow line. If children have not comfortably resolved their earlier fear of other people's power, they are not going to succeed at this new stage.

In his letter, James claimed that he could play softball if he wanted to but he didn't want to. The unstated reason he did not want to was that he was intensely afraid of being hurt by something or someone beyond his control. The old preschool fear of powerful adversaries had not been resolved; it simply took on new dress. Fear was keeping him from participating, but its currents ran far deeper than just a fear of getting bopped by a wayward ball. The robber in the closet—his fear of powerful others—was stealing not just James's joy, but his growth experience as well.

But now, as he has become older, he has another fear and concern, the opinion of peers, especially those peers hanging out of car windows. That fear adds itself to the growing pile of unresolved earlier fears to give James a heavy, heavy burden.

Who the Power-Wielders Are

James has to feel he has the approval of other people on three broad fronts.

Parents. Mommy and Daddy have to approve of what James does. They need not approve of everything. But he must be acknowledged by them as a winner at something.

Other significant adults. Uncle Fred, his teacher Miss Hoy, the next-door neighbor (not Willard's side; the other side), some or all of these people, important in his life for one reason or another, must recognize some triumph, some superiority, that James boasts.

Peers. This is where James fell down. The kids his age think he's a scaredy-cat. It doesn't matter to them that he makes almost all A's. It doesn't matter that he's the class spelling champ. They don't really care if, at age ten, he has mastered touch-typing.

And yet (grade school is really, really tough, you know—all these complexities) his parents and teacher do recognize those achievements. So who defines what success is?

Everyone but James.

Success, in the eyes of a child this age, has little to do with actual achievement. Success depends on what those other people call success. James's achievements, if any, must be in the eye of the beholder. This is true of all children this age. James, with his near-perfect grades, was ridiculed because he didn't play softball. Gretchen and Craig and those other jocks didn't recognize academics. Therefore academics don't signify a field of achievement.

Up until now, what peers thought didn't mean diddly. In fact, two- and three-year-olds are the most selfish little people you can imagine. They will hoard toys and grab the biggest piece of cake without a care in the world that their peer group might think they are greedy. Now, in school, James and others his age put an enormous weight on what the others think. They must feel the experience of appearing successful and admirable by all three groups, the parents, the peers, and the significant other adults.

One or two out of three is not enough. It has to be all three groups.

As always, success is relationship oriented. It's how others feel about you and not what you actually did.

Remember our mention in Chapter 1 of the nine-year-old girl who liked to spend recess in the library? Her mother tried to move heaven and earth to prevent the teacher from forcing her into active play.

Her case appears similar to James's. Both children shrink from play contact with others. Like James, this girl was afraid of the power to hurt, which uncontrollable playmates possessed.

Dr. Warren explains. "Sure, you might get boffed in the face with a softball—every parent's orthodontic nightmare. But it's part of the price you pay for honing your skills and establishing your place in a competitive game or sport. James and this girl were both avoiding competition even though competition is crucial for growth at this age. Therefore, no significant growth could occur."

When the school counselor finally set the girl's mother down, she learned that the mother herself had avoided competition in her own childhood. Mom had not mastered that growth step either.

WHEN THE POWER GOES SOUR—FAILURE AND DISCOURAGEMENT

When James and his peers don't enjoy the approval and admiration of all three of these groups, thus allaying the fears inherent in this age, a new fear crops up. If the child could voice it, it would sound like this:

"I'm never going to make it in the world. I'll be a failure."

This one is particularly devastating because it becomes a self-fulfilling prophecy. If this one is not resolved, James will set himself up to fail. Oh, he certainly won't mean to sabotage himself. Throughout life he'll struggle desperately to resolve all those fears of the past while, beyond conscious level, he'll pull the rug out from under himself over and over again.

There is a middle ground, and it is by far the most preferred place to make a stand because it represents a wholesome balance. Elaine Tanner's brother Fred found that balance.

Balance of Power

"So tell me about this Uncle Fred." Dr. Warren sat back in his leather chair and laced his fingers across his middle.

"Uncle Fred?" James grinned. "He's amazing!"

"He's been six years old his whole life," Elaine said with a sniff. "If he ever grows up, he might make something of himself. He's certainly smart enough."

"He sells baseball cards," James explained. "He has this little shop on the strip by the freeway. He sells other cards, too, and comic books."

"Would you say he is successful?" Dr. Warren asked.

"Oh, yeah! He owns the best baseball-card store in the country. He has some of the first Batman comic books there ever were. He has comic books from before he was born, and he's *old!* He's gotta be thirty!" James's face absolutely glowed.

Elaine's did not. "Success? Hardly. He received a very nice scholarship when he graduated from high school. He could have gone through college and really made something of himself. But he quit after the first semester. Can you imagine that? Just quit. Since then he's been bumming around."

"Is this baseball-card shop his first enterprise since leaving college behind?"

"That and the restaurant. He and some buddies went together into a spaghetti restaurant. Not the big franchise with a famous name, you know. It's just a little hole-in-the-wall place. It's never going to amount to anything. They're so short of funds he ends up busing tables sometimes. The owner? Busing tables? That's not what I would call a success. Fred is wasting his life."

"We get to eat spaghetti there anytime we want," James elaborated. "And he let me help try out some new recipes once. We sat around in the kitchen eating these new sauces. It was great. And when I said I didn't like one he said, 'then scrub that one' and he didn't use it!" The boy sat back in his chair. "I like Uncle Fred and he likes me."

I like him and he likes me. James and his Uncle Fred had achieved a balance Elaine and Fred had not. It is that delicate balance between approval and a sense of worth separate from success. Here is the most difficult lesson of all that the child must learn:

You are worthy whether you achieve or not.
Worth does not depend upon success.

It is a lesson Elaine had not yet learned. She had not yet balanced the need for approval and success against the innate and God-given worthiness of a person. Many, many adults fail to do that.

I like him and he likes me. That, to James, was sufficient.

Helping the Child Reach Balance

"You're saying James has to feel that he is successful in the eyes of those three groups." Elaine shook her head. "I can't control any of that. How can I help him?"

"You can't control it directly, I agree," Dr. Warren responded. "But you can help in several ways."

One of those ways is by *setting the stage.* Dr. Warren told Elaine she could help James enter situations where other kids and adults approve. Is there a computer derby at school where a peer group of computer aficionados meet to compete? They will understand James; they value the same things he does. He need not win the derby. He can achieve success by participating and being appreciated for it.

Elaine can help by working on *placing relational expe-*

rience ahead of tangible success. This will probably be new for her. She must come to realize that it is not a matter of James's (or Fred's, for that matter) succeeding, but that she applauds his efforts to succeed. She has to adjust her own definition of success to emphasize achievement less and uniqueness and individuality more. She must recognize that, for James, success and achievement are not an end in itself. Approval is the end.

James will almost certainly discover what he can do well. But Elaine and Roger must be there to *tell him,* implicitly and explicitly (and mean it!) that his worth is not determined by what he knows or how well he does it. His worth is determined by unconditional relationships, starting with their unconditional love and approval.

Children who do not achieve that balance, who grow up thinking worth is tied up in achievement, never resolve the fears we discussed earlier. They will continue to fear that they are not good enough, cannot grow enough, cannot buy enough strokes with their behavior, to amount to anything—in other words, to succeed. That constant undercurrent of fear in life robs them of life's joy. It's a bomb with continual fallout.

Fallout—How the Fear Affects Later Life

Some say that the middle-age crisis so many people feel has its roots in adolescence, and there is truth in that. "Who am I? Is what I am and what I do of value?" Those questions need answering all over again, particularly so if they were never satisfactorily answered in the first place.

But the deepest roots of the problem extend earlier, right down into the fear issues that were unresolved in grade school. The same old unresolved fears take on new form. Typically, the persons work hard to perform, to present the appearance of success. They do not understand that worth is not tied to rote performance. Eventually, usually around thirty-five or so, they find themselves getting pretty tired of trying to please everyone else. They are tired of doing everything right, and for once, despite the fact that they'll feel incredibly guilty about being self-ish, they want to please themselves. It all goes back to that unresolved fear (of lack of others' approval), that lesson unlearned.

"As a case in point, let me cite a family we'll call the Joneses," suggested Dr. Warren. "The child in question—he's a man now grown, incidentally—is Rick Jones.

"Rick's parents were kids during the Great Depression, and both of them lost their own parents then. When Rick's mother was eleven, her father was killed in a construction accident. Her mother died soon after, essentially of a broken heart. That left the girl who would later become Rick's mother, then not quite a teenager, with the responsibility for four siblings. By strange coincidence Rick's paternal grandfather also died while his children were still young. His grandmother sank into a chronic depression, and struggled to provide for her three children. Her boy, Rick's father, became the man of the family.

"The adversity taught both of Rick's parents that you are self-made. You can depend upon no one but yourself. They learned the value of holding on tight. As Rick and his younger sister were growing up, the constant message, never actually verbalized as such, was that you must take advantage of every opportunity you can. Miss none. Struggle to achieve success, and when you achieve it keep struggling, because you could lose it all in a moment. Work!

"Rick's parents indeed worked very hard. They prided themselves, and rightly so, on how well they supported their family. But in the process they paid the heavy, heavy price of being unavailable. I remember Rick reminiscing about the many Saturday afternoons when he wanted to go somewhere. He would ride his bike by himself because his dad worked every Saturday. *Every* Saturday.

"What Rick was never taught, because his mom and dad never learned it," Dr. Warren concluded, "is that a person's worth is not determined by what that person does or how well the person does it. Instead, worth is based on *who* that person is—a child of God—and *whose* the person is—supremely loved by the heavenly Father. In other words, your job, or money, or how clean your house is, or even how often you go to church, or how well you behave—those are all important, but worth is worth. God created you worthy. Worth is not something you can earn, any more than salvation itself is. It is His gift.

The solution, the way to have joy and satisfaction in life, is to work through those ancient childhood fears. Put them to rest.

We emphasize this crucial point: If the parent has not resolved the fears of childhood, that parent cannot lead the child to resolution. That parent is inadequate as a journeymate. Roger Tanner was learning this, to his temporary discomfort and the lifelong benefit of both himself and his children.

Let's get personal. How are you as a journeymate? To answer that question you must gauge how well you have allayed the fears of childhood:

- The fear of abandonment
- The fear of powerful people and their power to hurt
- The fear of losing the power-wielders' approval
- The fear of failure, especially in a new situation
- The fear of facing the world alone
- The fear of never achieving success or value

Spend some time analyzing your response to them, your attitude toward them today. Search honestly!

To help in your analysis review some things about your childhood:

As nearly as I can remember, my grade-school peers admired this about me:

The significant adults in my grade-school years appreciated this about me:

_____
_____
_____

My parents praised this:

_____
_____
_____

And they nagged me to do better at this:

_____
_____
_____

I can see the effect of these approvals and disapprovals today in these ways:

_____
_____
_____

How did these approvals and disapprovals, these points of praise and friction, influence me as I matured?

_____
_____
_____
_____

Finally:
Am I successful today? _____ Yes _____ No
Why or why not (i.e., on what is my success based)?

_____
_____
_____

Do I have value now? _____ Yes _____ No

Upon what is that value based?

_____

_____

_____

Obviously, it's not just children who must come to grips with these fears. Adult children must do this as well, and their parents also. A major problem in our society is that so many parents are still stuck in that trap of childhood, the fear that they'll never be good enough. They try to achieve success and worth now through their kids, the next generation. They are doomed to disappointment because people must find their worth by discovering who they are in God's eyes, not in drawing from the successes of others.

In a way, thinking your kids can define your personal success in life is magical thinking—that is, *If I wish it hard enough, it will come true.* Children are masters of magical thinking. To them, reality is a flexible thing, shaped by will and desire. In the next chapter we'll see how that sort of thinking affects the child's response to innate fears.

9
Helping the Mind Deal with Fears

Dear Troid,
Wait til I tell you what Hannah did today! This is
amazing. I mean, Hannah is weird anyway, right? (I
had to look up weird again. I can never remember how
to spell it.) She's the girl who sits next to me in school,
and her desk is always neat inside with her papers and
books lined up just so, and you better not bump her
desk and get it messed up inside or she's all over you.
Willard shoved her desk once just to make her cry, but
she didn't cry. She started swinging, and she was so
mad and so wild old Willard got this scared look on
his face and backed off and ran. I never ever saw
Willard run away before. Probably won't ever see it
again, either, because now he stays away from
Hannah's desk.
Anyway, Hannah's mom came to school this
afternoon. I heard her talking to Miss Hoy because the
window was open. She was saying she just doesn't
know what to do about Hannah. She says Hannah
cleans her room <u>all the time</u>. Can you believe it?
Hannah's always cleaning her room! I'm never going
to tell Mom that because she's always yelling at me
about my messy room. It's not messy. It's just lived in.
I can't imagine living in Hannah's room.
Someday I'm going to be an important doctor who
studies people like Hannah. I'll fix her up. I'll make
lots of money. I'll make so much money, I'll just pay
Hannah to be normal. That will be the easiest way to

fix it. Nobody wants a kid like Hannah around. Mom would get ideas. I told you Hannah is weird.

Your friend,
James

Poor Hannah was trying to deal with her fears with magical or wishful thinking. Everyone does that to some extent. But Hannah carried it to destructive extreme. She was locked in obsessive thoughts that emerged as compulsive behavior.

OBSESSION AND COMPULSION

No wonder a popular fragrance is named Obsession. An obsession is a persistent thought you cannot seem to get out of your mind. It is not based on reason, and yet it sounds perfectly reasonable. It is not based on fact, and yet it is absolutely real. All persons in the throes of incipient love want the object of their affection to be obsessed with them, to be haunted by the memory of their utter perfection. Wear the right perfume and stand back.

A compulsion, often based upon an obsession, is a ritualistic, repetitive action that's out of control. James's schoolmate Hannah obsesses about the need to be clean, the need to keep everything in proper order. That obsession drives her compulsion to maintain a clean room, an orderly desk. Children in first or second grade don't often have obsessions or compulsions, but disorders of that sort may well appear around age nine or ten and on into adulthood.

In the black-and-white world of children, you are either perfect or totally out to lunch. There is no gray area in between. Contrary to what most parents would claim, children tend to lean toward the perfectionism end of the scale. They strive for it, and when an obsession or compulsion consumes them, it consumes them perfectly.

Hannah was plagued by persistent, intrusive, unpleasant thoughts that took up an inordinate number of her waking hours. Such thoughts may or may not lead to compulsive behavior. In her case they did. She did not get her homework done; she didn't have time. She could not play with the neighbors; they would only mess things up. Hannah's extreme, perfect neatness and cleanliness is a common manifestation of deep fears. *If only I can be neat enough and keep my world orderly enough, maybe it will not fall apart.* Hannah literally cleaned her room ten times a day. She got nothing else done. She was so obsessed with thoughts of germs and dirt she drove her mother to distraction. Her mother would have been far more distracted if she knew that Hannah, as part of her obsession, was preoccupied with the fears of growing up.

Understand when we talk about obsessive-compulsive behavior we are not talking about the perfectionistic child who worries because he or she doesn't get a hundred on all the tests all the time. Kids worry about things. It's part of growing up (part of adulthood, too). Children this age are dealing with the fear they will not succeed, remember. Perfection guarantees success. That's natural, not pathological. Obsession-compulsion becomes a disorder when children like Hannah can no longer function well because of it.

Children who are locked into compulsive behavior and obsessive fears and worries need professional treatment, usually including medication. Certain medicines are dramatically successful in breaking the vicious cycle of ritualistic behavior and thinking so healing can begin. They succeed because there is a biological component to the ritualistic behavior and obsessive thinking.

Another case example involves Alexandra, a girl of ten. Alex was pitifully plagued with fear that her younger sister would be kidnapped. She was totally convinced that she herself had done something very wrong; she just couldn't remember what it was. Whatever she had done wrong, the punishment was sure to be the loss of her little sister.

Alex washed her hands. Dozens and dozens of times daily. She would go through the house straightening the rooms. Everything, absolutely everything, had to be perfect. On and on she went, washing her hands and putting things in order, hoping to atone for that fancied wrong. When her father came home from work and took off his shoes, she would run over and instantly align them just so at the foot of his bed. He claimed that if the dog ever got fleas, they'd have to arrange themselves in a straight line down its back. Alex could not make friends. In fact, she could not do anything.

With treatment, she is 180 degrees different. But it took medication and intensive professional therapy to bring her around.

If your child displays disabling obsessive-compulsive behavior, the kind of problem that goes too far beyond the perfectionism inherent in children, seek treatment immediately. This is one wound time does not heal.

Extremes aside, wishful thinking provides much power to cope with fears. Akin to magical thinking, dreaming and woolgathering (daydreaming) are useful tools in children.

DREAMING THE DREAMS

"Jimmy outgrew three pairs of sneakers in a year," Elaine said as she stared in dismay at James's feet, which regularly ate up shoes. "And those cycling shorts Aubrey wears used to come below her knees. I can't believe that those estimates about children costing twenty thousand dollars to raise take the shoes and clothing into consideration."

And yet, as much as children grow physically, by far the most of their growth occurs internally, where you can't measure the size. Fears spur that growth and direct it. So do impossible dreams, and the dreams are, in a way, the resolution of the fears.

I'm Afraid I Might Not Get it Exactly Right

A disgruntled wife wrote a letter to Ann Landers, complaining about her husband's table manners. "He is being passed up for promotion," the lady claimed, "because he insists on eating with his elbows on the table."

Ann didn't buy the wife's theory, but the letter typifies our attitudes these days. The message of media ads, of magazine articles galore, of society itself, is, *You can totally master all the problems and struggles of life if you just have the right things and do the right things.* A perfect life supposedly is achieved through the perfect devices to correct all the faults and imperfections. If that gentleman simply gets rid of his lousy table habits, success in the business world is his for the taking. Bad breath? Use brand-X mouthwash. Telltale dandruff? Try so-and-so shampoo. Two left thumbs when it comes to patio cooking? Toss a prepared bag in the grill, light it, and enjoy a perfect charcoal fire in minutes. Dandelions? Have we got a lawn spray for you! And on and on it goes.

Children just devour that media-fueled drive for perfection. It appeals to their needs, rings all their bells. The flip side of their hunger for perfection is the fear that they might not get everything right. Two sides, same coin.

Hannah's fear had slipped over the line into disorder, but most children find this annoying, not crippling. And they manifest it in various ways.

Think about James's next-door neighbor, Willard. He feared neither God nor man, right? Wrong. Willard was actually a fear-filled child. Not only was he still struggling with his early-childhood fears, he had the fear of failure common to his age weighing down upon him too. His route to success was simply to circumvent the fear. Sidestep it. By creating his own rules and setting his own standards for success he could make success be anything he wanted and needed. He considered himself exempt from the rules of common men.

Not even the movie characters Thelma and Louise could maintain that ploy forever. Sooner or later, Willard will get whacked, either by reality or the sheriff's deputies.

The child who learns this very important lesson will deal well with the fear of failure:

> **The secret to succeeding lies not in
> mastering life's daily struggles but in learning
> to cope with them successfully.**

THE JOY OF COPING SUCCESSFULLY

No child can get everything exactly right, and his or her imperfection magnifies the fearful child's fears. If that child can come to accept the idea that imperfection will do, the fears abate. You, the journeymate, can teach the child through interaction and example that the secret to joy in life is not perfecting it but coping with it.

How does a journeymate do that? By talking to the child, and talking to the child, and talking to the child. And modeling. The talk and the modeling reflect the parents' own confidence in their ability to cope.

I Want to Take the World by Storm and I'm Afraid I Can't

Roger Tanner asked a telling and important question: "I'm having trouble with my own fear of failure. How in the world can I help Jimmy?"

"At first this may sound like a waste of time," Dr. Warren responded, "but I assure you it is not: Dream with him."

"You mean like 'hopes and dreams'?"

"Exactly. Hopes, aspirations, plans, yearnings. Sharing these dreams between parent and child aids enormously in dealing with the fears of this age. And not too coincidentally, it greatly strengthens the parent-child bond, also."

In fact, we'll state it more strongly:

It is crucial that parents form the habit of dreaming with their children.

Dreaming with children pays an added dividend beyond growth. It makes adulthood a desirable state.

"Many times," Dr. Warren says, "a child will say something to the effect that 'I don't want to grow up. When you're grown up you never have time for dreaming.'

"I try to work with children in the context of play. Recently a girl said, 'When you grow up you don't have time for fun or play anymore.' Another child said, 'When you grow up, you lose heart.' Much too often they're right."

Roger looked a bit dubious. "I'm not sure I'd know what to talk about if we just sat down and talked."

"Then I'm not being facetious when I suggest that you don't sit down to talk. Stand up. Children do not do well just sitting and talking. It's one of the problems with children sitting at a desk in school so much. Drive out in the country a couple of miles and take a hike. Tear your bicycle apart and grease it. Build a wheelchair ramp together for your elderly neighbor. I have no idea if you even have an elderly neighbor, but you see my point."

"I do. Talk while we're doing something else."

"If you pause in what you're doing and just talk, all the better. But giving yourselves something physical to do will help the conversation. That's why fishing is such a great pastime for parents and children. You're doing something, but you sit around a lot doing nothing. And if you get skunked and catch no fish at all, it doesn't matter much."

Dr. Minirth voices the same point when he takes kids, his own and others, horseback riding. "From the back of a horse, children spill things they'd never say in a clinical setting, much less to parents."

Stuff to talk about. Even at ages six through eight or nine, reading to children remains important. Sharing lore about the family and about your family's background and culture also ranks high. Grade school is the perfect time for children to blot up stories about their past, to link them to their ancestors.

But kids this age need to dream too. Participate with them in dreaming for the future. It's not good enough to simply swap a couple of dreams and wishes. During play and talk, actively listen and participate in a discussion about the things kids dream of doing.

"For example," Dr. Warren offers, "my son dreams about being a professional baseball player. So I encourage him in that with questions such as, 'What do you think it will be like?' 'What are some neat things you'll be able to do?' 'What are some of the less-than-neat things?'"

There is a flip side to talking; sometimes the wrong talk can inadvertently damage a child's ability to cope with life.

Stuff to avoid. So often adults don't listen to these wild imaginings. Because the kids have no life experience to speak of, their notion of how the world operates can range pretty far out in left field. Their ramblings can get so ridiculous they become boring. Keep in mind it doesn't have to be accurate. It's a dream. It will probably change a thousand times before the child reaches twenty-one.

A worse mistake adults make than not listening is to put the dream down and try to smother it with a blanket of practical reality. What ought Dr. Warren be careful not to say to his aspiring baseball player? "You're never gonna play for the Texas Rangers, so quit this nonsense and get back to your schoolwork."

Here are some other no-no's:

"Dear, a girl would never make it on the rodeo circuit. Don't even think about it."

"You? A paleontologist? Ha! Do you realize how much expensive college you'd need?"

Throw the dream away and stick to the hard cold facts, and you've crushed more than just an aspiration. Instead of alleviating fears, putting the dream down makes children far more frightened about the future. And the future is already very scary, even without your help.

One of the ways kids cope with the frightening uncertainty of the future is fantasy. If you, an adult, think the future is incomprehensible, imagine what it must look like from the perspective of a nine-year-old with no experience of the past to make sense of what might lie ahead. Kids' dreams are their bridge to the future.

As preschoolers, children physically act out their mental processes. By grade-school age, children can still do that, but they have a new capability for processing the world around them. They can perform the play in their minds instead of having to physically act it out. That's basically what dreams and fantasy are. A girl imagines how many horses she will have someday. A boy pictures himself working amid the tropical trees he sees in a *National Geographic* article, high in the forest canopy with other researchers.

A more insidious mistake is to try to make our dreams theirs. It's insidious because we don't realize we're doing it. This is what psychologists call "unfinished business."

"Curious you should say that," Roger said after scrunching down in the plaid sofa and considering the point a few minutes. "Do you know who Virgil Fox was?"

"A virtuoso organist—one of my heroes too," Dr. Warren answered.

"I watched him in concert. He wore patent-leather shoes that caught the stage lights. His feet were all over the pedals, and of course his hands were all over four keyboards. He was amazing. So amazing."

"His performance of Bach's *Fugue a la Gigue,* ah!"

"Yes!" Roger beamed like a halogen headlight. "Oh my, yes!" The headlight faded. "Until you started talking about dreams here, I hadn't thought about this too much." His voice paused.

Dr. Warren waited.

When Roger spoke again there was a heaviness to his voice. "I have always wanted to be a concert organist,

that kind of virtuoso. I didn't realize how . . . how pathological my dream was until just now."

"Pathological? Explain, if you can."

"I ached to play but never bought an organ or took lessons, even after I could easily afford any organ I wished.
I'd clip articles about the men I admire and save them in a
secret file. I'd buy albums and never play them."

"Just Virgil Fox?"

"No. E. Power Biggs. All the great ones."

"Pathological is not the word you want. Hopeless desperation is not, either, but it's closer. You never shared this
dream with anyone."

"Never. Not even Elaine. In fact, especially not Elaine."

"May I suggest you share it with James?"

"I'm not sure I could," Roger said, straightening.
"When you started discussing unfinished business, my
dream hit me in the face, you might say. I bought James an
electronic keyboard when he was five. He never touches
it. Now I have him lined up for organ lessons with our
church organist two days a week. I told Elaine all these
reasons James should take organ lessons. It will improve
his coordination, and heaven knows it can stand improvement. Musical literacy is important. He can always get
work as a church organist while he pursues other interests. There is a growing shortage of church organists. So
many reasons . . ."

Dr. Warren completed his thought for him. "But the
only valid reason is that you want James to fulfill your
dream."

"And I never saw that until just now."

The next afternoon, Elaine Tanner sat on that same
plaid sofa talking about James and his dreams, but she
didn't realize she was doing so. "He's going through this
materialism stage. It really scares me, you know?"

"In what way?"

"Well, let's see if I can explain. We get lots of junk mail.
Who doesn't? Clothing and equipment catalogs and a
hunting-and-fishing catalog, although I have no idea why,

because no one in the family hunts or fishes. We even got a reloading catalog once. Do you know there is a whole catalog devoted to building bullets? A whole catalog! And toy catalogs."

Dr. Warren refilled her glass and his from the two-liter diet-soda bottle.

She went on, "He absolutely fixates on those catalogs, reads them over and over and over. He'll bring me the toy catalog and talk about some gizmo I would never in a million years buy him. We are materially well off, Dr. Warren, but too much is too much."

Elaine looks upon catalogs, newspaper ads, and the ilk as sales gimmicks. That's understandable. But children see a great deal more than that. They see in pictures the world beyond themselves.

Stuff to reveal the world. Let us say James picks up a Toys R Us flyer out of the Sunday newspaper. It's eight pages, full color, displaying the newest and greatest merchandise the toy dealers want you to buy. Roger and Elaine see it as a crass appeal to James's material instincts. James, having no idea what is materialism and what is not, sees it as a smorgasbord of marvelous things and ideas, a glimpse into the world beyond. He wants as much as he can get of it.

James is going to be stumbling across sales flyers his whole life, not to mention the myriad ads with which the other media assail him. Any way Elaine and Roger can blunt some of the crass appeal will benefit James. Treating the catalog as something totally different from a sales tool is one way.

So what else might Elaine do when James burrows into a catalog? Sit down and explore it with him. The two of them might go through the catalog not as a sales vehicle but as a dream vehicle.

"Look. The description here says this truck is only five inches long. That's about this long. That's a lot of nice detailing on something so small. If we had a truck like this, full-size, with four-wheel-drive, we could drive up to Mustang Ridge, like Mr. Wickers does. What would it be like, driving cross-country without a road?"

"If I had a full-size boat like that, know what I would do? Take it up to the lake and explore all the coves, one at a time, and have a picnic in every one."

"Look at this fashion doll! She has her own pony. What's the difference between that kind of saddle and a western saddle? Let's look it up in the encyclopedia."

"This book looks like it would be fun to read. Let's see if we can borrow it the next time we're at the library."

"They don't have any waterwings in the pool toys section. I remember waterwings when I was a little kid. It's how I learned to swim. Imagine these two floats attached to your shoulder blades; you know, where the wings sprout? You can't sink, but you're so clumsy in the water. You just sort of hang there, like this."

"Here's a police outfit—gun, badge, handcuffs. What would it be like to be a policeman?"

In summary, ignore the commercial aspect, that this company is trying to sell you something. Go for the seek-and-dream value. Ask questions and let the child's imagination fly. Listen. You'll learn a wealth of things.

I'm Afraid of Sexuality, Especially My Own

Elaine wrinkled her nose when sexuality was mentioned. "Sex education? The birds-and-bees talk? Heavens! Jimmy is much too young to think about that yet. When he's into his teens his father can sit down and explain things to him."

"A friend, Carol, was talking to my wife and me after church Sunday," Dr. Warren related. "The day before, Carol had chaperoned a busload of kids on a field trip. Her daughter and her Sunday-school classmates. Carol says that before the bus got out of the driveway she heard spontaneous discussion and joking about the use of condoms, sexual intercourse, and swimming nude. Elaine, these were children just entering seventh grade."

Moments later Elaine recovered the presence of mind to pick her jaw up off the floor. "Seventh . . . yes but . . . I mean, that's just three years older than . . . surely . . ." She wagged her head, completely bewildered. "It's so young."

It's so young. In our practice we have come to see that children without appropriate, healthy education concerning the facts about maleness and femaleness will fear their own sexuality. Always. Those fears, left unresolved, will lead the children into difficulties both immediately and later.

We have good clinical grounds for this:

> **Children's sexual problems and doubts are based in fear, and that fear is based in the fact that the children are not comfortable with their own sexuality.**

We find that every child is afraid of his or her own sexuality. Every child needs information appropriate to the age, not just in the matters with which the term *sex education* is usually associated—the facts and information, if you will—but also guidance to help the child feel comfortable with being male or female. Children who are not comfortable with themselves often escape their fears and discomfort in addiction of some sort, just as adults do. It might be obsessive-compulsive behavior such as little Hannah's intense penchant for cleanliness. It could be sexual acting out, alcohol, whatever.

As Dr. Warren discussed all this with Elaine, she took on a sort of resigned attitude. "Well. I see. I guess, then, I'll just have to get Roger to talk to Jimmy a couple of years sooner than we had anticipated."

"Good start, talking."

She smiled and bobbed her head. The smile faded into a blank look. "So what do they talk about?"

An excellent way to talk about this or any other topic is to link it to what kids already know. And they know relationships best.

***Provide information in the context of relation-
ships.*** Children, remember, weigh their whole world
on the balance of relationships. They read the interactions
among adults like you wouldn't believe. What they see
between Mommy and Daddy shapes their understanding
of sexual roles and expectations. By this we do not mean
those rare, unfortunate incidents when the child stumbles
into something that should not be stumbled into. We
mean day to day. How do Mom and Dad treat each other,
see each other, accommodate each other?

Modeling wholesome respect for the opposite sex, as
well as for the same sex, falls primarily to parents. What
would be a bad model? Words and actions that degrade or
belittle the opposite sex. A patronizing attitude and an excessively subservient attitude are equally bad. Negative
views of the opposite sex are damaging to children of
both sexes.

"See? She has two car-lengths along the curb, and she
still can't parallel park. I bet she couldn't park that car on
a football field without bumping into a goalpost. That's
just the way women are."

"The average woman can fix a television with a fork.
The average man can't find the fork."

"You'll just have to put up with your mommy. Women
get a little cranky during their time of the month."

"Super Bowl Sunday is a genetic anomaly of the Y
chromosome."

Negative, negative, negative.

An aspect of relationships that children innately understand and absorb is the actions they see before them.

Promote healthy sexuality by modeling privacy.
Privacy in our culture indicates respect.

"Oh. You're in the bathroom? I'll wait."

At a closed door: "It's just me." (Wrong: barge right in.
Right: knock, and probably wait.)

Children are into privacy big time at this grade-school
age. The child who at age three strips to the buff and

heads gaily down the sidewalk will, at age nine, hide in a closet to change the rubber band in her ponytail.

Children clearly perceive that parents who display respect for each other in marriage are displaying respect, by extension, to all persons of their gender. When Mom and Dad respect each other's privacy (yes, the kids instinctively know if Mom is rifling Dad's wallet unbeknownst to Dad, and if Dad is reading Mom's mail) the children blot up that respect because it's couched in terms the children understand.

In summary, modeling means not just sexual information or situations but parents' basic attitude toward one another—what they say and do not say, do and do not do—and modeling is crucially important.

A recent case illustrates an extreme result of inappropriate parental modeling. Chad, now nearly ten, has been in and out of trouble for years. He's been picked up several times for shoplifting and a couple of times at school he's gotten in trouble for swiping small items he doesn't need. He suffers frequent accidents that seem to be escalating in severity. First it was little things, like riding his skateboard off a curb into a storm drain, and wiping out with his bike. He's been hit by a car and attacked by dogs on two different occasions.

For years Chad's mom has told him things like the following statement and then put her words into action:

"I won't tell your father about your stealing; you know how he is."

"You'll probably get a tetanus shot for the dog bite, so we'll just tell your father you went to the doctor for your shots. We won't mention the stitches. Don't wear shorts until they heal."

"Your father wouldn't understand. This is just between us."

For years, Chad's dad has ignored his mother's opinion regarding every major decision the family has made: what kind of new car to buy, whether to move to a new home, how much money to pledge to the church.

They brought Chad to us not because of the stealing or the dog bites or the accidents, but because Chad is genuinely uncertain whether he is a girl or a boy. That, both parents agreed, is not quite normal.

Chad is incredibly afraid of his father. There, you see, are those primal fears of early childhood, still unresolved. But now Chad displays a lot of fear of his own sex too. Rampant fear. In desperation, his mother eventually talked to him about the birds and bees. Sort of. But Chad's true sex education has been Mom's constantly running Dad down and undercutting him, and Dad running Mom down, failing to show her even casual respect.

How are we helping Chad? We start first by helping the parents shore up their marriage. Then the standard formula, with variation, comes into play. This is the same formula you yourself use to allay children's fears: empathy, countering fear with facts, figuratively walking through them with the child. In Chad's case the therapist becomes the journeymate until his parents have healed themselves enough to take over. If Chad were denied professional help (and if his problem were not so extreme), a trusted adult would serve: a Sunday school teacher, school counselor or mentor, relative, or friend. That adult—a male would be best in Chad's case—would have to possess a healthy, respectful attitude toward the sexes and toward his own sex.

Empathy: "It must be terribly scary to not know for sure."

Facts: "Here are the physical differences, the hormonal functions, and the emotional distinctions, and what they mean to you."

The walk: "I will not laugh at you; this is serious business. I will not abandon you; when you need me I'm available. Let us talk when you feel like it. When I can help, I will do so."

Helping Chad now is wise. The sooner the better, because as the next few years unfold, Chad will begin naturally separating from his parents, seeking his own identity. And Chad has nothing upon which to build that identity. Social anxieties, triggered and exacerbated by a hormone surge around thirteen, make the teen years hard enough without adding the burden of all those childhood fears.

We gave Chad facts about gender differences. By middle childhood, children can relate better to facts too.

Provide appropriate facts. Elaine is right. James is not really ready to learn the nuts and bolts of sexuality. But he needs more than Elaine realizes. She and Roger may convey information through conversations, written materials they provide, or some other means to ease the situation and get the data across. Look at the matter this way: If you think you're uncomfortable about it now, you're going to be *really* uncomfortable about it later.

The victims of inappropriate or nonexistent sexual teaching parade through our offices constantly. Most of the girls we see incarcerated in jails or alternative residences had bad relationships with men, almost always with the father. In boys, the results may not be incarceration; they usually take other forms. But the end is the same: tragic consequences.

Opportunities for providing facts do not always come at convenient times.

"I read about this in a magazine, but I forget which one," a friend named Ron recalled. "The author told how one of his kids used the 'F word.' So the father asked, 'Do you know what that word really means?' Apparently the kids were all ears. This gave the father a perfect opening to talk about sex, about God's intention regarding marriage. Great idea! I could hardly wait for my own kid to use a sexually related word so I could do the same thing."

Ron snorted. "My big opportunity came when two stray dogs used our front yard for their liaison and my son asked me what they were doing. That was embarrassing."

"Did you use the opportunity anyway?"

"Yeah, but it sure wasn't anything to write a magazine article about."

Often the parents can set up an appropriate venue for

discussing sexuality. One of our friends took his elder son out on a father-son weekend of fishing and goofing off in a cabin near the Guadalupe River. Just the two of them. They talked about love, sex, sexuality, and God's gifts. The boy was about twelve. It worked so well, the man took his other son out in the same way at about age eleven. These days, eleven is probably not too young at all.

Discussions of the realities about sex and about sexual drives and responses are not a one-and-done occasion. As children grow and mature, they develop a more sophisticated knowledge of the differences between men and women, and what those differences mean. You will have to adjust your sex education for kids of different ages. More and more you will emphasize not just sex facts but God's plan for sexuality. The fact is, God made us sexual beings for our benefit. This is one area of your beliefs you do not want your children left in the dark about.

As children receive a clearer and clearer understanding not just of the facts of life but of the nature of sexuality, they will become more comfortable with their own sexual identity. They will see the picture and see how they fit in that picture. Their fear of the powerful thoughts and forces inside them will abate. Their uncertainties about their sexual identities will dissolve. Again, the fear is the catalyst for growth. Its resolution is the growth itself.

THE POWER OF THE WORD

This one is so obvious, people keep missing it.

"Everything great that was ever done started as a thought. Everything terrible too. Control your thoughts, and you control it all," says Dr. Minirth. "We are limited only by our thoughts. Read the scriptural account of the Tower of Babel. God said the builders could do it because they thought they could. I can do anything by thinking through Christ. The poet Virgil said, 'They can because they think they can.'

"The brain, like a huge computer, is filled with annals and stored messages. We think at between four hundred and twelve hundred words per minute. If you can control that, you can in large measure control your destiny. Storing healthy scriptural messages in your brain has an unbelievably powerful effect."

What messages? There are over three hundred Scripture quotations that relate directly to overcoming fear and anxiety. They reassure us that God is on our side and He will take care of us. They say, in effect, "Cast all your fear upon Him because He cares for you."

The subconscious can receive and respond to these messages below conscious level. You need not bring the memorized Scripture fully to mind (though that is certainly a comfort). These memorized assurances of God's love and protection work the same as all the other messages our brain processes below conscious level, the many rooms it explores without our conscious knowledge.

Scripture memorization, therefore, is not merely the province of Sunday school children out to win gold stickers and a pin at the end of the year. It's not a harsh duty. It is an exciting and powerful tool for dealing with fear and anxiety.

Children approaching their early teens are ripe and ready to make good use of this means of allaying fear. Younger children can certainly memorize scripture, and they should. They are in some ways better at it than their older peers. But older children grasp that these passages mean something important.

Appendix A provides a few of the many direct references in Scripture that can allay fear. Do not limit yourself to these. Find others. In a concordance, look up "fear" with special attention to the many "fear not" passages.

This method of dealing with fears doesn't just come overnight. It requires the repetitive use of Scripture memorization and review, over and over. The more you repeat it, the more the brain stores it, and the closer to the "surface" of your thoughts it remains.

I WAS A TEENAGE DOOFUS

These grade-school years are not the age when parents really start sweating bullets. If you think Mom and Dad look good with gray hair now, wait till the kids turn thirteen! Teenagers know everything and parents know nothing. Teenagers dress well; adults wear nerdy stuff. Teenagers are ready for sex, credit cards, drivers' licenses, and ownership of the Dallas Cowboys, and it's only the stuffy, antediluvian adults who are holding them back.

Next we'll explore how you, too, can hold some teenager back.

The Deep-seated Fears of Childhood

INFANT AND TODDLER
(THE BOTTLE AND BANKY SET)

- *I fear being abandoned.*

- *If I am abandoned, I fear I will lose my meself.*

- *I fear I can lose Mommy and Daddy's love and approval.*

- *The Oedipal phenomenon*

LATE PRESCHOOLER
(THE SANDBOX SET)

- *I am afraid of the power to hurt that big people possess.*

- *Nightmares and Night Terrors*

GRADE-SCHOOLERS
(THE SKATEBOARD SET)

- *I'm afraid I'll fail competitively.*

- *I'm afraid I won't succeed in life.*

- *I'm afraid I have little or no value.*

- *I'm afraid I might not get it exactly right.*

- *I want to take the world by storm and I'm afraid I can't.*

- *I'm afraid of sexuality, especially my own.*

PART FIVE

Teenagers

The Mall and Car-Keys Set

10
I'm Not Me but I'm Not You

THE TERRORS OF THE TEEN YEARS

Dear Hector,

I am a grown man. This is absolutely, utterly stupid. Foolish. I am writing a letter to a dog.

Can't help it. My son has the cat sewed up.

Speaking of sewed up, Hector, how are your stitches? You haven't been scratching them lately, so I assume they've quit itching. The vet assures us you're just fine. You'd better be, after all that money for spaying.

I guess Paul Warren is doing a good job on Jimmy. I mean James. Apparently he prefers to be called James. Maybe he's reading Ian Fleming. You know: "The name is Bond. James Bond."

No you don't know. Of course you don't. You're a dog, for crying out loud.

Warren says I can help James by doing this, so I shall. I'm supposed to air my feelings with these letters. Anything I want to write. There's some TV show about a teenager who's a doctor. Talk about fantasy! And he puts all his thoughts on a computer. The new medical criterion, apparently. Very well. Here I go.

James was telling me about the way the kids mock him and call him a scaredy-cat. A sissy. He can't possibly know how deeply his stories hurt me.

Because I am James. His stories are my story, his youth my youth. I remember, and ache. Their jeers echo in my memories.

You look at your newborn baby, hold him tight against your heart, and picture him growing up to conquer the world. Invictus! *He will become all the things you dreamed of being and never were. All the heroic deeds you imagined for yourself, your child will accomplish in your stead. I never foresaw when James was born that he might merely repeat my own painful childhood. Will he repeat my pitiful adulthood too?*

O God of deliverances, I pray You deliver my son from the misery of my own youth!

Dr. Roger Tanner

GROWTH AND CHANGES

James's father was finally coming to terms with his own unresolved childhood fears. He recognized them now. As he worked on them, he would be able to tackle the fears of the teen years too.

I'm Afraid of Growing Up

They were *goyim*, these two gentlemen—men outside the Jewish faith. They were watching a synagogue from across the street as the happy participants of a bar mitzvah came streaming out.

One man shook his head. "Look at the kid. He's what? Thirteen? 'Today I am a man.' Hmph. He was a kid this morning and he'll still be a kid tomorrow morning, and no religious mumbo-jumbo will change that."

The other man nodded sagely. "Say, doesn't your son get his driver's permit soon?"

The first man beamed. "Next Monday I take him down. He can't wait and neither can I. My kid, behind the wheel." He paused and smirked. "Think I'll look okay in gray hair?"

Every culture on record has a death rite. A marriage arrangement. And a rite of passage from childhood to adulthood. For example, the bar mitzvah ushers a Jewish boy into the beginning of a man's life. It is a door, a step, a chasm jumped. It is definite. Other cultures observe a wide spectrum of rites, but each, in the end, becomes that very same door. The two gentlemen observing the bar mitzvah from afar did not realize they were also discussing the modern American's rite of passage: the driver's license.

The neophyte driver whose father beamed so proudly will be a kid on Sunday. He'll still be a kid on Tuesday. Getting his permit on Monday won't change a thing. Rites of passage do not perform magical transformations. They mark progress, exactly as do the milepost markers along a hiking trail.

That does not keep either them or the progress itself from being very scary.

Let us look at the underlying fears experienced by children from eleven to about fifteen. We will examine how to resolve those fears and concerns. Then we'll discuss the noble task of setting the child up for the future, planting the seeds for separation years hence, and providing emotional support from ourselves and from others.

I'm Not Me Anymore and You're Not Who I Thought You Were

Observe the progression in a child from infancy to now. From fear of slogs of slime through fear of others, then fear of others' opinions, and fear of personal success, now comes the ultimate fear: the child's fear of himself. A lot of life-changes herald that fear. Hormones, both growth and sexual, change the body and the thoughts. The emotions change, wildly swinging side to side on their way to adult stability. Well, semi-stability.

Change is scary! I am not the same person I was two days ago.

Children this age joke a lot about how nerdy their parents are, and how parents are so behind the times. Beneath the veneer of joking lies fear.

Two major blows in the child's life generate that fear. One, the child is entering adulthood uncertainly, without a track record of adult achievement with which to evaluate success as an adult. For a hypothetical example, let's imagine a young man who wants to be an illustrator. He dreams of creating artwork for magazine stories, for book covers, perhaps for fantasy-film promotion. But as he begins to pursue this career he has no portfolio, no work he can cite to show, "this is what I can do."

He takes any job that comes along, building a portfolio, a track record. As his name becomes known in the business he no longer has to carry his portfolio into an art director's office and sell himself face to face. He can phone the art director with an idea. Once he has proven himself across a span of time, art directors phone him.

Similarly, children on the cusp of adulthood have absolutely no way of knowing whether they will succeed as adults, or how well. Ideally, as they build their track records as adults—achieving the grown-up successes of living independently, driving a car, getting a job, advancing, falling in love—they become more confident in their adulthood. The fear abates. But that comes later. How does one deal with that fear now? One way is to build oneself up at the expense of someone already built. Thus the jokes about parental incompetency.

Another is to stay little as long as possible. For example, recently a worried mother brought us her twelve-year-old daughter, Renée. Renée ate ice compulsively. Mama feared for Renée's teeth ("You know what your dentist says about eating ice cubes!") and her very sanity ("It's just not normal!").

When we probed to the seat of Renée's fears, we found her terrified of growing up. The ice tightened her alto voice into a more child-like soprano. She had no conscious desire to sound younger. The gimmick was a ploy to prolong her childhood and avoid the unknown terrors of being an adult.

The second major blow in a child's life is the inevitable, devastating realization that Mom and Dad aren't perfect. Only a few short years ago, they were. They were not always obeyed, not always listened to, but that was the child's shortcoming, not theirs. Now the child learns to his or her horror that Mom and Dad perhaps ought not to be obeyed in every single matter. Just when the child needs perfect, divine guidance most, the traditional guides are proved fallible.

Santa Claus has been unmasked and he is a government bureaucrat. The tooth fairy is dead. Life is bitterly unfair.

A lot of children at this stage fear they won't make it because they feel they don't really have parents walking with them anymore, leading the way. They are afraid of what they might do without perfect parents to offer guidance and control. Children are very black and white, right and wrong, remember. Parents are either right or wrong, black or white, perfect or poops. No shades of gray. No middle ground. No partial guidance or limited relationship.

This is an age where chronic problems such as serious health impairments, dyslexia, epilepsy, cerebral palsy, attention deficit syndrome, and other difficulties gouge their deepest wounds and scars. Children are already uncomfortable with who they are, and if they have a measurable, visible difference, they will have a difficult time both internally and externally with self-image. In our counseling we find that this is the classic time when kids with chronic problems become resistant to treatment. They have an emerging sense of omnipotence, and they will use that powerful feeling to handle—rather, to mishandle—their future.

Omnipotence is a universal coping mechanism to deal with the fear of inner changes every child suffers. *I can do what I want. I'm diabetic but I don't need insulin.* Denial is a dandy response (and potentially deadly at times) in children and adults both to that nagging fear of what may come tomorrow, and of what may forever stay away.

Will Rogers said, "We're all ignorant, only in different areas." What children fail to realize is that every single child has some disability. If all emergent adolescents were omnipotent, no one would be hampered by a disability. It's not rational, but then so few attitudes are.

"I tend to have trouble with mechanical things," Dr. Warren admits. "Call that a disability, if you will, compared with the mechanical prowess of many people. But I could still get through school being a mechanical klutz. A few laughs, some jokes and teasing—but I made it. It's embarrassing now and then, but not debilitating. But if you have trouble with letters and words and numbers, you're in real trouble. My mechanical clumsiness is nothing like the kid who is in a wheelchair or dyslexic. The only criterion adults see is school, and if your disability affects you academically . . ." He wags his head.

"When children have a disabling situation, their parents are going to have to be prepared to go through the whole grief process to deal with problems because there is very real loss. Omnipotence won't save the day."

How can someone who is not a trained counselor see these fears that are hidden so deep?

Recognizing Fears in Their External Forms

"Yes, I know the law requires Burton to go to school until he's sixteen. Yes, I know if he doesn't get a diploma he's not going to do well in life. Yes, I know it's not good for him to sit at home all day watching TV." Burton's mother, frail as a songbird and thirty pounds underweight, perched on the edge of a chair in the police precinct's booking room. Her discolored cardigan hung listlessly from sloping shoulders. She looked from face to face at the officers around her.

"I tried everything," she continued. "I begged and pleaded, I teased him, I threatened him. I yelled at him till I was blue-faced. Couldn't bribe him—I don't make enough money but to buy food and rent. But I doubt that would've done much good. Burton flat out refuses to go." Her voice dropped to a murmur. "And Burton's bigger'n me."

At age twelve and a half, Burton presented an extreme

case of school phobia, a common manifestation of fear. Burton and his mother had other problems also, severe problems. Sadly, although a brilliantly competent social worker tried to help them both, in this case the problems won.

Why does school phobia peak around Burton's age? As Burton entered junior high he faced a new school with new teachers and a new way of attending classes (moving from classroom to classroom for the different subjects). His old fears of childhood were still largely unresolved, making change and strangeness especially fearsome. Most of all, this is the beginning of individuation time, the close of childhood as Burton makes the shift from Mom's little kid to independent adult. Individuation is scary under the best of circumstances. Burton's circumstances were chaotic. He and his Mom lived in a small apartment, his father having long since abandoned them. To that situation add Burton's fear of self just now developing, a natural and necessary part of growing up.

But Burton's mom had just as many problems. She feared letting go of her boy, the only person close to her. Her voice and her actions said, "Go to school." Her heart and her subliminal attitude were, *Don't leave me. Don't grow up and go away.*

Burton's case was larger than life, but the kernel of his problems exists in every child. Thus we so often find a reluctance in children to move away from their parents by attending school.

The fears of this age also manifest themselves in rigidity. The more rigid the child's attitude, the more we worry about him or her.

" 'Not only do I not do drugs, I would never be tempted to! And I'd like to beat up every kid who does,' " Dr. Warren says, quoting a boy in his counsel. "That boy was thirteen when he spoke those words just about verbatim. He was rigidly, adamantly against any idea that drugs might be a temptation to him. We are seeing him now because he is hopelessly addicted. He'll be fifteen next month."

The young man desperately feared himself and all the terrible things that the world's temptations and his own impulses might lead him to do. He feared his own unpredictability and vulnerability. He no longer knew himself. He adopted a rigid, inflexible stance to build a stone wall between himself and destruction. His attitude might be pure, but his defenses were not flexible enough to guard him against being human. Assaulted, they shattered.

"An appropriate approach," Dr. Warren explains, "is an attitude flexible enough to give a little when it has to, to mold itself to the human being. One way to put it into words, perhaps, is: 'I'm not going to do marijuana, but I know it's a temptation, and I recognize that I could.' The kid who recognizes both the danger and his fallibility will probably be all right."

Kids may build a rigid defense against any temptation—sexual acting out, alcohol, or other deviant behavior. Their parents and society may even applaud the solidity of their convictions. But beware the defense that disregards human nature.

Kids so rigidly guarded against any of these experimental behavior impulses are depending upon internal defenses. Parents form the primary external defense. They play the major role in helping their children survive this time and thrive and grow, and they do so in several ways. Their attitudes toward rules, toward oversight of their children's lives, toward the eventual wrenching pain of letting go, all help or hinder the child's growth.

The Lure of Lockstep Rules

Talk about rigid. Two recent cases in our counsel come to mind.

Joyce was fifteen when her parents brought her to us. Her mother sat ramrod straight on the sofa as she talked rapid-fire staccato, like a typist putting out 150 words a minute. Call her Mrs. Jones.

"Everything was fine when Joyce was growing up." Mrs. Jones looked like a woman who had not washed her own hair in twenty years. She had it professionally styled, probably several times a week. She wore designer-perfect clothes and maintained a designer-perfect complexion. Every detail of her appearance suggested she left absolutely nothing in this world to chance.

Across from her, Joyce slouched in the wing chair. A charming girl with her mother's clear skin and rich brown hair, she scrunched in a corner of the chair with her legs crossed demurely and her long, graceful fingers gripping the chair arms the way Scrooge clung to his gold.

Mrs. Jones continued. "Joyce made very good grades. All A's. Then she went into junior high and things sort of fell apart."

"Explain," we requested.

"Well, uh, it sounds so trivial now. But . . ." Mrs. Jones frowned. "It seemed so incredibly important then. She started being late getting home to supper. School is out at 3:10, and she wouldn't get home until 5 or 5:30 sometimes."

"Did she offer some reason for not coming straight home?"

"Oh yes. One night she stayed after for some club she was in, and another night, she said, all her friends went to this burger place and so she went along."

"Why did you feel this was unusual or wrong behavior?"

"Well, uh . . ." Mrs. Jones laced and relaced her fingers in her lap. "I called the school to verify the club meeting, of course, and that Joyce had been present. Her father investigated and it seemed like an appropriate club for a girl. But the friends. The burger business. No way to check that. We could just see her being led astray. The age, you know. Those teenage boys."

"She worked within a rules system?"

"Oh yes! Doctor, a child that age knows nothing about the world, or about—you know. It is our duty to protect her. All these girls running around unsupervised, it's no wonder there are so many teen pregnancies."

Joyce sat before us seven months pregnant.

Joyce's parents had set up an airtight control system. After school was out, Joyce was required to check in every fifteen minutes by phone—just in case, her mother explained, she would get some impulse to do something she shouldn't. She was forbidden to sit next to boys or to talk to them on the phone.

Supposedly, this young lady in a family way never had a date or talked to boys.

The mother of another of our cases, Margaret Rissoto, was absolutely convinced she was being fair with her Robert, aged fifteen. She let him ride his bike anywhere within half a block of their house but he had to come home every fifteen minutes to check in. He was not allowed to talk on the phone, to have friends over, or to go to others' houses lest he be contaminated by kids who weren't very good.

"The only way Robert Rissoto could grow," Dr. Warren explains, "was symbolically to get into a Mack truck and drive over the rigid boundary. He ran away from home. When the police finally found him out in Midland he had hooked up with a marijuana dealer and was doing drugs."

Unusually gifted with words, Robert told us, "I learned a long time ago, when I was twelve, that it was far easier to come home with my tail between my legs, begging forgiveness for breaking Mother's rules, than to ever ask her permission for new rules."

Emerging adolescents are volatile and unpredictable—unknown personalities to both their parents and themselves. Parents are understandably tempted to lay down close, solid strictures.

Obviously, a rigid system controls an emergent adolescent like a picket fence controls an angry bull. The more they try, the more parents find themselves out of control and alienated. By trying to keep a lid on everything about this budding teen, they sabotage any chance of a healthy relationship. Growth is inevitable. It's programmed into the child. And yet, parents may be tempted to sacrifice growth for rules.

COPING WITH THE FEAR OF GROWING UP

Children this age will cope better with their fears if the parents take three important steps: letting go, monitoring surreptitiously, and allowing other adult journeymates into their children's lives. None of the three is easy.

Letting Go

Researchers conducting an ambitious survey in Richardson, Texas, schools asked kids this age, "What would you like parents most to know about your opinion of rules and limits?"

Their response, paraphrase, was: "We would like them to understand that at our age we need parents who let us go and at the same time watch us carefully."

Wise children.

"Think about a child—let's say a girl—growing up on a small farm," says Dr. Minirth. "She doesn't really have time to worry about whether she's getting appropriate responsibility. In her childhood she's out weeding in the garden, taking care of the chickens. Her parents taught her how to do it by modeling and showing her how. Years before she's old enough for a driver's license she's out driving the tractor. If for some reason she can't handle that, let's say because of a physical problem, she's shunted into other jobs. She always has something to do that's basically an adult job. She's learning the same skills her farming parents use every day.

"Letting go won't be quite as hard for her parents because she has a good handle on the future. She knows what the job is and she knows she can do it. So do they. Her parents see her as a child but also as a co-worker."

"I've said this before, but it's worth repeating," adds Dr. Warren. "Parents have to be able to let go by degrees while kids are young and failure isn't going to be as terrible as it would be later on. And every child, every family, is different. What's too liberal in one situation might be too conservative in another. It's a case-by-case situation."

Monitoring the Child's Choices and Well-Being

When Mr. and Mrs. Jones called the school about the club their daughter attended and investigated its aims and structure, they were monitoring. Monitoring is everything from keeping an eye on the odometer and gas-gauge readings if the child drives to running background checks on all the kid's acquaintances. Not all monitoring is healthful or helpful.

Mrs. Jones, trying to piece together what went wrong, looked confused and dubious. She shook her head. "I can see where letting go and monitoring are sort of a balance . . ."

"Exactly. A very delicate balance, requiring wisdom," Dr. Warren said, nodding.

"And I was a little fearful of letting go. We both were."

Dr. Warren knows the value of not agreeing out loud with everything a patient says. He listened.

"All right, I can see now where we were monitoring Joyce a little too closely. What is too close? Where's the line?"

The line varies with every child.

"Common sense," Dr. Minirth constantly preaches. "Stop and think and use your native common sense."

"Common sense," Dr. Warren agrees. "To find an acceptable line to draw—not necessarily the best and not the worst, but an acceptable one—give the matter some perspective. Sit back and think about it. Would your control measures have been appropriate a year ago? How about a year from now? When you were a child would you have considered it appropriate, or at least livable?"

Mrs. Jones winced. "I would have felt suffocated."

"Compelled to do anything to get out from under?"

"Anything!" And then insight hit her right between the eyes. "Joyce did anything to get out from under it. I asked her so many times why she did what she did, and she wouldn't tell me. She didn't know, did she?"

"I doubt it. She felt compelled but didn't know why.

Children don't do well analyzing their own motives and actions; they haven't had enough experience yet with human nature to understand what goes on inside. They do things, sometimes precipitously, and don't always know why they do them."

"But what would be too little supervision?"

"You tell me."

"I suppose setting no rules at all."

"Allowed to come and go whenever she wishes, you mean?"

"Allowed to do anything."

"If you had been given that freedom, so to speak, in your own childhood, how would you have felt?"

Mrs. Jones had to think about that awhile. He gave her the time. She frowned. "Frightened, I suppose, with no guidelines to work within. I wouldn't know what was okay and what was dangerous. But you've talked about letting her fail. What do you mean, let Joyce fail while it's safe to do so? Obviously, she made a wrong choice and it wasn't safe."

"Good question."

Monitoring does not mean protecting the child from failure, from the consequences of wrong choices (within reason). You monitor to keep a potentially dangerous situation from getting out of hand or causing lasting harm. Pregnancy and parenthood, drug and alcohol misuse, riding a skateboard on Route 30, getting in with a crowd devoid of ethics—from these the child needs protection and a wise guide. But for his or her own growth, the teenager must learn to handle all the non-ruinous slings and arrows of outrageous fortune, painful though they may be.

During our conversations, we learned that Mrs. Jones wanted everything just right for Joyce. The mother operated from the best of intentions. She and her husband worked hard to protect Joyce from many dangers. But they neglected to give her the necessary experience of responsibility while it was safe to fail. Specifically, they interviewed not just Joyce's friends but the friends' parents before she could talk on the phone to them. Joyce was allowed to associate only with kids whose parents were friends of Joyce's parents. Mrs. Jones worked so hard at protecting Joyce from failure that she would call around before school to find out what other girls were wearing so that Joyce would be dressed like the others that day. *Honey, we don't want you to feel the pain of other kids rejecting you,* she said not with words but with actions.

Ultimately, Joyce was unable to fend for herself. She was easily swayed by smooth words and got her feelings hurt by rough ones. She felt depressed and lonely with her life. Kids—yes, even the children of her parents' friends—joked around with her and about her, tittering over her naivete, acting like geese, as kids that age will do. Joyce wasn't prepared for real life. Thoughtlessly—that's how peers treat you. Because she could not experiment with friendships early, taking her knocks and learning about the thoughtlessness and perversity of human nature, by the end of early adolescence Joyce was critically damaged. The window of opportunity to learn had passed unused, never to pass again. Joyce would play catch-up, but she would never quite succeed in actually catching up.

Mrs. Jones presented another important question. "Very well. We monitor from a distance, so to speak. And we find something very wrong. How do we handle it?"

"Actual wrongdoing?"

"For starters, yes. Let's say actual wrongdoing."

"Let me tell you about Brandon."

Brandon was what his harried mother called "all boy," Dr. Warren told her. Into everything. Inquisitive. Creative. Inventive. Those attributes are dandy if you're Thomas Edison, but in a fourteen-year-old they can cause havoc. One night Brandon and some buddies did a tour through an alley behind Eighty-fourth Street, pegging rocks through garage windows. All six kids got caught.

In the past, Brandon's transgression would have earned him a spanking, but a fourteen-year-old is too old to spank. His father demanded restitution. With Dad waiting and watching from twenty feet away, Brandon knocked at each door on Eighty-fourth Street. He confessed his deed and promised to make good. Placing himself in financial debt to his father up to his ears, he borrowed to buy the replacement glass. His father helped him reglaze the garage windows—thirty-seven of them. Brandon learned the most important lesson a child this age can learn: You are responsible for your actions.

"I read a magazine article once about appropriate enforcement. That's what you're talking about. Discipline, right?" Brandon's mother said.

"Right," Dr. Warren agreed. "But at this age, discipline is also another tool to dispel fears, an important one."

"How?"

"Remember, children fear themselves, fear they'll lose control of these uncontrollable urges. They fear what they might do if they stray from the limits; they might even lose their parents' love if they stray too far. Discipline says, *You just blew it, buddy, but I love you anyway.*"

"That's like Brandon's father did. He stayed with him right through his discipline." Mrs. Jones shook her head. "But if Brandon's father had kept a closer eye on him and set an earlier curfew, Brandon wouldn't have done it in the first place, maybe."

"Maybe. But quite possibly he would. Had he been prevented from misadventure, he would not have learned the lesson in responsibility. It was costly, yes. And embarrassing. But by seizing the opportunity, his father helped him through important growth. Brandon feared what would happen if he went out of control. Then he did go out of control and he did not lose his father's love. That was an even greater lesson than that of responsibility."

"Can't you supervise closely—stringently, I suppose, is a good word—and just teach the precepts? Does it have to be object lessons in life all the time?"

You don't have to look for object lessons. Kids being what they are, the lessons will come. You yourself know that a child can get into serious trouble despite the closest supervision. Our advice is control what you can control and drop the rest."

"What can I not control? Obviously, behavior."

"Right. You cannot control what your child says, her attitude, or what she does when you're not there. But you can control the consequences of behavior, as Brandon's father did. Particularly at this age, when you try to control what you cannot control, you reinforce, in a funny sort of way, their fears of growing up. By trying to control what you cannot control, you're saying, in effect, 'I don't trust you to mature; I don't trust your control of yourself.' Kids have got to face who they are, which means they have to feel they are in control of what they do and say."

Mrs. Jones wagged her head sadly. "I'm still in the dark about how to respond when Joyce does wrong, or does something I don't like."

"Again, there are no absolute rules. Every child differs. Let me suggest a repertoire of responses."

Responding to the Inevitable Goofs

One response is, simply, no response. If you can keep your wits when friction erupts, pause to think, *Why is the kid doing this?* The child may simply be frustrated or out of sorts, as we all are on occasion. It might be wise to let a minor infraction (such as speaking disrespectfully) slip through, particularly if you sense the child is trying to hook you into a battle. Children may pick a fight to let off steam, just as older people (who ought to know better) do.

Another response is to invoke a loss of privileges. If the child chooses to engage in certain behavior, so-and-so privileges are forfeited as a direct result. Cause and effect. The opposite cause-and-effect is even more powerful: the child who behaves in a positive way gains specific desirable privileges. In short, children receive the fruit of their choices. Is this bribery? Not really. The lessons of cause and effect are crucial to responsible behavior now and later. Children need those lessons.

A third response is grounding. Many parents use this response much too broadly.

"Dad, I'm sorry I threw my brother through the back screen door. While it was closed. It was an accident. Sort of."

"You, son, are grounded for the rest of your natural life."

It's better to reserve grounding for when children say with their behavior, *I feel like I'm out of control,* or, *I feel I am trapped in circumstances beyond my control,* or, *I'm in over my head.* In other words, when the children need help and protection. What behavior says this? Every time a boy is allowed to be with a certain group, he becomes involved in a fight or in trouble. Every time a girl associates with a certain boy she comes home in tears. A child is caught joyriding in a "borrowed" car, a potentially lethal situation. Grounding is *always* for protection, not for punishment. With grounding the parent sends the message, *I don't think you can handle this; therefore I need to protect you.* It helps immensely here if the parent and child enjoy an open relationship in which to talk about it.

An ultimate measure may include professional help. A child who is out of control may require no less. Some options are counseling, hospitalization, unusual discipline, placement elsewhere (such as in an alternative residence or group home), or restitution handled by a third party (for example, a court may require appropriate community service of a teen convicted of vandalism). The underlying feeling is, *I'm going to do whatever I have to do to help this kid, to turn it around.*

We caution parents never to *threaten* kids with drastic action. The mind-set must be, *This child has big problems. I'll go all the way to help.*

There are a number of actions that should never be in the repertoire of responses.

One is physical, corporal punishment at this age. Brandon's father did not spank him, although Brandon had received his fair share of spankings when he was small. Children become more physical in their reactions during this early adolescence. Boys are pushier, girls are more into movement and contact. When you push an early teen, the teen pushes back instinctively. Besides, you want to teach teenage children ways to solve problems themselves, and a swat teaches nothing. Kids this age say, "I don't worry about getting in trouble. I'll just get some licks and burn it off." Not a good lesson. Negative consequences alone may extinguish inappropriate behaviors but do nothing to teach the child appropriate behaviors.

Positive restitution, such as Brandon's father used, beats physical response because it is physical in some way but is nothing the child can react to. "So you got in trouble for spray-painting fences and smashing bottles, eh? We won't spank you. We'll make you responsible for picking up the glass and for repainting."

Mrs. Jones wrinkled her nose, not in disdain but in serious thought. "Now what about this adult journeymate business? I mean, Brandon's father was a journeymate. He walked through it with his son. What more does the boy need?"

Encouraging Other Adult Journeymates

"Quite a bit," Dr. Warren explained. "The child is starting to move from the dependence of childhood into the independence of adulthood. It's not a smooth transition. It happens in fits and starts, just as the child's growth and maturation occur by fits and starts. Children this age are not ready for strong peer relationships, yet they're pulling away from their parents. During this lag time, so to speak, a healthy adult best fills the gap. This is someone who's willing to invest time in the child. Also, we hope, it's someone the parents do not feel jealous about."

A few days later, Elaine and James Tanner were in for a periodic visit. Elaine, James's mother, did not take well to this idea of other adult journeymates. Why? Because Elaine's brother was John, the baseball-card shop owner who never grew up, the one person in the world James should not have as a role model.

"It's not like John is a convicted felon or a bum out on the street or a shark in the business world. It's just that he's so . . . so flaky. So immature. What if James latches on to him a couple years from now?"

"James very well might. I perceive that he idolizes his uncle."

"Oh, Doctor! You could have talked all day without saying that. I mean, really. What would we do? This is serious!"

"Not quite as serious as you see it, perhaps."

"Oh, no? You don't know John. He makes his whole living off baseball cards and comic books! You want a 1957 Batman? He can get it for you. Did you know that in the early fifties, there was a line of comic books about the Lone Ranger's horse? Not the Lone Ranger. His horse— Silver. Before he met the Lone Ranger, I guess. John didn't want anyone handling them; they're collector's items apparently; but he photocopied them all for James. Every page."

"Wholesome comics?"

"Well, yes. How many adventures can a horse get into? But that's beside the point. You see, James and his father are not close, not really. But James and John could be. Frankly, they're the same age, as far as I'm concerned."

"And you're secretly afraid that if Roger doesn't spend more time with James, he'll abandon you, his parents, in favor of Uncle John. At least, emotionally."

Elaine gaped a moment, then sat back. She drew a deep breath. "I keep forgetting that your profession is knowing what makes people tick. Yes. That's what I'm afraid of."

"The first step for a child reaching out to other adult journeymates is having his own parents as journeymates. The picture is getting much better, but up until now, James hasn't had that."

"He's behind."

"Way behind."

Elaine brightened. "Like you say, that's getting better, though. Roger and James are going out on a hike in the country this weekend. Remember, you recommended that?"

"Something of that sort. I'm glad to hear it. Little things will make a big difference in James's attitude toward himself—things perhaps as simple as going down a scary water slide, jumping in the deep end of the pool, playing ball. The journeymate relationship, whether it is your husband or Uncle John, can validate the new feelings about himself. Soothe some of the old fears. Give James new experiences. Ideally, Dad is the one to do that, now and later."

She darkened again. "But about John . . ."

"I urge you to relax, Elaine. As James enters adolescence and begins the process of separation, and then adopts an adult journeymate other than you, his parents, his uncle will do just fine. You see, the adoption is temporary—a few months, a year at most. It's a stepping-stone, a transition. The outside relationships do not take the place of parents but augment them.

"This, too, will be in the interest of allaying James's fears of himself. James will need affirmation that he really is okay, and that affirmation should come from people other than his parents. Or rather, in addition to them."

"An outside opinion."

"Exactly. Parents have to approve of you. But as you move into adolescence and separation begins, you think you don't want their approval. James will need other adults—other kids, too—for approval."

In addition, some fears are too scary to share with one's parents. This is part of God's plan to help children fledge the nest, to spread their wings and leave home. If they could always talk about everything with their parents, the camaraderie would pose a powerful temptation to never grow up.

In other words, these new journeymates must enter the picture, not just to provide approval, but to talk deeply.

Forging Friendships

Elaine's worries about the influence of Uncle John aside, Elaine and Roger are the primary teachers of friendships in their children's lives. With their own adult friendships they model what friendship is all about.

Here is where "like father like son" can be literal. A recent example is a girl we'll call Melanie. Melanie's mom brought her to us because Melanie, excessively shy, had no friends. Mom was deeply concerned, for although she could get Melanie to school, the child remained essentially isolated. She never went to others' houses, never played in others' yards, never invited others home. "How," Mom wanted to know, "can I get Melanie over being so painfully shy? She seems so fearful of social contact."

As we got to know Melanie's mother, we learned that she literally sat at home all day. She herself had no friends. Melanie's father worked all day and had no friends, either. Although he did not act withdrawn or shy, Melanie's older brother had no real friends either. He played team sports and knew none of his teammates except on the most casual, shallow basis.

Here were four separate people in this house with no outside contacts. But the problem ran deeper because the emotional growth in the parents was stunted as much as it was in the kids. Inwardly directed, the parents were shy, themselves, though they claimed they were not.

Parents need friends for many reasons. A major reason is to teach the kids of this age how to be friends by modeling adult friendship. However, it goes a giant step past merely modeling. Because outside friendships are stimulating—the catalyst of other people promotes growth—parents who are committed to friends are committed to growth itself. This is what the child "hears" below conscious level.

Parents also make an important contribution by guiding their children into choosing healthy friendships.

Joyce Jones's distraught mother insisted, "But that is exactly what my husband and I were trying to do! What went wrong?"

"I suggest," Dr. Warren responded, "that you were trying to control what you could not control: every specific friendship, every social contact, every minute. You can't choose your child's friends, but you can control what you can control. The method of that control is to teach children about positive and negative friendships."

"Kinds of friends, instead of specific friends. Generalization."

"Exactly. Consider this: You might say 'I'm not going to give you permission to be with that kid or this kid.' But you can't follow your child around to enforce it."

"You can say that again."

"Neither can you say, 'It's that nasty other person's fault if you get in trouble.'"

"I understand. We have to hold her responsible for herself, for her own actions."

"Right. So, although you cannot choose your child's friends, you can say, 'Such-and-such child is not welcome here in my home,' and you can have a reason for saying so."

"Being social. Do you realize how many problems are linked to being social? We would escape so much heartache if everyone were normally solitary."

Dr. Warren laughed. "On the other hand, good friendships are one of the ways children conquer their fears about their changing bodies and personalities. The friends accept them. The friends treat them like real people, hurting and helping. The friends present a united defense against the buffeting of the world."

"What is a good friend? How do I teach Joyce to tell good from bad?"

"Another excellent question!"

When we discuss friendships in counseling with young clients, we offer the children these criteria for a good friendship:

- Good friends tolerate each other's weaknesses instead of tearing each other down because of those weaknesses.
- Good friends, especially at this age, enjoy an active sense of humor. They appreciate a good time, with lots of laughing and fun and being silly.
- Good friends express a healthy respect for parent-child relations. Good friends don't encourage you to get in trouble with your parents; they don't try to destroy or damage the parent-child link. Your biggest asset in getting through this life is a strong bond with your parents, even if it doesn't seem that way on the surface, and good friends honor that. Good friends have that bond themselves.
- Good friends are supportive. They stick by you.

We find that children understand and react to these criteria pretty much instinctively. "Yeah," we hear again and again, "that's the kind of friend I want. Except maybe about the parent part."

"You want someone to wedge in between you and your family?"

"Naw, I guess not."

In these sessions we also characterize bad friendships:

- Bad friendships are centered around negative things. What holds these friendships together is not fun but negative, destructive behavior and hatred. Skinheads and gangs are two examples.
- Bad friendships are based on poor boundaries. It is not the job of one friend to carry another's burden completely. It should never be the responsibility of one kid to keep another alive. For example, we frequently see, mostly with girls, a case where a girl will tell her supposed friend, "I'm going to commit suicide but don't tell anybody." Where does that put her friend? The friend carries a terrible burden. If she tells anyone, she betrays her friend, and if she doesn't her

friend might do something awful. What does she do?
It's a problem to vex older people, and this girl has no
life experience to help her make a wise decision.

• Bad friendships damage the parent-child relationship. For example, a so-called friend might say,
"Don't pay attention to what your parents say."

The Prime Advocate—the Parent

But amid all the friendships and significant other adults
and guidelines and lessons, the child's biggest support remains the parents.

We have in our counsel now a young man of fourteen
named Josh. Not Joshua. Josh. He insists on that. His personality shines bright even if his scholastics don't. He has
a gap in his front teeth, "like Terry-Thomas and Omar
Sharif," he'll be quick to tell you. "Movie-star stuff, huh?"

Josh's scores run under the rug clear across the floor.
His years in schools have taught him only that it's all his
fault he's disruptive. His disruptions aren't vicious or bit-
ter; he's a pain in the patoot for teachers, but in a genuinely kindly way. He's certain he is dumb. He thinks all he
can do at school is be the troublemaker. It's the role he's
always taken because he can't handle symbols of any sort.

He has survived because his mother won't quit. He's
welcome at home regardless of the grades he makes. The
school hates her; she's always in there. She holds Josh accountable to get certain jobs done around the house. She
does not hold him accountable for things he's not capable
of doing.

He's great at doing stuff with his hands. He can do just
about anything that does not involve marks and symbols.
With Mom behind him, we're helping him see that he has
strong points—they just don't show up on the tests—and
value. In a few years he'll be able to go into vocational
training and find a spot for himself. Right now, his strongest advocate is a mother who won't give up.

James had a strong advocate, too, although neither he
nor his mother realized it at first. Elaine Tanner almost

became a dentist once. It was what she had always dreamed of doing. She pictured herself in a clown suit, serving little children who were afraid of the usual dentist in a white tunic. She pictured herself on an Indian reservation or in some emerging third world nation, serving as a missionary dentist to people who needed the service desperately. She pictured herself as the boss of a support staff, paying them all a little more than she had to, giving them their birthdays off, keeping morale high with her gentle spirit and servant's attitude.

Elaine Tanner never told anyone about her dream, not even Roger. It takes money and dedication to complete the schooling.

She got married instead—the safe way out for a woman. It takes guts to travel out into a hostile world. Elaine couldn't quite bring herself to do that. It takes poise and self-confidence to practice in that profession. Elaine was hardly a powerful authority figure.

And so the dream withered, leaving a residue of bitterness deep inside her, the dry, scratchy little remnant of a flower gone with the season. Fear, like a killer frost, had nipped her dream in the bud.

Now fear stood a good chance of nipping James's dreams too, and Aubrey's, just as it had destroyed hers. Through counseling, Elaine was beginning to see how her children's primal fears had not been allayed, just as her own had not. One night when Roger was late at work and the children had been put to bed (now that Aubrey was doing better about monsters, life was so much more pleasant!) Elaine sat by the fireplace sipping tea. She thought about fear, and about its effects.

And that night she determined that fear would not cripple her children. She was uncertain yet just what she would do about it, but she would not let history repeat itself. Her children would flower, frost free.

Let us look next at the later teen years and how the devastating results of unresolved fears can be minimized even later in life.

11
What Am I Getting Into?

A FEAR OF LIFE ITSELF

Dear Hector,
  Here I go again, an adult of reasonably sound mind writing to a dog. And anyway, where were you when I needed you?
  When I was a kid I used to watch "Lassie" on television. In Lassie's adventures, the dog always saved the kid, and sometimes Grandpa, and occasionally the mother, and even the whole farm once in a while. Single-handedly. Single-paw-edly. You, you big lunk, you could have helped us. Lassie would have. Lassie would do all that wonderful, heroic stuff. You hid in the bushes. Gutless mutt.
  If only Warren didn't say, "Take your son for a walk, out in the country perhaps. Get to know him. Just go somewhere. Talk. Don't talk. Simply be together." Then we wouldn't have gotten into that mess.
  And like a dolt I took him at his literal word. That's why we drove out through the farms along those back roads Saturday. I admit James really got a kick out of all the stuff we passed. He talked about the cattle and horses in the fields, the trees, that dead jackrabbit flattened on the road. And you, with your head out the window and your ears blowing straight back—you seemed to be enjoying it also.
  The problem, of course, was the walking part. As long as we were cruising along in the car, everything was great. It looked like a simple, innocent little

*pasture. Gentle hill, some scrub trees scattered across
it. A rock here and there. Really picturesque. Bucolic.*

*The blankety-blank bull had to weigh three thousand
pounds! I've never before seen an animal that size. He
was bigger than a schoolbus. I wouldn't dream two
people could climb a scrub juniper, either. I never
prayed so hard or so fast in my whole life. How long
did James and I sit up in that blamed tree? Three
hours? At least. Until that giggly girl in the pickup
drove by and then went off and got the rancher.*

*Three hours in that tree gave me time to think. The
situation was unique, true. But the feelings it created
in me were not. When that bull charged us and we
scrambled up into the tree, it felt the same as when I
was in high school and some bully would come toward
me or one of the teachers approached me. In volleyball
(how I hated gym class!) the ball would be coming over
the net toward my position and I felt as if my whole
team was charging, very much like that bull—coming
right at me, ready to trample me.*

*And now that I think about it, it wasn't just big
people charging toward me; life itself seemed intent on
crushing me underfoot. Here it came at me, ready or
not, rushing in on iron hooves, and all I could do was
cower.*

*I relived a lot of ugly memories. No, more precisely
speaking, the bull gave form to the deep, ugly fears I
felt in high school. The fears have always lurked in my
memory. The bull simply expressed them in a physical
way. For the first time my fears were something I could
see, hear, and smell. They had always been real in a
vague, abstract way. That Saturday they became real
in the concrete—"in the now," as the evangelist used to
say.*

*It's the last time I'll ever venture outside the city
limits, I don't care what Warren suggests.*

*You could have at least barked at the bull, you
deadbeat, before you high-tailed it through the fence.*

*With malice aforethought,
Roger Tanner*

Roger's vivid allusion to life's attempt to trample him is a manifestation of a major fear of later adolescence. Most teens could not express it as he did, but it is there.

THE LATER TEEN YEARS

A generation ago, teens gave fresh meanings to English words such as *cool* and *groovy*; now they've added terms like *chill out, Dude* to the lexicon. Thanks primarily to teens we now have a new generation of meanings for whole groups of words. For example, *crank, meth, snow, crack,* and *black tar* come courtesy of the new drug culture. Once the province of gangsters in old movies, *drive-by shootings* are now a teen phenomenon. A vehicle slows along a city street, guns fire, and the vehicle speeds off into anonymity. Growing up is tough these days. So much, including the teens themselves, seems to be out of control.

And that is the very fear plaguing the teen years. *Man, I'm out of control. I try, but I lose it. I can't keep up; I'm in over my head. My parents are imperfect and they can't help me. I'm on a roller coaster and I can't get back to solid ground.* Life comes at them like that bull roaring down on Roger and James Tanner, and there's no tree around, no safety.

Ideally, the teen has already learned the important lesson that if you do get out of control, you can handle the consequences. You can manage the restitution. Those lessons about accountability were important in grade school and crucial in the early teens. Ideally, the early teen learned about the balance of privileges and responsibilities, the essential economy of cause and effect.

Now, in the later teen years, comes the payoff from lessons well learned. And yet, even with those lessons, later teens are afraid they can't handle life. They need frequent affirmation. They'll blame their parents for failing a class;

after all, Mom and Dad didn't help enough. They'll blame their parents for getting grounded. Mom and Dad shouldn't have let them out that night when the eleven rolls of toilet paper ended up draped all over Mr. Thayer's chinaberry tree. Dig to the roots of these posturings and blame and you'll see a deep, dark fear of self.

But there lies an even deeper fear below that, a fear of life itself. Soon they will actually have the vaunted autonomy and independence they've been begging for for years. On their own, they'll have no one to fall back on, no one to bail them out, no one but themselves to blame. Can they handle it? Can they cross the threshold into adulthood with all its dangers and responsibilities? What if they won't make it once they are apart from family? So far, there's not a lot of evidence to assure them they can.

As teens rapidly approach adulthood, at the deepest level they fear life itself.

I'm Afraid of What I'm Getting Into

Rarely do teens recognize these feelings for what they are. Rarer still is the teen who can articulate them. But we have found in counseling that until teens can resolve these feelings, at least to an extent, they cannot function happily, cannot mature comfortably. The thief in the closet is still at it, stealing the joy.

Since kids can't recognize and express these fears, the fears surface in various ways. The kids then handle them in their mutated form as best they can. Remember that none of this is rational thought on a conscious level. It's all going on in mental rooms the conscious mind doesn't even know exist.

Kids bring this inexpressible fear to the surface, or nearly so, and try to deal with it in any of three ways.

One Approach: Skip It

Grace Walters beamed proudly. "She's wonderful, just wonderful. I wasn't too sure I wanted to do it, but her teachers all assured me that she's incredibly grown up for her age—that Marri is mature enough to handle it. So we went down and got her a work permit on her fifteenth birthday."

Mrs. Walters was one of those people who would be struck mute if you handcuffed her. In her right hand she swung a tall glass of iced tea the way an orchestra conductor swings a baton. Her left hand did aerial acrobatics a soaring barn swallow would envy. She stood on the patio amid fifty other guests, so radiant with pride that the sun wasn't needed.

"That's the earliest a child can obtain a work permit in your state," Clay Walters, Grace's brother-in-law, remarked as he sipped his own iced tea.

"That's right. And a driver's permit is fifteen and a half. Fifteen years, seven months, actually. We go down to DMV and get that next week."

"So Marri has been working now for about seven months."

"She started at this fast-food place, noon hours and weekends. You know, busy times. Pretty soon they made her assistant manager on the weekends. As soon as she can drive, the company will put her on as weekend manager. They say her work habits are exemplary."

"It sounds like her teachers and her bosses all like her."

"Oh, they do. And no wonder. She works very hard and makes certain she does everything just right. They all agree she's amazingly grown up for her age. I do too. Don't you?"

Yes, Clay did, but for different reasons. A school counselor and psychologist, Clay saw this a lot. Marri Walters was an excellent illustration of one way kids deal with the fear of growing up. They simply hop right over the difficult part of maturing and land smack in the easier part, the actual maturity. Fear generates a certain energy. Kids like Marri invest that energy in overachievement or perfectionism. They invest themselves in becoming adult without making the painful transition. Usually they are afraid they can't make the jump, so they transplant themselves into instant adults. Needless to say, if rough waves start breaking, they quickly find themselves in over their heads.

For obvious reasons, the significant older people in their lives love them. That pseudo-maturity—and that's what it is—is very attractive to grown-ups who want to see the kids turn out perfect.

Were Clay to suggest this to Grace Walters, she probably would say, "What's so wrong with pseudo-maturity? It will ripen into true maturity before long, will it not?"

And his answer would have to be, "Maybe. But probably not. More often, it cracks, with detrimental consequences."

We have found that the child who is pseudo-mature will get through life only so long, investing all that energy into pleasing others. Then the importance of the race will pale, the runner will flag. The child-adult will then either adopt a high-risk lifestyle or live a miserable life.

Mid-life crisis will hit the pseudo-mature child-adult like a mallet taking out a Twinkie. By his or her middle years, the child-adult will almost certainly do both—live a miserable life *and* take on high-risk behavior.

Another Approach: Cut Directly to the High Risk

Dr. Warren surveyed the board a moment before sliding his castle forward. Gregg made what looked like a meaningless move with his knight. This was the second chess game between Dr. Warren and Gregg Holland. Dr. Warren knew from experience the move was not random, but he could not yet see Gregg's strategy. With his bishop he took out another of Gregg's pawns. Gregg seemed to hold pawns in unwholesome disdain.

At age seventeen, Gregg had been placed in counsel by his parents because he seemed bent on killing himself, or at least mutilating himself spectacularly. He was, literally, a skinhead. His hair was shorter than the fuzz on some peaches. He wore camouflage pants, shirt, cap, and belt.

Did they make camo underwear, Dr. Warren wondered idly, and was Gregg wearing that too?

"Ever use an AK-47?" Gregg asked casually.

"Nope. How does it feel?"

"Well . . .," Gregg paused, his attention zeroed on the chess board for a moment. He slid his bishop in close to his queen. "It's a bigger kick than you're expecting. Hard to aim—it just stutters all over the target. Not as bad as Darla's Airweight, though."

"Darla is the young lady your parents mentioned—your girlfriend?" Dr. Warren could see parts of Gregg's war strategy, and things did not look good.

"Sorta, yeah. Her or Liss, depending on whose parents you listen to. Her little .38 has no heft to it at all. You know much about inertia?"

"From college physics. I understand you get straight A's in the sciences."

"Yeah. I like to find out how the world works. I'm taking physics this year, chemistry and biology last year. Anyway, a big, heavy handgun has enough inertia to absorb most of the kick when a bullet is fired."

"Kick: action equals reaction." With some trepidation, Dr. Warren took out Gregg's knight with his castle. Gregg was a terror with his knights; getting rid of one of them was worth losing a rook.

"Right. But her Smith & Wesson Airweight is so light, there's nothing to absorb the recoil. You aim at your target, you fire, the next round's aiming at God."

"You mean it kicks so badly it's pointing straight up."

"Right." Gregg ignored Dr. Warren's rook and shoved his queen over one. "Check."

Dr. Warren was having trouble keeping enough distance from this intriguing game to guide his conversation into useful avenues. He moved his own queen in to protect her king. "Have you always had an interest in weapons?"

"Yeah, I guess. Watched *Rambo* and *Terminator* and all them when I was growing up. They had some happening guns in those movies."

"I agree, though I wouldn't think to employ 'happening' in that context, as an adjective. I'm still not used to your ultra-modern jargon."

Gregg cackled. "At least you admit it. My old man thinks he can understand me. Nobody understands me unless I want them to."

"And sometimes not even then." Dr. Warren was probably going to lose this game, but he'd go out swinging. Throwing caution away, he shifted his queen forward. "Check."

Gregg's parents, Democrats to the core, prided themselves in their liberalism. In contrast, Gregg had shifted to the far right of the political spectrum. Gregg played chicken on his skateboard with cattle trucks. He was implicated in a drive-by shooting, although he himself was not accused of either driving or pulling the trigger. Gregg courted death half a dozen different ways. When he baited a suspected gang member in the high-school cafeteria and was stabbed for his efforts, his parents brought him in for treatment. They held life in such sanctity that they picketed fur salons. Why was their son trying to snuff his own life?

Dr. Warren's conversations eventually came down to that. "Why, Gregg? What is your motive?"

And Gregg answered with total honesty, "I don't know."

In Gregg's case, as is the case with many other subadults in their late teens, acting out is based on that deep, deep fear of growing up. The mechanics of the phenomenon, we believe, is not a simplistic, "I'll wreck myself before I have to grow up and go out into the world." The factors are much more complex.

Distraction and escape form part of it. These kids choose exciting, stimulating, challenging things to distract themselves from their unspoken fear. They don't want to deal with either the fear itself or the difficult struggle it takes to grow up well. Television and films play a large escape role here, as the child hides in fantasy. Gregg used violent action movies both to escape and to distract him. He considered *Rambo, Terminator,* and such to be training films for his alter ego, a devil-may-care soldier of fortune.

Invulnerability is another factor. Unfortunately, an immortality complex is innate in these kids. A teenager feels incredibly unique. These days they are educated in the dangers of drinking, drugs, wild driving, and casual sex, but that's all cognitive. Head only. It's not emotional, not of the heart. The heart murmurs, *You can beat the rap. You're not like everyone else. You're smarter, luckier, quicker. Do what you want; you can pull it off, Dude.* And the heart wins, hands down, for that is where decisions are ultimately made. Even in their late teens, kids truly believe, as they have for years, that the dangers grown-ups preach about won't happen to them personally.

"If you join a gang, you're probably going to get hurt," says the prevailing wisdom (in Gregg's case, his guidance counselor).

But that won't happen to me, thinks Gregg smugly. Rambo lived to fight again. The Terminator keeps coming back from the parts shop to fight anew. Teens escape into unreality and magical thinking, all to avoid dealing with fear and the pain of making the transition, and our modern media do nothing to discourage them.

In counsel with Gregg, we brought the subject around to fears, surface fears and underlying ones, and talked, talked, talked Gregg's underlying fears to the surface. Once he gave them spoken recognition, handling them became possible, though difficult. It was a giant step toward growing up whole (or, considering Gregg's somewhat suicidal lifestyle, growing up at all).

The approach is by no means employed only by boys. Girls can use it too. Back in the first chapter we cited a sixteen-year-old girl who, when riding the family's all-terrain vehicle or driving the family car, kept colliding with inanimate objects. It was her response to the fearful uncertainties of leaving the nest.

Incidentally, a medical workup on the girl indicated extreme near-sightedness. Corrective lenses helped the situation somewhat but did not eliminate it. She still flung herself recklessly through life. When you are considering the actions of others, children in particular, never ignore such possible factors as sight or hearing problems, health abnormalities, and other external influences.

A Third Approach: Experiment with Lifestyles

"I swear, Lucia has the attention span of a honeybee— never the same flower twice." Grace Walters discussed her other daughter, Marri's eighteen-year-old sister, with Clay. "She went away to school for a semester, decided to drop out and work awhile—it certainly didn't bother us. College is exorbitantly expensive, even the state schools. Then she got a job nurse-maiding a group of senior citizens traveling to Argentina, of all things. Now she's talking about going to some business school in Pennsylvania and then joining a mission society as an office worker." Grace wagged her head in disbelief; her expressive hands flapped even harder.

Just as very small children use play to work out fears and questions about life that they cannot express verbally, teens use experimentation. They try on different lifestyles and attitudes much as a customer in a dress shop might try on fashions. They are working out unspoken fears and unexpressed questions in, at the very deepest level, the same way those preschoolers do: nonverbally. In a sense, they're role-playing.

Psychologists say that healthy children "achieve a good balance between their experimental lifestyles and hostile-dependent struggles, that is, ambivalent situations with their parents." In English, that means most kids work their way through their fears successfully without stepping on Mom and Dad's toes too badly. *Hostile-dependent* means "I can't live with you and I can't live without you," and all teens and parents reach that point to a greater or lesser extent now and then.

Experimental behaviors vary from the ridiculous to the sublime.

"You can say that again," crowed Grace. "We were beside ourselves with that girl. For instance, Luci went through a period of swearing like you wouldn't believe. I don't know where she came up with that language—certainly not under our roof!"

Clay watched Grace's iced tea slosh gently onto the patio bricks. "Did the episode last long?" he asked.

"Well, no. My mother kept saying, 'Let her go. She'll outgrow it.' I hate to say it but my mother was right. Luci seemed to. She hardly ever uses an unseemly word anymore." Grace frowned at the dark wet spot on the bricks. "Where do you think she heard such language, anyway? Some evil, dangerous place?"

Clay nodded. "Schoolbus, probably. I wouldn't worry about it. Was that the extent of her experimenting?"

"Don't I wish! There was the time I found cigarettes in her book bag—and these terrible love notes from some kid named Edgar. And the night we caught her when she sneaked out the window . . . Ellis swore he was going to ground her until her hair turned gray and her major form of transportation was a rocking chair."

Grace waxed hot on the subject of experimental behavior for a few minutes more, then wandered off for an iced tea refill.

What she described of Luci is the normal way kids cope with the fears of growing up. "I can make my own choices," the emergent teen fumes. "Don't tell me to get my homework done." And the homework fails to get finished.

Fortunately, unless something down deep is seriously awry, kids possess an internalized monitor that makes the experimentation only episodic (a term we'll define a little later). These internal regulators prevent the kids from going too far or getting locked into destructive habits. At this age, their whole life appears to be one big risk-taking adventure, ameliorated, of course, by inherent invulnerability. Life is a magical thinking experience.

Not all this experimentation involves the physical. Kids play head games with themselves, too, as they figure out who they are. For example, their politics or morals might just flip over to the opposite of what their parents do. Even worse off than the daddy from Dixie whose daughter dates a Yankee is the Dallas Republican whose kid comes home a Democrat. Again, the kids are experimenting with what it's like to be different. They have found out that the rest of the world is not just like their house and their family.

With clients, we sometimes compare this stage of life with a walk-in pantry. During childhood, the child ate whatever was served, sometimes under protest, sometimes with gusto. The menu was limited to the parents' interests. If Dad hated liver, little or no liver showed up on the table. Mom loved scalloped potatoes, so she served them a couple of times a week.

Now the child is walking into that pantry himself, able to choose foods he never knew existed. It's scary, facing a wide world of unfathomable options. Better to taste before eating the whole serving. Pick and choose. Reject some and adopt others. And the foods the child discovers may not be the same the parents serve.

There are problems with this hit-and-run-with-the-tastebuds experimentation, this cautious testing of what life has to offer. It desensitizes children to a lot of things they probably should be sensitive to. The child who has gone over the line and adopted the whole experimental lifestyle will certainly be desensitized to the world as his parents see it.

Problems aside, these spates of experimentation serve another role. Grace described it without realizing it.

"There's one thing about Luci," Grace said, her tea glass filled again, as she settled into the garden swing. "She's very poised, sure of herself. Marri is, too, but Marri seems so frantic about it—anxious, in a way. It's not right out in the open, but a mother feels these things, you know. Luci simply cruises through life and lets the rain roll right off her, so to speak."

"Does your mother have any theories about that?"

"She has theories about everything," Grace sniffed. "She said she knew Luci would come into her own. Said they all do. Of course, Luci is the firstborn grandchild on both sides. She's right up there next to apple pie and the flag, if you talk to her grandmother."

Luci, we could have pointed out, followed a normal path to discovery of herself. She avoided being what she was, trying on roles that were not her usual self. By so doing, she learned what she actually is, by seeing what fit and what failed to fit. To describe an abstract concept as a visual image, she defined herself by the shape of her psychological container, and she determined that shape by groping around until she learned where its walls were.

When Experimentation Goes Over the Edge

What is the line between healthy experimentation and dangerous experimentation, between trying on a lifestyle and adopting it? Grace Warner and Greg Holland's parents worried about that.

Marri, Grace's younger daughter, avoided experimentation, carefully sticking to whatever line the adults in her life expected of her. And yet we just said that could cause her major problems later. Where are the lines between healthy and unhealthy?

"When Luci was messing around with smoking and swearing—and beer I'm sure, though I could never prove it—I was frantic," said Grace. "What if she, you know, stayed that way?"

When Gregg was released from the emergency room, his superficial stab wounds bandaged and his costly antibiotic prescription in hand, his parents were distraught.

"Let's define *episodic*," suggests Dr. Minirth. "It's a matter of investment. How deeply is the child investing himself? Episodic means the child is investing little pieces of his or her life in the experiment. This applies equally to girls and boys. The child with a problem is investing his or her whole life in the new lifestyle."

"Yes, but how does it *look*?" wailed Gregg's mom, when her son showed up at an anti-fur rally wearing a coonskin cap.

Gregg loved it. Appearance meant so much to his mom, and he delighted in rubbing her the wrong way by appearing outlandish. Appearance means everything to kids too. Because they've not had enough life experience to understand deeper aspects of human behavior, kids understand the surface best. They look at the outside and assume it to be a reflection of the inside.

Appearance is easily changed. A few snips of the barber's scissors, some different clothes, the right accessories—anything from shoulder-duster earrings to an ammo belt—and you can outrage anyone you wish, of any persuasion. You can look like any lifestyle without investing any more than your surface in that way of living. This also, in part, is what we mean by episodic.

Dr. Warren, too, separates out the child who experiments from the one who has adopted the new lifestyle, and he adds another dimension: "The hardcore no-longer-an-experiment lifestyle encompassed by the child with a problem almost always is based on hate. Gang membership is founded on a hatred of non-gang institutions and people. Of other gangs. Far-far-right political associations feed on hate. So does the far left, equally so. Even the extreme rock lifestyle has its roots in hate."

Rock music. The kids listen, and yet they don't. Most teens don't care what the words to their "happening" songs really say. "It's an art form, man; lighten up." Likewise, most kids don't live a rock lifestyle, even though they may taste it and move on. To bury oneself in that sort of life can be fatal. Ideally, children's natural survival instincts kick in. When they don't, the line has been crossed.

"It's sad," Dr. Warren muses. "Almost all punk kids over the edge have a father who is still struggling with his old fear that worth is wrapped up in how you perform. Here's Dad working his tail off, trying to get his kid to squeeze into his own mold of what he thinks is valuable. He's afraid to let his kid be anything else."

Illustrating this is a boy who was in Dr. Warren's counsel several years ago. The father, a prominent executive in a Fortune 500 company, struggled mightily to present his son to the world as a model child. "The father tied human worth to output, not to being: *Produce and look good doing it or you're not of value.* This was a mutated specter of the father's own childhood fears about inadequacy and the pitfalls of growing up. The father had been a pseudo-mature child, incidentally.

"In the process of struggling with his own problems, the father lost the boy. I don't know that he'll ever get his son back. I couldn't help him. The boy has adopted a destructive, sordid lifestyle," Dr. Warren said.

As teens turn inward to examine themselves, to explore the inner boundaries of their own beings, exemption and entitlement come naturally. For awhile they are almost totally self-absorbed. Exemption and entitlement (being spoiled, in other words) waltz hand in hand with invulnerability. Pathology exists when the kids get stuck in the fatal waltz full time.

"Spoiled teenagers who think that the normal laws of man and nature don't apply to them are no fun to be around," says Dr. Warren in a stroke of understatement. "Their attitude is extremely difficult to change. We find it very difficult to treat entitled, narcissistic (that is, self-absorbed) patients. They simply can't see life any other way but their own."

GIVING 'EM THE BOOT

If these, then, are the fears and problems of kids this age, can parents and other interested adults help teens ease into adulthood? For that matter, can the kids be helped at all? Is this a road to be traveled alone, this coping with the fear of life and the struggle for self-discovery? In other words, is senioritis curable, or must it play itself out, possibly blunting the child's happiness and productivity the whole life long?

Life is coming at these kids like the bull came after Roger and James. Can loving adults at least provide a tree for the kid to climb?

12
The
Shift to
Adulthood

Dear Troid,

James here. Have you noticed the difference in Dad lately? He's home more and he sits around thinking a lot. I got up for a glass of water last night—you saw me, I almost stepped on you. You have to quit curling up by the bedroom door. And Dad was just sitting in the living room, watching a fire in the fireplace. I was afraid to interrupt him, so I just got my drink and went back to bed.

You heard me and Dad telling Mom about the bull, how it chased us. You know I wasn't scared. I guess it's cause Dad was there. I knew we had to run, and he shoved me up in the tree ahead of him. And that bull probably could of knocked the tree over, but I wasn't scared. Cross my heart.

Dad says he's no one to trust when it comes to being scared because he's scareder than I am, but he's just saying that. He's the greatest, Troid. Absolutely the greatest!

I wish you were there instead of Hector. You would of shredded that stupid bull.

Your friend,
James

James's father, searching his own soul and ferreting out the fear he found there, was becoming a powerful journeymate for James. But the day would come when James, a teenager, would leave the immediacy of hearth and father and strike out in the wide world. Most children handle the transition smoothly. Sometimes, though, things go roughly, as they did, for example, with a young woman named Fiona.

I'M AFRAID TO CUT THE CORD AND GO OFF ON MY OWN

What a jewel was Fiona Murphy! Her mother said so as Fiona, sweet sixteen, breezed through high school. At the senior banquet she was voted most likely to succeed at anything she put her mind to. They phrased it just that way, pointing out that she prepared for the future so well that the future would lay itself obediently at her feet (the senior-class yearbook writer planned to become a poet). Fiona had absolutely huge smoky gray eyes and absolutely gorgeous wavy red hair. Well, not quite red. Auburn. Dark red. Vivid. Copper, in sunlight. A jewel? A ruby. A garnet.

Preparation was indeed her watchword. She prepared for tests, prepared for research papers, prepared for guests, prepared for school events. Preparation is fine, to a point. But three months prior to her graduation, preparation started getting in the way of her future. An outside observer might say Fiona was dragging her feet. Her sudden indecisiveness and inaction bothered her dad, but Mom defended her. Fiona developed a crippling habit. She constantly prepared for the future, but she never actually stepped forward into it.

After graduation she planned to attend the University of Texas, but she never filled out a college application. All her plans were for the year after graduation. She needed the interim time in which to prepare, she explained.

And then she met Arthur. A high-school dropout with a ponytail, Arthur was every father's nightmare. He lived in one room above a furniture store, took pickup work down in the warehouse district (when he worked at all), and could identify by taste forty-seven different brands of beer.

At age twenty, Fiona was still living at home, taking one

course at a time at the local junior college, preparing herself for a really splendid college experience. Her entry-level job at a carwash supported Arthur. When her parents, said "Don't bring that bum around here!" she, ever dutiful, didn't. But her life revolved around her ardent love for her misunderstood Arthur.

Her parents brought Fiona in to us, ready to do anything, they said, to help her get in gear and start realizing her vast potential. She was going to waste, hot-waxing cars when she could excel in any of a number of professions. And that Arthur . . . They were upset enough that they claimed to be ready to change their own lives to help Fiona.

And that—changing everyone—was the key to helping Fiona.

The Steps to a Healthier Life

First, we asked who or what was to blame. What was the reason for Fiona's stalling out? We asked Fiona and her parents to consider both surface and sub-surface causes. Second, we asked how the underlying causes and surface problems might be resolved. Third, at the practical level, we talked about ways to get Fiona unstuck and rolling again. By taking a big problem one small step at a time, Fiona and her parents worked out a solution that was satisfactory—and healthy—for all.

We worked with Fiona and her parents for several months, dealing with denial, digging down to the motivations and fears below conscious level. As you might guess, parents and child were very closely linked in ways they did not realize.

When assessing blame or cause, it is tempting to blame the boyfriend for all of the problems. Fiona's father did. "If she hadn't started dating that squid," her father fumed, "she'd be a fine stellar college student now. Arthur did it to her."

The father focused all his anger on Arthur; and in truth, Arthur was certainly a handy target. Dad spent a lot of his waking hours trying to find ways to break them up—with the best of intentions, of course. He knew, as we could see, that Fiona's relationship with Arthur was destructive for them both. Arthur used her, encouraged her to mother him, and remained totally irresponsible himself.

It was inaccurate and useless to lay all the blame on Arthur, though. Arthur was a surface symptom. Dwelling upon him was much like shooting at a rabbit's shadow and hoping to hit the rabbit. We had to dig out the real fear, the bottom-line cause: Fiona was terribly afraid of taking that final step into adulthood. She so feared leaving the nest, she refused to really spread her wings and fly.

We learned that in this family, Mom never discussed how scary it was for her when she finished high school. She had gone on to college, where she almost immediately got involved in a destructive relationship that developed quickly into an abusive marriage. Within a year the man walked out. Mom felt helpless and victimized, but she never dealt with it. She quietly picked up most of the pieces and within a year had met and married Fiona's father. She never did complete college.

Mom had shared none of this with Fiona. By pressing our questions and probing sensitive areas that Mom, at first, did not want probed, we opened these old wounds. It was a matter of being cruel in order to be kind. Only when Mom dragged them to light and began grieving the pain of her past could she help both herself and Fiona move forward.

"Unfinished business" is what we call problems that a preceding generation failed to deal with. Those problems and pains almost always haunt the next generation. As difficult as the transition from teen-at-home to adult-in-the-world might be for Fiona, it was just as difficult for Fiona's mom, who feared changes and passed on that fear of change.

Also, Mom was excessively attached to her only daughter. In her deepest heart, she didn't want Fiona to leave. Her surface message was, "Get out and on your own. Go to school." Her unspoken message was, *I need you here. Don't leave.*

Fiona could have resisted the unspoken messages and stepped out on her own if her fear of leaving home had not been so intense. The robber lurking in her closet stole her bright promise.

Mom began sharing her past with Fiona, talking about the struggles and difficulties. Then Fiona, her liquid silver eyes as big as compact discs, told us how amazed she was by her mother's complexity.

How did we get Fiona unstuck, so to speak? Her father suggested they should, "apply pressure. Order the college catalogs ourselves if Fiona won't." He recommended conveying in the strongest terms, "We gotta get going here." But that wasn't solving the problem.

Some parents might simply kick her out of the house. That's getting closer to a good answer. It's hard to do, though. Fiona, after all, is such a nice girl.

First, we helped Fiona and her parents address their fears in a personal, empathetic way. By getting them to talk together about the problem we could get them to work together. We advised the parents how to gently, appropriately, escort Fiona to the front door and get her out and going on her own. For example, we suggested they go on apartment-shopping tours with her. They talked about the apartments they considered, revved up enthusiasm for them, and gave her some excellent insights regarding what to look for in a dwelling and in a rental contract.

Mom proceeded with her own grieving. For years she had said she wanted Fiona to go to college. But when college time finally arrived, the mother learned that that was not what she really wanted down deep inside. For quite a while Mom could see no bright spot in her life, no life for herself apart from worrying about, watching, and henpecking Fiona.

Incidentally, four years after she met him, Fiona broke up with Arthur spontaneously. She had grown. He had not.

Fiona is not alone. Her case was a bit extreme, but regardless how they tackle their plunge into adulthood, the late teens almost invariably display the symptoms of a hound dog on a sultry day—just too lazy even to scratch fleas. We refer to this as:

SENIORITIS

Fiona's fear was a magnification of the fear in every late adolescent, the fear of leaving home. Children of this age reveal that fear in several common ways. We call the syndrome *senioritis*. Technically, the term is *separation anxiety*. That's right! It's the same term that describes preschoolers faced with separation from Mommy. Again, the same primal fears surface repeatedly through life and must be re-resolved in ways appropriate to the age. If Fiona never came to terms with her preschool separation anxiety, imagine the load she was carrying now. All the old fears would pile up on the current ones. And they were!

Typically, the senioritis symptoms start showing up during the final months of high school. The kid who for months or years has enthusiastically talked about getting out of school, who can't wait to leave home, all of a sudden turns ambivalent. As graduation nears, the underlying fears lead to mixed feelings. The child realizes life is about to change dramatically.

James's mother, Elaine Tanner, had suffered a sort of senioritis as devastating as Fiona's, though she never realized it until years later, when we asked her to make a list. We suggested she catalog all the things she wished she had done in her youth, beginning from about age twelve, when dreams of the future start becoming do-able.

She settled onto the plaid sofa and proudly whipped out two single-spaced pages of dreams. "Some of these I hadn't thought about in years. Not just about being a dentist. There were a lot of little things I always wanted to do." She handed the list over. "You can mark on it. I have a copy at home."

"So you're going to keep it?"

"I think it might teach me something. Am I right?"

"Almost certainly." Dr. Warren scanned the list and smiled. " 'Write a novel.' Do you know, that shows up on almost every list we see. Explain this one: 'baseball angel.' "

"My best friend's brother was on a minor-league baseball team—a farm team. The booster club had a secret angel program. During the season the angels—that's what they call them—each adopt a player anonymously. The angel bakes cookies, leaves cheap little gag gifts in the player's locker, writes notes of encouragement, clips articles about the team out of the newspaper for a scrapbook, collects photos for the scrapbook. Then at the end of the season, the player learns who the angel is and they meet for the first time. It's a darling program."

"You wanted to be one. For your friend's brother?"

"For any team member. They were all cute guys."

"Why didn't you?"

Elaine pondered the question a long time. "I can't really say. I just never got around to filling out the application; it was my senior year, and I was very busy."

"This item: 'a scholarship at Southern Methodist.' "

"Silly to mention it. Obviously I didn't have any control over who is chosen for a scholarship. I just threw it in."

"Did you apply, or ask a sponsor to nominate you?"

"Well, no . . . but then, my grades slipped a little my senior year. I probably wouldn't have qualified."

Dr. Warren went down through another half-dozen items, forgotten dreams that would not remain forgotten. He laid the list aside. "What characteristics do all these have in common? Let's speculate."

"They're all goofy."

"Dreams are never goofy. That's how dreams are defined: out of the ordinary."

"And unrealistic. No one could do all that."

"True. You have several lifetimes of wishes here. Let's analyze the list two ways: one, what factors do they all have in common, and two, how do they compare with the dreams you've realized?"

Elaine's face went blank. "What do you mean, the dreams I've realized?"

"These are the things you wish you could have done. What about the dreams you actually achieved?"

She started out brightly enough. "Well, I wanted to have a nice family, and I do. And I decided to be a dental assistant, and I am one. And I married well. I mean, Roger is very nice and takes good care of me—supports us well." And the brightness faded. "And I always wanted to own a Mercedes. We do."

"It mentioned here you wished for a little convertible, a sports car."

"Someday." She smiled. "It's not practical now, of course."

Item by item, using the two criteria, she and Dr. Warren weighed the list of dreams against reality. The major characteristic linking nearly all of them, although many had been within her reach, was that Elaine had procrastinated so long they slipped away. She never did send for Southern Methodist University's bulletin. She planned to see some of the West before she settled down to get married, but she never found time to make the trip. She still hadn't seen the Grand Canyon; it must be an amazing place, she thought.

In almost every case, when the dreams she had realized were matched against the dreams she had once dreamed, she found that the reality had been dreamed after the fact. For example, in high school she didn't really dream about having a nice family (although the Mercedes wish was real). Her nice husband and nice family and nice job all happened to her *before* she considered them a dream come true. She turned them into dreams retrospectively.

In short, time and ambition robbed her of all the real dreams and wishes.

But did they?

How about You?

In high school or college, most of all, I wanted these things to happen after my graduation:

1. _____
2. _____
3. _____
4. _____
5. _____

During my first years on my own, or in my profession, I most of all wanted these things to happen:

1. _____
2. _____
3. _____
4. _____
5. _____

What did all these dreams and aspirations share in common?

_____
_____
_____

In the lists I wrote above, these dreams never came close to realization:

1. _____
2. _____
3. _____
4. _____
5. _____

Of those unfruitful wishes, procrastination played a major part in my failure to realize these:

1. _____
2. _____
3. _____

Of my "someday" list, I could probably realize these dreams right now, in part at least, if I were willing to throw myself into it:

1. _____

2. _____

3. _____

4. _____

5. _____

If procrastination can be one of the mechanisms for coping with inner fear, as it seems to be, an underlying fear below all these dreams might be, for me at least:

_____

_____

_____

And this fear might lie deeper still:

_____

_____

_____

Deep down, Elaine was afraid she wouldn't please her baseball player enough, or do the angel job well enough. Her fear was nothing more than a mutated version of the primal fears from long ago. So she avoided the possible failure by never starting. To this day she has no idea whether she could have found a place for herself at the school of her choice, pursuing the career of her choice. It is certainly possible that she would have failed, had she tried. But fear kept her from even trying.

Fear saved her from failure. It also prevented her from making her dreams come true, of seizing her life wishes during their windows of opportunity. That monster in her closet scored again. And again. And again.

A Reversal of Behavior

Senioritis is also manifested by a reversal of behavior—from regression to more juvenile behavior and from lowered grades to increasingly irresponsible actions. Suddenly this supposedly mature semi-adult is not keeping curfews, not meeting expectations; he or she is acting like an eighth-grader. Friction with the parents heats up to the temperature of a dragging brake shoe. There may have been no such friction before. Now what's getting into this kid? We also may see an increasing sense of depression and anxiety.

Indecisiveness and inaction also plague this age. The child who talks about going to college hasn't actually taken the first step. He's going to get a job, but he hasn't started looking, has yet to schedule an interview. Her arguing, fighting, and frustration with her parents escalates. Fiona acted out with a lot of these symptoms. One of them was Arthur.

"In most cases, it's greatly preferred that the kids move out to go to school or get a job," says Dr. Warren. "If they continue to live at home, they should either attend the local college or work at a job and pay some rent to parents. And all this should be under the banner that dependence is only temporary."

But what about farm kids? In a healthy farm family, the child may graduate from high school and stay on the family farm. Kids aged twelve and even younger are driving tractors, working other machinery, and doing what city families consider dangerous and demanding jobs. The situation is actually much healthier than it appears at first blush. By early teens the child is already carrying a fair share of the adult labor and is considered an adult with regard to work. That aura of the adult remains. Although a twenty-five-year-old may still live in the parents' home, in practice and in common regard, that kid has grown up.

"The extended adolescence in our modern society may not be avoidable, but it's not good." Dr. Warren recalls, "I was an adolescent until twenty-six. I moved out of my parents' home—I made that separation—but they paid for college. I worked part time at first but I couldn't work at all in medical school. Being supported by my parents created extreme conflict.

"Being financially dependent so long increased the fears of growing up; it didn't alleviate them. About the only tool I had to keep my separation and identity was argumentiveness. I had to oppose my parents' opinion in order to establish my own identity. At age twenty-five or twenty-six to be an adult physiologically and physically but not economically—that's extremely stressful for both parent and child."

Fiona's stall-out might have been minimized or avoided altogether if her parents, her mother in particular, had talked about their own fears of that age: communication. Also, she and her parents should all have begun the separation process years before, as Fiona was entering high school or even earlier.

Fortunately, parents *can* help resolve the fears of this age.

Instilling the Truth, "You'll Be Moving On"

For years preceding the child's graduation, parents should be delivering the message in an optimistic way that "when you graduate from high school you'll be moving on." And they must mean it. This should be a seed planted since early childhood. In Fiona's situation, that seed was not planted.

The longer an adult child's dependency lasts, the harder it is to make the break. Where the seed is not planted early, both parents and kids struggle intensely with the fear of leaving home and entering independence.

The parents should be emphasizing that dependency in the family is temporary but the family relationship is permanent. "You will never lose the love of your parents after you leave home residentially and emotionally."

It is in some ways even more difficult for the parent than for the child when the parent says from the heart: "When you grow up and finish high school, you'll move off on your own (to a job, military service, college, marriage, whatever), not because we're kicking you out but because that's the expectation we and God—and you, yourself—have. That's the way it's going to be. That's the way it should be."

Parent and child both must realize that God did not create that special person to be a little child forever. Its corollary is that "child of my parents" is not the child's only identity.

In counseling we constantly encourage and remind parents that the child is not the only one making a difficult transition. The parents are too. They must come to grips with the fact that they no longer have a child. Many, many parents will do anything to avoid losing all control of the child to the big, bad world. They still feel they have the right to approve or disapprove of adult children's choices and that kids should base certain decisions on what the parents think.

Such parental attempts at control can cause serious problems in the adult children. A woman named Jennifer, in counseling for acute depression, listed some of the constantly repeated orders that irked her most whenever she visited her aging mother. "Sit up straight. You're slouching." "Don't walk pigeon-toed like that." "Put on your jacket; it's freezing outside."

As a result, she says, "I find any excuse I can to stay away. Then my mother calls up and says, 'You don't come visit anymore,' and she's right. Then the guilt kicks in. And yet every time I go over there she treats me like a seven-year-old. She always has, my whole life."

We responded, "What does the Bible say?"

"Honor your father and your mother," Jen replied bitterly.

"And what does 'honor' mean?"

"You know—honor. Don't talk back. Obey. Behave. Toe the mark."

We hear that so often. The Bible indeed obligates us to honor our parents. But that does *not* mean we must agree with them on every point, or seem to. We need not cater to their whims and opinions, nor need we serve them as little children would. We are not obligated to remain little children.

We are required to respect their opinions, whether we

accept them as our own or not. "To honor" demands that we cherish their love and love them in return. Most especially, we must always act in what is their best interests, particularly in their later years when they cannot always handle their own affairs skillfully. A good question for Jen to ask when contemplating interaction with her mother is: "Is this an act of honor by an adult for an adult?"

How do parents and children together develop a healthy regard for each other as adults? How do you break a child out of senioritis so that both parents and child can move on to a stage of mutual regard?

When advising victims of senioritis we pose some questions, not so much for them to answer for us as for them to ask of themselves. The biggie is:

"Why do I do what I'm doing?"
We encourage people this age to use that
question as a watchword for this time of life.

We asked Fiona, "Why are you washing cars?"
Other questions might be:
"How long do you really want to remain in limbo like this?"
"Exactly why are you doing what you're doing?"
The final stage before adulthood consists of being able to answer that kind of question.

If the honest answer is, "I'm doing this to please someone else. My mom and dad want me to (or my girlfriend/boyfriend wants me to)," there's a problem. If the honest answer is, "I'm doing this to displease someone else, to show someone else what for, to get back at someone else," that response is flat out wrong.

The honest answer must be, "because this is in my best interest."

How about You?

When I left high school, I next:

_____

_____

The reason I did that was:

_____

_____

_____

If I had it to do over, I would:

_____

_____

_____

Because:

Knowing all this, I would advise _____ (my child or a child I know well) to do this after high school:

_____

_____

_____

We urge adolescents to recognize the power of peer relationships. Late adolescents relate to others their own age with even more depth than do early adolescents. Fiona spent all her time with Arthur, even though her experience with him was almost exclusively negative. They shared many things; sexual acting out (which was pleasurable to both on the surface) and indecisiveness (an identical fear of becoming an adult). Their intense preoccupation with each other also answered an unspoken challenge neither realized they had: *Adults don't have fun. We have to have all the fun we can now; we don't want to grow up yet.*

The Final Step

The last challenge the emerging adult must meet in order to conquer the fear of transition is to come to grips, once and for all, with the fact that he or she has imperfect parents. Only then is that child truly free to go on, knowing that he or she need not leave a perfect home behind.

Ideally, the process began in early adolescence. There was a great dawning day when this child suddenly realized that the god-like parents who could answer every question, *couldn't.* The knee-jerk reaction to that horrible truth was joking and a strong feeling that the parents were stupid. Kids are black-and-white, remember. The parents are either geniuses or idiots—if not perfect geniuses, then perfect idiots.

By late adolescence, the message should be sinking in. "So my parents aren't perfect. I survived anyway. It's not as bad as I thought." This message doesn't come easily.

First comes *denial.*

Denial tells the child the parents are perfect and wonderful after all and never make mistakes. Denial demands that the child will do anything, just anything at all, for these marvelous people. Denial puts the parents on a pedestal. But you simply cannot have a personal relationship with a pedestal.

Denial keeps you the parents' little child.

A man now twenty-three was still bogged in this denial phase until just recently. John had always been the perfect oldest sibling, the one who could do no wrong. It was a mutual admiration society between him and his parents. Besides, his parents really were very good. Dad was an orthopedic surgeon who made sure he had time for his family. Mom was a successful political figure, a state representative and later a state senator. She was widely respected for her intelligence and depth of insight. Peers sought her opinion on complex issues.

John was graduating with a bachelor's degree in business administration when he finally, finally realized that this lovely couple who held him in high esteem, who carved prominent careers for themselves, actually bumbled from time to time. Breaking the denial threw him for a loop.

John became exceedingly and (to an outside observer) illogically angry with both parents. He fussed and fumed that they had ruined him with their harsh, insensitive demands when actually they had given him a remarkably free rein to follow his heart (he really liked business administration). He complained bitterly and constantly. Bewildered, they and his grandparents simply blinked in disbelief. "This is John?" they asked themselves. But *anger* is a part of the grieving process too.

Anger is an initial stage of *grief*, which comes next. Grief is the only response possible to learning one's parents are imperfect. So the child grieves the loss of perfection, grieves the loss of innocence. And the first phase of the grieving process is anger.

Unfortunately, John got stuck there.

Anger wasn't a bad deal, actually, for John's subconscious. By investing all his energy into being angry with his parents, he didn't have to go through with the rest of the grieving process. True grief is painful for a while, so he was simply saving himself a lot of pain. By remaining angry he could project all his own fears and shortcomings onto them. "It's your fault!" is a whole lot easier than "I must make some basic changes in myself."

Of course, neither was that anger healthy. Instead it was destructive, blocking his progress to a more positive outlook.

Lynn, a twenty-year-old in a local business school, did not have the same problem. She had to say, "My parents' unhealthiness is harming me and I must distance myself." Both her parents are alcoholics. They hide it well, and her father holds down a responsible job. Lynn refused to believe there was a problem until a few months ago—that old denial was kicking in. When she finally took a good look at her parents and realized what had been going on for years—the fights, the constant arguing, the bickering over who had how much to drink and who should go out for the vodka—her common sense won out over the dream of every child to have perfect parents. Denial faded and anger stepped in.

Then the anger faded enough that Lynn could see that her parents' presence was toxic for her. She was a nervous wreck every time she came home from school for a visit. Her holidays were disasters. She decided to choose not to be around when they were drinking. She distanced herself, not out of anger or even pity, but for self-preservation. She was on the road to healing. Her parents were not—not yet. Lynn's situation was not the same as John's, with his raging at how horrible his parents were.

At the same time, along comes *options*. The child figures out, or is told, that life doesn't have to be the way it has been all along. The young child has to follow with whatever the family, or fractured family or foster family, does. No options. Once a child gets into middle and late teens, life can be different. This transition phase from childhood and early adolescence into adulthood is the first time the kid realizes that near-adult kids have choices the little ones do not. They can walk a different path from their parents' path.

And that is extremely scary.

Sometimes fear outweighs opportunity, and the robber rustles around in that closet yet again. The familiar is reassuring and comfortable even when it is painful, even when the child can accurately predict the painful consequences for going along as things are. The choices themselves are too scary to grab. The child goes back to the abusive or chaotic home, unwilling to exercise options, unwilling to step out into the fearsome unknown of a different lifestyle.

Lynn could avoid healthy confrontation with her parents, choosing instead to invest all her energy into anger. Obviously, she would be justified, in a perverse way. They really did ruin her life with their alcoholism, at least to this point. They certainly altered her forever, and not for the better. They forced her into painful battles of the psyche that she should not have had to fight.

Unlike John, though, she has not given way to anger. When her parents ask her why she got herself a little two-room place in a retired lady's attic, she explains why. When they whine that she never visits much anymore and wasn't home at all on Thanksgiving, she tells them why: Coming home hurts. Watching her parents drink themselves to death hurts.

Lynn, you see, answered the questions "What shall I

do?" and "Why am I doing it?" with healthy responses. "It is in my best interests to separate, and it is in my parents' best interests that I no longer enable them and ignore the destruction they're working upon themselves."

Eventually there must come a *resolution*. This is the middle ground, the balance between denial and rejection. The near-adult child comes to grips with the fact that he or she has imperfect parents, grieves out the anxiety, commits to the truth—that is, acknowledges that the way things are is the way things are—suspends blame, and lastly, looks honestly at his or her own feelings. "This hurt. That made me angry."

All this requires a lot of processing, and it does not all occur at the conscious level. John has not yet taken all these steps. He is still mired in his anger. The counsel of others, plus self-realization, should work together to bring him through it eventually. He faces rough times until then, for anger eats both the accuser and the victim.

"This phase didn't occur for me until I was in my thirties," Dr. Warren confides. "It can occur anywhere from the twenties on, and for some people it never occurs. Some at forty or fifty are still stuck in that fear of transition, that fear of getting on in the world, because they never made peace with their actual parents. Their mind's image of their parents is either still perfection or unforgivable imperfection."

Lynn is well on her road to resolution. She tries to observe her parents as if she were an outsider, a person without an emotional stake. She's trying to get perspective, to see their strengths as well as their flaws. That helps her immensely as she seeks to complete grieving and leave anger behind.

Lynn's step, then, is the step every child must take, but perhaps on a much less dramatic scale. Each child must, in a healthy and true way, forgive the parents. The child is not to condone, enable, or reinforce imperfections. The child is to forgive, just as one day that child must be forgiven by his or her own children, and move on.

Lynn's whole view of her parents includes the positive,

not just the negative. It is an integrated, truthful view.

Her ultimate step, then, is to come to the realization, in her heart as well as her head, that the strengths and weaknesses of parents have nothing to do with whether she loves them.

Earlier in Lynn's life, she failed to learn the lesson, "You are worthy; worth is not dependent on your accomplishments, perfection, or productivity." Here, it raises its head again. In Lynn's case she finally came to grips with that truth. She finally absorbed the lesson she should have been able to learn years earlier. She can now take that lesson a step further:

True love—mature love—is not based upon worth. It is unconditional.

This unconditional love will itself conquer the primal fear of transition. John, in his anger, is still a long, long way from the peace and contentment of unconditional love.

The Parents' Part—Recognizing a New Relationship

During this difficult time, the parents are in transition also, or should be. They are called to put aside the parent-child relationship and adjust to an adult-adult relationship. That's a profound step. To this point, their whole lives have been invested in the parent-child union. If they can make the shift, their children reap the benefit.

That old fear, once resolved (Lord willing), crops up in the kids one last time: *There may be something I can do, somewhere, sometime, that will cause me to lose my parents' affection and love.* When parents manage the transition from parent to friend, they give their children a big boost in re-resolving that lifelong fear in this way: Their love is not based on a parent-to-child relationship. The child need not remain a child in order to continue receiving their love. It waxes just as strong in the adult-adult relationship. The child cannot lose that affection after all. The child can grow up safely.

"Easy for you to say," a friend commented. "Your kids

are still small. Every time I see my Charlie out on the road crew driving heavy equipment, I keep thinking, *I used to change that kid's diapers*. How do you get over that?"

"Charlie works for the highway department?"

"Yes, she does."

Love is a Choice and other books in this series delineate the stages of separation a child must make—residentially (leaving home physically), financially (cutting the parents' purse strings), and emotionally. The books point out that these stages do not all happen at once. As they occur, the parent also makes the separation. We suggest you review this series for more information on making the step from parent-child to adult-adult.

NO FAMILY IS AN ISLAND

Roger Tanner sat in the office on the plaid sofa, absently chewing a pencil to splinters. "The more I think about it, the more I see a problem with my own parents."

"Haven't made that separation yet, you mean?"

"That, in part. But it's more their meddling. No, I guess you wouldn't call it meddling. I don't know . . . Maybe I'm wrong."

"Give an example."

"A couple of days ago, James came to me with this problem." Roger quit attacking the pencil a moment. "Hey, that was great! That was the first time James ever just came to me right away and volunteered that something was worrying him. If you never do another thing for us, you've done that. Anyway, some kid at school is shaking him down for peanut-butter cookies. I was able to sit with him and talk about it awhile."

"Told school authorities?"

"Absolutely. I was on the horn first thing the next morning, and then dropped by later to talk to the principal. Apparently the kid who's giving James a hard time is a spoiled brat and general troublemaker. They have their eye on him."

"What about the grandparents?"

"Oh, yes. Granny Tanner volunteered to keep James supplied with peanut-butter cookies, just to keep the goon off his back. She didn't just tell me. She told James too. He was going to take her up on it. Now I look like Scrooge, saying she shouldn't do it."

That will be the focus of our next chapter. After a quick review we'll take a look at the grandparents' role in the conquest of children's fears.

The Deep-seated Fears of Childhood

INFANT AND TODDLER
(THE BOTTLE AND BANKY SET)

- *I fear being abandoned.*

- *If I am abandoned, I fear I will lose my meself.*

- *I fear I can lose Mommy and Daddy's love and approval.*

- *The Oedipal phenomenon*

LATE PRESCHOOLER
(THE SANDBOX SET)

- *I am afraid of the power to hurt that big people possess.*

- *Nightmares and Night Terrors*

GRADE-SCHOOLERS
(THE SKATEBOARD SET)

- *I'm afraid I'll fail competitively.*

- *I'm afraid I won't succeed in life.*

- *I'm afraid I have little or no value.*

- *I'm afraid I might not get it exactly right.*

- *I want to take the world by storm and I'm afraid I can't.*

- *I'm afraid of sexuality, especially my own.*

TEENAGERS
(THE MALL AND CAR-KEYS SET)

- *I'm afraid of growing up.*

- *I'm afraid of what I'm getting into.*

- *I'm afraid to cut the cord and go off on my own.*

- *Instilling the Truth: "You'll be moving on."*

PART SIX

The Extended Family and Other Situations

13 Granny Knows Best?

THE GRANDPARENTS' ROLE

Dear Troid,

Well, what do you think? You were lying on Gramma's lap all curled up, so I know you heard everything. Personally I don't think it's such a hot idea after you think about it awhile. I mean when Gramma said, "Wouldn't it be nice to have a baby brother, Jimmy?"

In the first place, she keeps calling me Jimmy, but I'm tired of reminding her. Mom says old people get set in their ways and I have to go along with it. That's okay. I don't mind. This is Gramma we're talking about, right? Besides, she calls Dad Tootie, like he says she used to when he was my age because he tooted on a trumpet in the school band. I think it's a howl. Tootie!

The baby business is what I mean. She said it last week, too, when she and I were out back in the yard filling in the holes in the flower bed where Hector dug. Then we put up that little white wire loopy-loo fence. It's short enough to work in the flower beds but tall enough maybe Hector won't dig anymore.

I didn't want to contcherdict her but no, it would not be nice to have a baby brother. I went through all that once with Aubrey and I don't want to hafta go through all of it again. Gramma seems to think there ought to be more kids around the house, I guess. I already think there's maybe one too many.

But never too many cats, right, Troid?

Your friend,
James

Grandparents, even when they don't see their grandkids frequently, exert immense influence. That power can work for good or for ill. In James's case, the grandparents weren't helping family matters a bit. What is meddling and what is succor?

THE THIRD GENERATION

There sits the artist's mother in her rocking chair, staring benignly off into space as Whistler paints her picture. Despite the fact that their stereotype bears no resemblance to reality—nor does Whistler's mother, for that matter—grandparents are often viewed as gray, doddering, simplistic, old-fashioned, cookie-loving, warm, cuddly, overweight optimists.

Hardly.

Some grandparents are multi-faceted, complex, politically active, child-intolerant realists on high-fiber diets. Others are not. But all of them by definition were once parents, and many of them are loath to abandon that role completely.

The Problem

"It's the classic example," says Dr. Warren, "and I hear it a lot. The grandparents talk to the grandchild, particularly an only child, saying 'Wouldn't it be wonderful if you had a brother or sister?' or, 'Tell your mom and dad you want a brother or sister.' They're not actually talking to the grandchild, of course. It's a clear message to the adult children."

Grandparents, having lost direct control of their adult children, may try to maintain parental sway by manipulating the grandchildren.

Dr. Minirth relates an example. "Two of our friends decided to buy a new house. The grandparents weren't real sold on the idea, but they were committed to not interfering. Every time the grandchildren (cute little children, about, oh, I think one's six and the other's nine) come over to visit the grandparents, Grandpa or Grandma will say, 'Isn't your new house wonderful! But it's so big. Are you sure your parents can pay for it?'

"The children are totally confused. They're getting one message on one side and another message on the other side. They're asking their parents, 'Can we pay for our house? Are we going to lose our house?' "

That particular example typifies the problem in several ways. Manipulation of that sort creates worries in the minds of the children. The last thing grade-school children should be worrying about is house payments. The grandparents are inadvertently laying an unwise burden on children who are too young to carry it.

Too, the grandparents' remarks undermine the children's sense of security, particularly in this case. Their home should be their haven, their refuge, their redoubt. But the grandparents seem worried that that sanctum could be ripped away. Is anything safe? Perhaps not.

Even worse, the children's trust in their own parents is subtly being eroded. Did the parents make a good choice by moving here? There's some question. Note that the grandparents would not have to voice their concerns out loud. Children are experts at picking up subliminal, unspoken messages.

A little piece of these grandparents' comments is legitimate concern. A big piece is manipulation as they attempt to maintain parenthood over their own children. If you asked these people about their motivation in speaking to the grandchildren as they do, they would quickly assure you their motives are pure. And they would mean it. The mental rooms to which they have conscious access would all hold rational concerns. The rooms actually controlling their actions, however, would be those nether chambers holding the need to control, the desire to make the kids turn out exactly the way the parents want.

The big losers, of course, are the grandchildren. They

find themselves with two sets of loved ones to deal with, and they, the kids, are stuck in the middle. With that double set of important adults comes a whole new body of fears.

Small children, such as these two, don't really try to weigh who is right and who is wrong when a difference of opinion or principle crops up between parents and grandparents. It's not a matter of taking sides. It's the relationships they're concerned about. What is material to the children is, *How can I avoid displeasing any of them?* That means the child must assiduously avoid taking sides so he or she does not lose the approval of one set of loved ones or the other.

And that, too, is a burden children should not be forced to carry.

More than any significant adults in a child's life (other than the parents), grandparents hold the key to harmony in their grandchildren's lives. Children who get caught in the middle of a control issue, getting mixed messages as the children in the examples above are, find themselves in a terrible bind. They desperately want to be loyal to their parents, of course. And at the same time they want to be loyal to their grandparents. Thoughtless or manipulative grandparents set up a situation where the child must choose, yet where choice is impossible. How dreadfully unfair that is! There can be no harmony where conflict of that sort exists.

One other knotty problem causes disharmony. The values of the parents, shaped by the mores of the last few decades, may not be those of the grandparents, whose life attitudes were forged on the anvil of the 1930s and 1940s. Children cannot understand the philosophical ramifications of this conflict of values; abstract differences mean nothing to them. But they get caught in the pincers, nonetheless.

Dr. Warren cites a recent case in his counsel. Seven-year-old Jason Mains was a somber boy. When he received a box of crayons of his own ("Now these aren't school crayons, Jason. They're at-home crayons"), he colored only when urged by his parents to use his new coloring book. And then he used only dark colors—browns, black, purple. He hardly ever smiled and during the last two years had never laughed, that his mother could recall. When she offered to play a game with him one afternoon and he responded, "No, I'd better go see if I have homework," she brought him to us.

Mrs. Mains, well dressed and pleasingly plump, wagged her head. "We don't have what you'd call a dysfunctional family. Not in the least. The kids are normal and my husband and I are normal—well, as normal as a postal carrier's life ever gets. We can't understand what's bothering Jason, but something obviously is." She lowered her voice. "Frankly, Doctor, I fear the worst. You know these stories about things like incest and secret molestation and . . . We want to get to the bottom of this now."

The more we talked to Jason over the next month, the more we found nothing wrong. Mrs. Mains's assessment of her family was accurate: normal people in a normal neighborhood. Loving and close. They regularly enjoyed picnics, reunions, and holiday events with aunts, uncles, grandparents and various hangers-on; all the younger kids seemed to have best friends who wanted to join in the Mainses' big, happy gang gatherings.

Then we talked to the Mains grandparents. Both of them were Depression-era children, whose families had lost it all in the thirties and survived, barely, by dint of ceaseless hard work. They bore their children, Mrs. Mains's husband and four others, in the fifties. Their work ethic was, to say the least, very strong. Further, they had expanded that work ethic to include play: Work hard and behave hard. Have no fun.

The Mains grandparents were ecstatic about becoming grandparents; Jason was the first of a string of eight grandchildren spread among the five siblings. The granchildren were truly loved. But whenever they stayed at Grandpa's, the grandparents spent, essentially, too much time correcting them. The children laughed too loudly, talked too loudly, had too many toys. The grandparents were afraid to buy Jason another toy because, as they pointed out to him, he already had so many and there's more to life than toys. They were concerned that the seven-year-old didn't have enough chores around home.

When we talked to Jason, we learned he had two fears. One, he was preoccupied with the fear that his grandparents might die. We asked him why.

"Because they're afraid to have any fun. Toys are fun; that's not good."

Does that sound logical to you? It doesn't have to. Children's fears are never shaped by logic as adults use it.

His second fear was a fear of being silly and happy. It might be phrased, "You're not supposed to play. You're not supposed to have fun. If you have fun, you're wasting time. That's bad."

Bad to whom? To his grandparents. He loved his grandparents dearly and loathed the thought of disappointing or displeasing them. Jason, the firstborn, happened to be a bit of a perfectionist anyway. He felt driven to perfectly please his wise old grandparents.

This attitude of his grandparents is not uncommon. Obviously, it is completely different from that of the indulgent grandparent, who strives to spoil the child, hand it back to the parents, and go home happy. Actually we find a lot of grandparents, children of the thirties and forties, who are convinced that godliness means, essentially, working your tail to the bone—or your fingers off, or whatever the trite expression is. There are just as many Mains grandparents out there as there are indulgent grandparents; perhaps more.

"Make every moment count!" the popular battle cry, has been reinterpreted to mean, "Never spend time on yourself. Never relax! Shun recreation!" That's not redeeming the time at all. Redeeming the time means keeping a good personal attitude and emotional health, so as to serve better. And that requires relaxation and play as well as work. Recreation breaks the grip of work, lest you burn out. Jason had none of the joy Paul promises in Philippians. And Jason was still just a tender little boy.

As we explored the background of Jason's family, Jason's parents came to realize that the grandparents' fears were based on their Depression experiences so many years ago. They found laughter, toys, and fun very threatening. They were deeply afraid they would somehow lose everything and the only protection, skimpy as it was, was constant hard work and sobriety.

Jason's parents had to come to realize also that the grandparents were not bad people. They were very good people, full of love. How then to restructure the relationships and attitudes that would release Jason from his gloom?

The Solution

Roger Tanner grimaced as if he were sucking in a string of spaghetti in acid sauce. "You don't understand about my parents. Elaine's, either, for that matter, but mine especially. They aren't going to reexamine their actions, not by any stretch of imagination. They're certain they're perfect grandparents. They want only what's best for the children. Just ask them."

"Have you talked to them about their habit of using James and Aubrey as middlemen?"

"I tried. Zero. Zip."

"Talking to them, working it out, is by far better than letting it ride. But if talking fails, you need a plan B to fall back on."

"Lay out plan B for me."

"Plan B consists of prepping the kids."

When Elaine explained to James that Grandma tended to be locked into certain ways of doing things and that calling him "Jimmy" was one of those things, she was prepping him.

Elaine was not reasoning with him. Reasoning would not work well with a grade-schooler and would not work at all on a preschooler. She was simply explaining, in black and white so to speak, how Grandma operates. She asked for tolerance. She did not require some rare level of understanding. She simply voiced how things are.

In the case of Dr. Minirth's friends, in which the grandparents indirectly questioned their adult children's wisdom in buying a large home, the adult children would first try to talk to their parents. If that failed to produce the desired result—in this case for the grandparents to cease raising doubts or even discussing the matter at all—they might take the children aside in advance of a visit.

They might explain that Grandpa and Grandma gave a great deal of attention to financial matters such as buying houses, and that sometimes caused them to worry about other people's financial matters. Their concerns did not indicate a problem. Their concerns indicated rather that they loved the children very much and were worried they might be disappointed. Love is a very positive and desirable thing for grandparents and the parents are very lucky that the grandparents care so much. With further reassurances, the parents might reinforce the basic thought now and then.

The problem is deeper and more insidious in the matter of Jason Mains. The adult children tried talking to the grandparents, and again met limited success. The grandparents, understandably, had lived their whole lives under their no-play mindset and the adult children could not realistically expect them to change.

The parents took three different routes to the same end. These roads involved some changes of lifestyle themselves, but they turned out to be healthy changes.

First, they modeled recreation, knowing children learn by imitation. Both parents deliberately carved out some extra free time to do more leisure activities such as visits to the zoo and the Renaissance Faire in a neighboring town. The whole family rooted together for the old classic John Deere and the bright red 1950s Farmall in a tractor pulling contest. At the science museum they marveled at the wonders of electricity and played in the discovery room. They took care to prevent these jaunts from becoming a let's-hurry-and-do-it-all sort of thing. Their attitude was relax, enjoy. Stop to smell the flowers.

Second, they reiterated their love for the grandparents, while pointing out that different people have different ways of looking at things. Different people have different likes and tastes. That is very good. Someday Jason would have his own preferences and they might not be the same as the grandparents' or the parents'. That is good too. In a very important way, you see, the Mainses were planting that seed for the future, preparing Jason to leave the nest. By word and deed they showed Jason that it's okay to be different, even from a loved one. Because of the situation, it was helpful to Jason that the seed began to sprout a little early.

Finally, they physically curtailed somewhat Jason's contact with his grandparents. They cut no ties, but they watchfully sought out ways to minimize the grandparents' adverse effect on him. They monitored visits more closely and did more activities as an extended family rather than simply turning Jason over to the grandparents and making a swift exit.

Jason laughs now. He's a silly little boy again, at least as much as his natural perfectionism will allow. But the big dividend came to the parents. They discovered how much they themselves followed the all-work-no-play mind-set and how close they had come to burning out. Their lives, now more balanced, are also more productive.

THE THREE-GENERATION HOUSEHOLD

"You can't imagine how often it happens," says Dr. Warren. "I suppose it was probably more common ten years ago when divorce was less acceptable. But it still happens so much. The couple get a divorce. She has custody of the kids and moves in with her parents. I have never once seen a situation of that sort that did not cause

incredible frustration and anger across all three generations. The whole fear thing gets stirred up anew for everyone."

The fears and concerns may never be voiced. They may
not even rise to a conscious level to be recognized for
what they are. But they're there. The grandparents fear
they will get stuck being parents again for not one generation but two. The adult children fear coming under the
parental thumb again, or perhaps never being able to get
out and become autonomous again.

The fears in the kids, exacerbated by the fact that their
world has just been shattered, reflect the fears of the other
two generations visited upon them. In addition, the kids
fear, and rightly so, that by having two sets of parents they
won't be able to please them all. Like their parents, the
children fear that this means a permanent change in their
lives, to be trapped forever, never to have a normal family.
Rarely can the children give voice to their fears, but that's
what lurks inside.

On the surface, living with the grandparents can be fun
for the children. Fun, yes—but ultimately destructive.
Grandpa and Grandma feel intense sympathy for the innocent children, whether or not they feel any sympathy
for the parents. It matters not whether the grandparents
have chosen sides in the divorce dispute; it's the children
that matter. *Pity the poor children, who have no say or
control.* To feed that sympathy, they very, very frequently
bend over backward to pamper the innocents. As a result,
the children become damagingly entitled—that is,
spoiled.

Willard, next door to James, is just such a child. His
grandparents overgratify him. His mother remarried and
went off without him. Old Willard, the terror of the town,
is terrified. Beneath the abrasive, belligerent exterior, a
confused little boy is unimaginably scared about his future. He has no idea what it's going to be.

Willard has no journeymate, and certainly no parenting. Gratification is not parenting, and that's what his

grandparents are concerned with, meeting the needs they think he has and he thinks he has—very rarely what his true needs are. The over-gratification itself produces tension inside Willard; he loves it and he hates it. His mom doesn't parent at all, and no one knows where his father is.

But everyone knows where Willard is. In the principal's office. Again.

If a Three-Generation Arrangement Is Unavoidable

How could Willard's mother have avoided the situation? She had no financial choice other than moving back in with her parents.

Both adult generations agree that it's temporary. Sure, Willard's mom was devastated. Newly divorced people almost always are. Sure, she needed help getting back on her feet. Before she separated, when she was first determining that she would have to move in with Mom and Dad, she should have set up a schedule, a timetable, for leaving there again. Six months? Eight months? What would it take to become reestablished? Put it in writing. Commit it to paper. This is a master plan.

When they learned that Willard and his mom were coming, the parents, too, should have sat down and made a plan. Once Willard and his mom actually arrived (ideally, it would occur before she moves in, but that never happens), all three adults would then compare plans. What is realistic? What is workable? What is the time limit?

"No time limit," Willard's grandma said. Her heart was filled with love. Her head was filled with fairy dust. There *has* to be a time limit, a line drawn. Draw it ahead of time.

The child's parent remains the child's parent. "I shall remain the rearing parent of my own children." The adult child returning to the nest must make that pledge.

And the grandparents must validate that pledge. "Our child is the parent. We are temporary landlords."

What does this mean specifically? The parent makes the decisions about discipline and scheduling (bedtime, for specific example), and handles personality conflicts.

"This means I shouldn't get into it at all? But I see such needs the child has!" the grandmother would argue.

"Common sense," claims Dr. Minirth, "draws the line between help and meddling. By all means step in and help when you can. Help when it's appropriate. But allow the reins, the primary control, to remain in the parent's hands."

A system will be in place to help the child emotionally. The parents' separation has just torn the children's whole system apart. That wrenching destruction produces unspeakable fear in children. The parent is in emotional upheaval, true. But still, parents and grandparents together must be sensitive to the children's new and special needs. Make certain both the parent and the grandparents have in place a method for dealing with the kids' fears.

"I was seeing a child in the hospital whose parents were divorcing," says Dr. Minirth. "The kid had sad eyes. Such sad eyes. He had attempted suicide. I said, 'It must be pretty rough.' He said, 'Yeah, I guess so.' His utter sadness got to me. His whole world had been destroyed."

Part of any system is simply persons to spend time with the children. Children can make great strides toward working out their fears just by talking to trusted adults. Adults earn trust by spending time with the kids. That may mean putting aside something else that is clamoring for the adult's time.

Dr. Minirth smiles at one of his own memories. "I was going to work one morning when my little one asked to go four-wheeling. She loves four-wheeling. I thought to myself, *Forget doing the radio broadcast; the other will do fine without me.* And we went four-wheeling."

Now, not all people can leave their job at a moment's notice, but we can all plan relaxed, fun time to spend with our children. And Dr. Minirth is not dealing with divorce issues, of course. He is firmly and happily wed. But his course of action with his children is a model for parents and grandparents with children of divorce. His advice is to, "Find something the kids like and are good at."

His daughters are into horses big time. Many Saturday mornings, he gets up with them at 3:30. Then they load the horses and head for a cafe for a substantial breakfast of biscuits, gravy, and sausage. Then they go to a local horse show or trail ride.

"It's been wonderful," he says. "It's so positive, and great for their identity and self-image. It's important to spend that time when they're younger. The older they get, the less they want to be with you. Carrie, ten years old, wants to be with me most of the time. Renee, the thirteen-year-old, is still with me but I have to work at it. Rachel is almost seventeen—it's harder to get time with her now. She has her own schedule and things to do."

Is Alicia, at a year and a half, included?

Dr. Minirth grins. "She has her own horse named Suzy.

"One thing I've done with my daughters is take father-daughter trips. Every three months or so we take a trip, *usually* to Arkansas. We camp out, ride horses, sing hymns of the faith. It's a great chance to share fears and anxieties—to bond. For dealing with fears and insecurities, and for building and confirming their faith, it's probably one of the most valuable things."

The happy smile fades. "I counsel many people who never enjoyed their children while they were young. They'll ask me, 'Is it too late?' So I quote Joel 2:25 for them, 'I will restore to you the years that the swarming locust has eaten.' No, it's not hopeless anytime. But the younger your children are when you spend time with them—and I mean significant time—the better."

The older we get, collectively speaking, the stronger

our defenses become, and the harder it is to train us. The efforts spent helping a child deal with fear and pain in the early years multiply themselves as the child grows.

When children are in a divorce situation, with the added tension and confusion of living in the grandparents' home, they need even more of this closeness and attention. They need a journeymate.

"Kids will spill it all from the back of a horse when they won't talk to you otherwise," says Dr. Minirth.

Again we say, find something the children like, and do it with them.

These general concepts transfer well to any child-adult relationship. Many kids today, children without a closely bonded adult in their lives, need big brothers and sisters. The church should be leading in this area with wholesome mentors.

"There was a boy in my church," Dr. Minirth recalls, "who had no male models at all. None. He and I would go down to the creek and skip stones. I taught him how to walk like a man, how to throw rocks, do boy things. You never know how far that will go; it might be the spark to keep a kid going. A little attention goes a long way.

"God placed great value on kids. We ought to too."

14

Single Parenting

Dear Hector,

What a morass is modern America.

What a waste is poetic alliteration on a stupid mutt.

You know Michael Roberts down the street. He's the nine-year-old who feeds you dog biscuits. I suspect he also feeds you the whole wheat bread from his sandwiches at noon. He told me once he doesn't like whole wheat. Apparently his mother serves it regularly.

I referred her to Dr. Warren for Michael's school phobia. She says that's getting better. But helping Michael—and herself, too, apparently—would be so much easier with a man in the house.

You don't see a man around their house because his mother is divorced. And that's very sad. Her Michael needs a man, a buddy. I suppose you could say a substitute father. I'd like to be that person. His mother would be grateful. James wouldn't mind; he and Michael sometimes do things together anyway. But Elaine doesn't want me to get involved. She's afraid if I get started, the demands on my time will escalate, that Michael will need more and more. I don't have free time anyway. Also, she points out that I'd be opening myself up to a lawsuit maybe years in the future. The way America's going, she's probably right. Our propensity to sue has created a morass of fear and hostility. I feel that hostility and especially the fear.

I feel trapped, afraid some harmless overture will be misinterpreted, afraid someone will misconstrue an innocent gesture. The gutless wonder, that's me. Always has been.

You're lucky you're a dog, Hector. Nothing to be

afraid of. No hard choices. In fact even fewer, now that you're spayed.

> *In my usual state of confusion,*
> *Roger Tanner*

HOME ALONE

The single parent. Thousands of people in America annually become instant single parents through the tragedy of the spouse's untimely death. Statistically, though, the far larger source of single parents is divorce. The statistics also show that this pattern is by far the most typical: Following the divorce, Mom takes the children. Within two years Dad has almost no contact. Statistically, he will enjoy a higher standard of living single than he did when he was married. Meanwhile, Mom's standard of living will drop significantly. Mom will be frustrated and depressed and the children will have difficulties. That's another statistic: The percentage of children of divorced parents with serious emotional problems is far greater than one would predict from the raw divorce figures.

These single parents are desperate for answers. Even more, they are desperate for someone who simply knows what it's like. They'd love to find books with pat solutions to their unique problems, but there are none. Now they'll settle for anyone who understands.

The Problem of Finding Support

One of the most serious issues with which singles must deal is lack of support. Not only do other adults fail to offer practical help to them and their children, the other adults stand wary. To wives, a divorced woman seems, undeservedly, to be a threat to their marriages. Husbands instinctively don't like a divorced man anywhere around their wives. Plagued with jealousy and fear, surrounding adults back off, offering nothing more substantial than platitudes and pity, if anything.

Single parents suffer fears unique to their situation. They greatly fear being inadequate to the job of rearing healthy children. They fear their children will go through the same painful marital experiences they are enduring now. And they know their situation has bred a new colony of fears in the children.

Anything that threatens a child's world produces fear. This is true of all children, not just those of divorce. If a parent becomes ill, if Dad loses his job, if the parents fight, the kids know it. Worry fits children like a puppy fits people's laps.

The healthiest of children in "unbroken" homes harbor a secret worry that they might lose a parent. It's a remote concern, not a threat as such. But that fear pops right up to the surface when the child of divorce actually does lose one resident parent. Can the other parent, the custodial parent, not slip away just as easily?

"Concurrent with this fear is the dream," says Dr. Warren. "The child also dreams, hopes, wills, prays—whatever you want to call it—that somehow his parents will get back together again. A very devastating thing that can happen to a child of divorce is the remarriage of one or both parents. Then reconciliation is no longer possible. The dream has been destroyed."

Quelling fears.   Fern, you'll remember, was afraid to separate from her children, Michael and Gail; she had become too firmly enmeshed with them. We worked with her to root out and resolve her fears. But she must be working on the children's fears as well. That means time spent with them—reading books, playing games, taking walks, pretending.

Fern snorted. "Peachy. So who does the housework? I come home every night to five hours of laundry, cooking, cleaning, and getting the kids ready for something or other. And I'm not a fussbudget about the house. We're talking minimal cleaning here, shoveling up the big stuff, straightening up, cooking non-gourmet meals. I just don't have time for anything else, and I barely make grocery money, not money to hire a maid or something."

Enter the support system. If Fern must choose between spending time with her kids or with her vacuum cleaner, friends should be helping out with the vacuum cleaner.

Friends should be helping out with the kids too. Men should be taking Michael along on jaunts with their own sons. The mothers of Gail's friends should be making special efforts to include Gail and to provide both children with loving, secure, significant-other adults.

Here's where Roger, as a neighbor, can help. Michael and James are close together in age, so Roger has an open door to becoming a mentor and male model for Michael. This would be very difficult for Elaine, who feels threatened because Fern is a sharp lady, and, technically, she's available.

Elaine must come to realize that being available does not mean being predatory or wanton. Elaine must picture the situation from Fern's point of view, or from her own if she were suddenly cast into the role of a single mother. What would Elaine and her children need most? That's what Fern needs now.

The Long Haul—As Children Grow

A mother named Rita talked about the problems of her eight-year-old son Bucky. "His father and I divorced five years ago. We saw a counselor. Bucky seemed to do real well. There were no problems, at least not serious ones. Now this problem is occurring all of a sudden. He's getting into fights, arguing, crying, irritable . . . I just don't know what's happening."

"Does he mention the divorce?"

"No. We worked out the divorce years ago; we parted friends, more than most couples do when they split. Bucky sees his father every other weekend. No, it can't be that."

As we worked with Bucky, we could see that the divorce was indeed the problem. The difference was that he was no longer three years old. His cognitive thinking, his feelings, his perceptions, and even his needs had all matured. And that was good and natural. Bucky was thinking in ways he could not think before. He was gaining insight and cognitive skills. He was learning about abstraction and the difference between fantasy and reality. He saw things in new ways appropriate for his age. He was looking at the divorce in new ways too.

The issue of Dad and Mom not being together, and Bucky's wishing they weren't divorced, was the same old issue, but now it had to be addressed again. Bucky had to reprocess those things in the new context with his new skills.

Whether or not the primal fears are allayed, circumstantial fears rarely go away totally. They slip into the background if they are managed well, but they will come again from some different direction, possibly from the same sources, over and over as the child grows up.

The single parent needs help, a little extra to fill the gaps, not a place to dump the whole job. Sometimes a stopgap is all that is needed.

Garth, a twelve-year-old boy, illustrates what we mean.

Garth's father died after a car wreck four years ago. At the time of his death, everything was done right, so to speak. Garth saw his dad in the hospital before he died and was able to say good-bye. He did well. His mother got a good job and then a transfer to Dallas. So Garth, his mom, and his three sisters moved down from their family home by the water in Barnstable County, Massachusetts. Then, suddenly, Garth was falling apart at school, acting moody and withdrawn.

He cast gloomy eyes at Dr. Warren (very attractive eyes, actually, deep blue with huge lashes, but Dr. Warren wasn't about to say that). "I think about my dad all the time," he admitted. And he broke down, weeping and wailing.

Dr. Warren supplied the tissue and the empathy until the crying subsided. "You don't tell anyone, though."

Garth shook his head. "I'm afraid if I tell people how sad I am, they'll think I'm not strong. It'll mean I'm not a real man."

"Mmmm. Ever talk to your mom about this?"

"I can't. I'm afraid it'll upset her too much. Her and my sisters. I can't."

There were two fears right there. Dr. Warren started digging for the deeper ones. "Have you always thought about your dad all the time?"

"No, not much." Garth shook his head. "When I was little I never thought about it at all. Until we moved."

Moving is traumatic for kids, at least to some extent. It placed Garth on uncertain footing—could he make new friends and find acceptance in Texas with his Boston accent and eastern ways?—as well as in an alien environment. Dallas isn't the least little bit like the Back Bay. Garth was deeply afraid he couldn't handle all this, much less life itself, without his dad. He feared he could not make it growing up without a dad.

But even if he had never moved, Garth would still need help. Now much older, he was able to realize far more clearly how much he missed his dad. He could perceive more deeply how much he had lost.

Dr. Warren empathized. "When you're twelve you miss your dad a lot more than when you're eight because you need a dad a lot more when you're twelve."

"Think so?"

"Absolutely. Thinking about him so much is the way it should be."

We also uncovered a deep, hidden fear in Garth that he would die when he became a man. That, too, was natural. He identified closely with his father, as all sons do, and his father did not survive manhood.

Garth's story has a good ending. We took him through the grief process all over again, helping him regrieve the loss. That grieving in itself addressed much of his fears. In that process his mom and sisters made good journeymates.

But as females, his mother and sisters were not adequate to initiate the grieving process. Garth, afraid he'd not be manly, needed a significant male in his life to give him permission as a male to be scared, fearful, and angry. Dr. Warren assumed the role of authoritative, empathetic male and showed him by example as well as by talking that grieving and weeping and anger are all right for men. Then his mom was able to take over. She carried it splendidly, responding exquisitely to the cues. She was no stranger to grief herself.

Garth needed a significant male figure in his life for only a few months while he learned the lesson that grieving is not effeminate. But when he needed the male, he needed him in the most intense way. He could not have undergone healing without one.

Were Garth not in counsel, another male—perhaps a pastor, coach, teacher, friend, or neighbor—could have met that need. Note that it was a temporary need, not one that would lock the adult into Garth's life forever.

As children of single parents grow, and as they process and re-process old fears and wounds with new skills, they need specific kinds of adults from time to time. If the single parent is not the required adult of the moment, it is crucial that another adult step in. So, although ministering to singles and their children is a long-range proposition, the ministers need not become entangled in their lives constantly through the long term. Being available when needed now and then serves also.

And Then There's Willard

Ah, yes, Willard. If only his mother had not married and moved away without him, Willard wouldn't be messed up now, right? And now nobody is going to be able to un-mess Willard, so why try?

"I can't begin to tell you the number of older kids, eight to fourteen, who suffer as Willard does even though their mothers did not actually leave," says Dr. Warren.

"And then there are the 'dry' divorces," Dr. Minirth adds. "These are the cases where the relationship ended without an actual divorce. Mom and Dad are all wrapped up in their misery and not relating to each other, but they're not relating well to the children, either, even though they're all living under the same roof."

The golden triangle we discussed in Chapter 3, with

Mom and Dad relating to each other and also down to the child, doesn't exist in these cases.

So many times, when divorce actually does divide the parents, Dad leaves. When Mom takes her baby to live with her parents, the child loses his or her own mommy. The grandparents become the parent figures, just like in the old days before the marriage, and Mom loses her authority, her position as Mom. She becomes a kid again, and yet the grandparents are not parents of the child. Even with all those adults in the house, the child is virtually parentless.

Typically, Mom is devastated. Mom has become such a child herself because of her devastation, she can't set up any structure for herself. Her natural child becomes, in essence, a possession—a factor in an ugly equation, but no longer a child to be nurtured.

Mom and child in this situation relate to each other in an infantile way, each existing to gratify the other. The mother may be either the child's closest friend or unavailable, but she's not the mother the child needs. She certainly is not the father, which the child needs desperately.

"The kids get to be fourteen or so and they're still messed up," Dr. Warren concludes. "In some ways Willard is no better off and no worse off because his mother left physically. I know a lot of children whose single mothers or single fathers have checked out emotionally— just as unavailable as Willard's mom—and they are with their children on a daily basis."

None of the primal fears were put to rest permanently. They crop up again. The special fears generated by the child's situation press down. If the neighbors think Willard is a terror now, just watch him in another six years.

The aggressive Willard needs significant adults just as much as does the polite Michael and the shy James. James's family is in place, providing a measure of help, and that measure is getting larger and larger as James's father grows. Michael and Willard have no resource except the attention of others.

A variety of agencies have been set up to help kids like Willard. Here is a partial list. You can add to it by asking your library about available community programs. The local United Way office can also make suggestions.

- The church, with youth groups, singles groups, youth activities such as Awana, Young Life, scouting.
- The place of the parent's employment, if it offers child care, counseling, flex time.
- Big Brothers and Big Sisters.
- Private social agencies such as the Salvation Army and the Red Cross.
- The school. Teachers may have the same single-parenting problems you do.

THE SINGLE PARENT'S SYSTEM

Let us now assume the case that usually exists. The single parent has no support system whatever. It's Mom, or Dad, and that's it. What might the single parent do?

Finding support people isn't easy, but it can be done. Use the agencies above to make and screen contacts. Seek out other singles, friends you can trust. As a single parent you need support for such things as babysitting while you take a break. If that's not possible, take the kids along on a break from the routine. Go to a fast-food joint that has a playground and turn them loose while you relax. Go to the zoo and take the tram ride. Visit a park with a playground and take along a book. The idea is to break out of your rut occasionally.

Keep in mind that you want to prevent the parent-to-child leg of your broken triangle from growing too thick. They are the kids. You're the parent. You're not a friend and playmate, even though you play with them. You're unique. Keep that firmly in mind. You're providing the guidance and role modeling they need to understand themselves and overcome their innate fear of their own growth.

"I have the kids doing jobs like taking out the garbage and sweeping the porch and sidewalks, but I pay them for it—a flat rate." Fern Roberts detailed some of the positive steps she was taking on her own. "Every time I give them something to do or start to talk to them about something, I ask myself, *Is this a grown-up's role I'm foisting off on them? Am I expecting them to do a parent's job?* The answer has to be no. Then I ask the biggie: *Would they be asked to do this if Roy were still with us?* That answer has to be yes."

Fern is now actively avoiding becoming so enmeshed with the kids. She's trying to keep them kids.

Swap Tasks

Get together with other parents in the same singles boat. Make an offer to swap babysitting or housework. Get tips from others on how to streamline chores and avoid time-consuming jobs.

"Did you know," Fern Roberts bubbled excitedly, "that if you spray your mop with the spritzer you use for ironing, it picks up the dust easier? Meg over in Irving told me that. I've started clipping those "Hints from Heloise" in the paper. We're getting together at lunchtime, about five of us at work, to get a babysitting co-op going. Hey, if I'm going to be sitting at home with my kids all evening, I might as well have Meg's kids too once in a while. Then she takes mine. Some of the other girls, and Randolph in shipping and handling, too—he's a single parent—are starting to join in. They like the idea of an evening without the kids."

Seek Spiritual Support

Fern had been neglecting her spiritual life, so wrapped up was she in the drudgery of getting through the week. Now she takes the kids to Sunday school without fail, using the adult Sunday school as an impetus for her own growth. The same teacher also handles the adults' Wednesday-night bible study, but Wednesdays Fern has

Meg's kids. So she gets the study materials and works on her own. She misses the discussion and cross-fertilization of ideas, but she gets the basics. She is planning to join a Tuesday-night class.

Perhaps the biggest benefit comes from the support Fern receives with members' prayers. Prayer is powerful! Many churches offer a combined Bible study/prayer group of dedicated people. Such groups are worth seeking out.

The quality and benefits of singles groups vary widely from church to church. Some churches have strong, active groups, while others provide little more than token attention to singles. Again, good singles groups are invaluable and well worth finding. Fern found an excellent group in her own denomination, but other singles might cross denominational lines.

Build a Separate Identity

As another gimmick to break out of the trap of over-involvement as a mother, Fern is taking an art course.

"An art course?" we asked.

She smiled wistfully. "I have always wanted to be a fashion designer. When I was little, in school, I'd draw beautiful ladies in evening gowns. In high school I designed the costumes for the junior class play. We did *My Fair Lady*. It's the most fun I've ever had. So now I'm taking an art class through the adult extension program at the local high school. It's correspondence, with homework assignments. This university graduate student does the grading and evaluating. I give half an hour a day to it, even if it means not doing housework. I do more if I can. And I checked out videos at the library on how to sew. Mom never did teach me how and my high school home ec. course was a dud."

Fern Roberts will probably never rival the fashion mavens of Paris. But whether she succeeds brilliantly as a designer or even succeeds at all is entirely beside the point. She is developing another identity that does not have "Mom" written all over it, building at least one element of her life that is entirely her own, in which the kids are peripheral. She's taking pleasure in something not household oriented.

This is not selfishness. It is survival.

Find Gender Roles in the Library

Fern needs a man to take Michael under his wing and show him manhood at its best. In short, Michael needs a role model. Let's assume that no man comes along who can accomplish that. Then what? Then it's time to use—again—the power of the story.

Stories are the natural medium for teaching children moral standards and values. They aren't bad for teaching gender roles, either.

Fern wanted to show Michael how a man is supposed to be. She sat down one day during coffee break at work and made a list. What attributes did a real man have? She wrote them down. What men in fact and in fiction displayed those attributes? She wasn't sure. There was the John Wayne type, but that wasn't all of it by a long shot. There was also Alan Alda on "M*A*S*H" and everything else from *The Scarlet Pimpernel* to *Lethal Weapon*.

That Saturday she took the kids to the library and turned them loose in the kids' section during story hour. While they listened to the story reader, she went to the video section. She asked questions of an assistant librarian, a young woman who had seen most of the films and knew about the others.

"Here's my list," Fern said, waving her coffee-break paper. She explained what she wanted by asking questions. "What male character would best display bravery? What males would provide a good model for how to deal with emotions?"

The librarian was reticent at first, uncertain how to proceed. But she warmed to the idea quickly. Five minutes later she was into it so enthusiastically Fern would have needed a wheelbarrow to cart off all the materials she suggested.

Fern left with several Jacques Cousteau videos, the Magnus Magnusson PBS video about the real Vikings, and a stack of books. The males in Walt Morey's stories, or Lee Roddy's, or even the Laura Ingalls Wilder *Little House* books also offered positive models. Fern and Michael watched the video of *Old Yeller*, which vividly displays the best attributes of both boys and men—bravery, diligence, responsibility, and wisdom. Over the next two weeks she and Michael would watch the other videos and talk about them, and read the books either separately or together and discuss them too.

The power of the story could teach Michael what Fern, as a woman, could not.

Learn Mental and Emotional Housekeeping

Fern, like any single parent, had to shift gears in her own life. She had to adjust herself to her present reality, and this was something she could do by dedicating herself in three ways.

First, Fern dedicated herself to talking about the trauma she'd been through with other people. This was not a case of rehashing old grievances, but of discussing her life in a therapeutic way. Fern's prayer group provided this support. It could have been a counselor, a pastor, a trusted friend. She talked about her feelings of anger and sadness, lest those feelings begin to dominate her interactions, particularly with her kids. Other words to describe this would be *catharsis*, or *cleansing*.

Second, Fern dedicated herself to clearing up the conflicts that had led to the divorce. It is always wise to do this as soon as possible. She had to make sure those conflicts got put to rest. It wasn't easy. She's still working on it. The purpose behind that need, experience and research tell us, is that the children's greatest need is stability. They need stability geographically—that is, knowing they have a safe place to live—and stability financially, knowing their situation is safe. They also need stability in their relationships and for that to happen, Mom and Dad must quit bickering and get on with life.

Fern needs exactly that same stability herself.

Finally, Fern dedicated herself to a realistic view of who she is now. And that was tough. Not who she was (a wife, a distraught person, a person struggling with problems) and not who she wishes she were (a happy wife, a powerful supermom, father and mother both to her poor children), but who she is.

No single parent can be both father and mother, and it was very hard for Fern to quit having that expectation. The kids' father would always be Dad and she would always be Mother. No less, no more.

It was especially hard for her to relinquish the dream that she could shape the relationship between her kids and their absent father. All she could do (and that was hard enough in itself) was avoid damaging, changing, mutilating, or undermining the children's relationship with that other parent. It was not her job to build it.

Control What You Can Control

Many singles feel trapped and powerless in a crushing role. Fern had to fight that feeling of powerlessness for two reasons. One, it was wearing her down. Second, in counseling she learned that the person who feels powerless is likely to try to control everything, whether it's controllable or not. Empowerment would help her take control of those things she ought to be controlling and, as the children grew, release control of them little by little. Now was the time to plant the seed—the idea that someday they would be equipped to leave home. Being on their own was their birthright and expectation.

Because control was such a problem for her, she had to work hard. Even then she was not entirely successful. With our help she wrote down lists of what she could reasonably expect to control in her life, such as:

- Her free time, what little there was of it
- Her attitude at work (but not her co-workers')
- Her mood and attitude at home (but not her children's)

- Meals at home (but only to a limited extent what the kids nibbled on when she wasn't around) and similar everyday matters

She also listed what she could control in her children's lives but *only while she was with them.*

- What they could watch on TV
- What they ate or did not eat
- Whether they got their homework done
- How much allowance each received
- What friends could be invited into her home

Then she built a list of what she could not control. The length of it startled her.

- Roy's abandonment of her. That was his choice, regardless that he claimed she forced him to leave.
- Roy's involvement, if any, with his children
- Her children's friendships beyond the home
- Her co-workers' and fellow church members' attitudes

She checks her behavior and attitudes against those lists periodically. She especially reviews control issues when she has a blowup with Michael. Kids control whatever they can too. So she asks herself, *Was this storm a contest of wills or just human error?*

The ultimate effect of these steps is to reduce greatly Fern's feelings of powerlessness. Before, she was a reactor. Something would happen and she would react to it (reactors have little power). Now she is an actor. She is taking the initiative in several areas of her life. Initiators have the power to change things.

Even more, her new spiritual life gives her confidence. There is immense comfort and power in a solid prayer life, a strong spiritual identity, a healthy, growing faith in God and Jesus Christ.

In Jesus Christ is the ultimate role model for every man and woman.

15
Fear
Strikes
Back

SIGNS OF GROWTH

Elaine marched into Dr. Warren's office, James and Aubrey in tow. Dr. Warren rose to greet her and waited as she seated herself on the plaid sofa. He greeted little Aubrey as she perched on the sofa edge, smiling. Then he glanced at James as he sat down, and did a double take.

He leaned forward, grinning, for a better look. "Seldom have I seen a shiner that perfectly magnificent. Your black eye has a few colors in it the rainbow doesn't know about." He sat back, still smiling. "Now there's a story I want to hear!"

James shrugged bashfully, grinning. "Here's my letter to Troid. It's a printout this time. Is that okay?"

"It's excellent. Thank you." Dr. Warren laid the letter on the coffee table by his knee and noted in passing that it was three pages long.

Elaine was not grinning. "When we determined to help James about his excessive fearfulness, Doctor, this is not what I had in mind. You know my feelings regarding competitiveness and violence."

"So this is a product of violence. Interesting."

Aubrey chirped, "She's mad at Daddy too. He laughed and said 'Great going, son!' when Jimmy came home with his black eye. He didn't ask him about it or anything. Mommy won't speak to him."

Elaine started to shush her daughter and caught herself. Her lips formed a tight, thin line. "I believe James has lost a little too much fear."

Dr. Warren laced his fingers together across his belt buckle. "How did this all come about, James?"

"Well . . ." James glanced at his mom and took a deep breath. "It was Willard. He was being cruel and I told him to stop it, and he said, 'Make me.' So I made him."

"I see. What was the cruelty?"

"There's this girl in our class, Gretchen. She's tough. She's the only girl on the softball team and she's really strong. Anyway, Willard grabbed her pouch and wouldn't give it back to her. Playing keepaway, you know? She has this pouch with medicine in it. She's diabetic. You know what that is?"

Dr. Warren nodded.

"She really needed it and she threatened to go tell the teachers. Willard said if she did, he'd throw it in the creek and she'd never find it. He would, too. Willard doesn't care about teachers or anything. She was crying and angry and she couldn't do anything alone, and we—"

"Where was everyone else?"

"I don't know, going home, I guess. It was after school, out on the Eighteenth Avenue side of the schoolyard."

"Continue."

James shrugged again. "That's it. I socked him and he socked me. But he let go of the pouch to do it, so Gretchen grabbed it quick and then she started swinging at him, the two of us. He fell down. I don't think we hit him hard at all; I think he tripped. He's pretty clumsy. And we ran."

"I recall your telling me you don't like Gretchen."

"I don't. She's one of the kids that laughs at me a lot and calls me a scaredy-cat. But you should have seen her crying, Dr. Warren! She was so . . . uh . . ." James searched awhile through his mind, seeking in vain the right words.

"Beside herself? Distraught? Upset?"

"Yeah! Really upset. Choking, she was crying so much and yelling. I had to do something."

"You were very brave. I know how much you dread Willard."

"Please, Doctor," Elaine sighed. "Don't encourage him. I will not countenance fighting."

"James," Dr. Warren asked, "do you remember we talked about people like Willard? Do you remember what we said?"

"Sorta."

"Are people like Willard always brave and fearless?"

"No. Usually they're scared inside and putting on a front."

"Were you brave and fearless?"

"No!" His one eye grew big. The other stayed pretty well puffed shut. "I was scared inside. I didn't want to mouth off to him but he was going to cause Gretchen a lot of trouble if he threw her pouch away."

Dr. Warren turned his attention to Elaine. "I neither recommend nor encourage violence. But, in fact, I see an even more positive sign that your son is coming to grips with his fears." He picked up the letter on the side table, a gesture. "At first your son would not bring the letters he wrote to the cat, Mergatroid. Then he brought them in the form of a floppy disk. You see, by bringing in a disk, he didn't have to look at a printed paper. He could divorce himself completely from the thoughts he was expressing. They were very frightening to him.

"Now he brings in the printed letters. He's no longer keeping his distance, symbolically, from his innermost thoughts. It's a great stride forward, an external indication of important internal growth."

She frowned. "There's that much difference between a paper and a floppy?"

"Children are very big on symbolism, remember. Not consciously perhaps, but they pick up on it and use it well. He earned himself a shiner by confronting the schoolmate he fears most. He defended a person who holds him in low esteem. Those are all exciting symbols of his growth—his release from fear."

"Exciting." She grimaced.

"How is Aubrey coming along with her monsters?"

Elaine brightened. "The problem has subsided wonderfully. It's not really a problem anymore. In fact, sometimes I just send Roger in and don't handle it at all."

"Last night Mom and I read a book after Aubrey went to bed." James glowed. All but the one eye. "It was a story about a cat. Troid was perched on the back of the sofa with her paws tucked in while we were reading. She heard the whole thing but she didn't prick her ears up at the funny parts or anything. I don't think she's into stories."

"Cats, as a rule, seldom are. Shall we spend some time in the playroom?"

Both children bought that idea instantly. Aubrey slid off her perch and James jumped up.

"Go ahead. I'll be there momentarily." Dr. Warren watched them leave.

"Doctor," Elaine said, smiling at last, "I don't want to encourage James's fighting in any way, so I couldn't say this in front of him. But I'm so glad we were able to work out his problems so well. Last night, after the children were down and we had gone to bed, Roger talked a long time about his childhood, and how he would never have had the courage to do what James did, and how he would have hated himself afterward for his cowardice. Until our conversation last night, I never dreamed how heavily Roger's childhood weighs on him. I can't tell you how happy he is that James isn't following the same path anymore—even if it did get him a black eye."

Dr. Warren considered that thoughtfully a few moments. "I don't believe I am telling tales out of school here. Willard was in earlier today for his weekly appointment."

"Willard?" she sighed.

"Willard, Mrs. Tanner, was sporting two black eyes."

Appendix A—
What the Bible Says about Fear

Here are a few of the hundreds of verses in Scripture that reassure the believer. Over and over, God reminds us there is only one necessary fear: a heart-in-the-mouth, awestruck, worshipful fear of God Himself. He'll take care of all the rest.

You may wish also to use inspirational and reference books that will lead you to the lovely promises of God. There are many, such as *Healing for Today, Hope for Tomorrow*, a Bible promises book by Thomas Nelson Publishers, and *Jesus said,* the words of Jesus arranged topically for inspiration and comfort, by Ronald Philipchalk and Phillip H. Wiebe, also published by Thomas Nelson.

* * *

"Be strong and of good courage, do not fear nor be afraid of them; for the LORD your God, He is the One who goes with you. He will not leave you nor forsake you. . . . do not fear nor be dismayed." (Deut. 31: 6, 8)

* * *

For the LORD will not forsake His people, for His great name's sake, because it has pleased the LORD to make you His people. (1 Sam. 12:22)

* * *

Whenever I am afraid,
I will trust in You. (Ps. 56:3)

* * *

But You, O Lord, are a shield for me, . . .
I will not be afraid of ten thousands of people
Who have set themselves against me all around.
   (Ps. 3:3, 6)

* * *

I will both lie down in peace, and sleep;
For You alone, O Lord, make me dwell in safety.
   (Ps. 4:8)

* * *

All of Psalm 23.

* * *

The Lord is my light and my salvation;
Whom shall I fear?
The Lord is the strength of my life;
Of whom shall I be afraid? . . .
Though an army should encamp
   against me,
My heart shall not fear;
Though war should rise against me,
In this I will be confident. (Ps. 27:1, 3)

* * *

I sought the Lord, and He heard me,
And delivered me from all my fears. (Ps. 34:4)

* * *

God is our refuge and strength,
A very present help in trouble.
Therefore we will not fear. (Ps. 46:1–2)

* * *

He shall cover you with His feathers,
And under His wings you shall take refuge;
His truth shall be your shield and buckler.
You shall not be afraid of the terror by night. (Ps. 91:4)

* * *

The LORD is on my side;
I will not fear. (Ps. 118:6)

* * *

The LORD shall preserve you from all evil;
He shall preserve your soul. (Ps. 121:7)

* * *

Whoever listens to me will dwell safely,
And will be secure, without fear of evil. (Prov. 1:33)

* * *

When you lie down, you will not be afraid;
Yes, you will lie down and your sleep will be sweet.
Do not be afraid of sudden terror,
Nor of trouble from the wicked when it comes;
For the LORD will be your confidence,
And will keep your foot from being caught.
  (Prov. 3:24–26)

* * *

The fear of man brings a snare,
But whoever trusts in the LORD shall be safe.
  (Prov. 29:25)

* * *

"For I, the LORD your God, will hold your right hand, saying to you, 'Fear not, I will help you.'" (Isa. 41:13)

* * *

"Do not fear nor be afraid; . . . Is there a God besides Me?
Indeed there is no other Rock." (Isa. 44:8)

* * *

"Do not fear, for you will not be ashamed; Nor be dis-
graced, for you will not be put to shame; For you will
forget the shame of your youth, And will not remember
the reproach of your widowhood anymore." (Isa. 54:4)

* * *

"In righteousness you shall be established; You shall be far from oppression, for you shall not fear; And from terror, for it shall not come near you." (Isa. 54:14)

* * *

"Do not fear, little flock, for it is your Father's good pleasure to give you the kingdom." (Luke 12:32)

* * *

"Peace I leave with you, My peace I give to you; not as the world gives do I give to you. Let not your heart be troubled, neither let it be afraid." (John 14:27)

* * *

For you did not receive the spirit of bondage again to fear, but you received the Spirit of adoption by whom we cry out, "Abba, Father." (Rom. 8:15)

* * *

For I am persuaded that neither death nor life, nor angels nor principalities nor powers, nor things present nor things to come, nor height nor depth, nor any other created thing, shall be able to separate us from the love of God which is in Christ Jesus our Lord. (Rom. 8:38–39)

* * *

Be anxious for nothing, but in everything by prayer and supplication, with thanksgiving, let your requests be made known to God; and the peace of God, which surpasses all understanding, will guard your hearts and minds through Christ Jesus. (Phil. 4:6–7)

* * *

For God has not given us a spirit of fear, but of power and of love and of a sound mind. (2 Tim. 1:7)

* * *

So we may boldly say: "The LORD is my helper; I will not fear. What can man do to me?" (Heb. 13:6)

* * *

. . . casting all your care upon Him, for He cares for you. (1 Peter 5:7)

* * *

There is no fear in love; but perfect love casts out fear, because fear involves torment. But he who fears has not been made perfect in love. We love Him because He first loved us. (1 John 4:18, 19)

Appendix B
Summary of Clinical Approaches

Taking care of bedtime fears and nightmares—as well as other fears—is not easy. But even harder is making a judgment call about whether the child is troubled beyond home help. When is professional clinical help recommended, if at all? The adult who sees a troubled, fearful child bumps into that question all the time. What's normal and what's not?

"In one survey of a thousand children, 90 percent had phobias of some sort between the ages of two and fourteen," says Dr. Minirth. "I don't mean the fears we've been talking about so far here. I mean irrational, intense fears beyond the expected. A similar study found that 43 percent of a group of children aged six to twelve expressed many fears and worries.

"In another study, 8 percent of males and 11 percent of females had clinically significant, diagnosable fears by age eighteen. And that happens to have been a conservative study, so we can call this a minimum. In still another study, 6 percent of children aged four to six and 2.5 percent of children twelve to fifteen years needed treatment. I mean clinical treatment, a full-scale professional effort."

SO WHAT'S ABNORMAL?

André LaFarge, age ten, was about as French as the American flag, but his mom fancied things French and things elegant, so she named him André. . . . with an accent mark that André's teachers and the school computers never used. André is scared to death of teenagers—all teenagers—but especially boys. Boy teenagers but especially big ones. Overweight boys. Wrestlers. Football players.

André's mother brought him to us because his father insisted. She had no intention of seeking treatment. She sought instead an evaluation to take home and show Dad, to demonstrate scientifically, as it were, that André was simply going through a stage.

Mrs. LaFarge, her golden hair stylishly cut, did look vaguely like a French film star. Slim and pretty and perfectly dressed, she curled up in an armchair with her legs crossed elegantly. "It's a bit of a problem," she explained, "because André's afraid to go to school. He doesn't mind school at all once he gets there. So Fred or I have to drive him. Other than that, it's nothing."

André, a tad overweight and undertall, was probably the only kid in his fourth-grade class with hair that was styled rather than cut. He wore snazzy cords and a tailored, button-front shirt. He sat quietly, melted like neglected silly putty into a corner of his chair.

"How long have you been aware of this problem?" we asked.

She pursed her lips, carefully made up in a tasteful shade of lipstick, Pink Surprise.

"I'd say two or three months now. Yes. I'm sure it's been less than half a year. Well, no, I suppose it started when he was asking us to drive him to school, and that was last September."

"Eight months ago. Describe the teenagers in your neighborhood," we asked.

"Dreadful!" Mrs. LaFarge wagged her head. "They're so noisy. They drive around all hours and play that music. You can just see their car windows pulsing. It's a shame, too. It used to be such a nice, quiet neighborhood. And they're rude. Incredibly rude."

"Have any of them ever threatened you or harassed you?" We directed the question at André, but his mother answered.

"No, not really. They don't seem to pay attention to

anything or anyone except themselves. They cut across our yard sometimes. We have a corner lot. Never an 'excuse me' or apology. As I say, they're rude." She shrugged helplessly. "You see? His fear is really quite silly. It will go away."

After we completed the evaluation we had to tell Mrs. LaFarge that if the fear indeed disappeared, it would resurface in some other form. It would not go away. It fit our informal criteria for abnormality.

• **It impaired function**. André was afraid to walk to school or ride a bus with high-school students on it. He was, we learned also, afraid to play in his own front yard because the neighborhood kids occasionally (as it turned out, only one family very occasionally) cut across the yard. His life was hobbled, his normal activities curtailed, not because of a real danger but because of his fear.

• **It lasted more than a month**. Kids get some pretty weird ideas. Normally, those ideas come with a flash, then fade. André could have talked himself into being afraid of teens; such momentary phobias happen. But he should have forgotten it, or at least learned to disregard it, over a period of weeks. The fear was not supported by any action on the fear-objects' part. It should have died a natural death.

> **When normal childhood fears take on abnormal proportions, impair function, and hang on for a month or more, it's time to sit up and take note.**

In a clinical setting, we find that many mental disorders have a fear element as part of them. A deep depression may include intense irrational fear. Schizophrenics fear excessively. Brain damage generates fear and anxiety. Autistic children are very fearful. The list goes on. In this book we are talking about fears, whether clinically significant or not, that stand alone. We are not considering fears that are part of another disorder.

To persons outside the profession, diagnosis of fears and mental disorders may seem haphazard—guesswork. Actually, there is a manual for rating and analyzing fears and other problems. It's called, simply, *DSM-III-R* (the III is soon to become IV). The full title is *Diagnostic and Statistical Manual of Mental Disorders (Third Edition-Revised)*, and it's published by the American Psychiatric Association. It provides general guidelines for judging which problems are near-normal and which need professional scrutiny.

The *DSM-III-R* guidelines classify problems based upon the symptoms you see rather than the causes. Not everyone agrees on causes, but everyone *can* agree on the symptoms. The manual is used by professionals both to diagnose problems and to be able to talk about those problems with other professionals. In other words, the guidelines set a common standard.

Although you, the reader, would not make a professional diagnosis, some familiarity with the guidelines may be helpful to you. Reduced to common language, we have cataloged here some of the points that professionals consider. The fears are arranged in escalating severity from near-normal to extremely dysfunctional. Remember that fear is normal. Only when it is carried too far does it become classifiable.

1. Separation Anxiety Disorder

• Anxiety about separation from loved one(s), as in kidnapping, death, accident.

• Manifests itself as intense worry about the loved one, refusal to go to school or to sleep, avoiding being alone.

• Headache, stomachache, nausea, intense distress with crying, pleading, and tantrums when anticipating separation. When separated, an excessive drive to return home, call home, etc.

• Separation anxiety is natural until eighteen months to two years.

2. Avoidant Disorder of Childhood or Adolescence

• Excessive, prolonged withdrawal from contact with unfamiliar people to the degree that functioning is interfered with.

• Occurs naturally after two and a half years, especially five to seven years and particularly in females.

3. Overanxious Disorder

• Excessive prolonged anxiety over future events, past behavior, competence, with attendant inability to relax. Accompanied by somatic complaints such as headaches.

• Marked self-consciousness and need of repeated reassurance from adults.

• Reassurance is a superficial treatment. It won't cure the problem.

4. Phobia (simple type)

• Irrational fear of an object or situation. Object frequently is an animal. The child, for example, may be scared to death of dogs and won't know why. (This is assuming the child was not bitten by a dog; that would be a generalized anxiety with some basis. A phobia is irrational with no basis.) Snakes are common objects of phobias. The snake and dog, in these phobic cases, represent something other than what they are.

• Common up to age ten. May just go away. No one knows why phobias come or why they go. May appear and disappear rapidly. Tend to be transient.

5. School Refusal

This is not a *DSM-III-R* diagnosis but may be related to several of the *DSM-III-R* diagnoses. The child refuses to go to school. Some official diagnoses may be:

• Panic disorder with sweating, trembling, racing heart, dizziness when forced to go to school.

- Extreme fear, anxiety, and panic. In some cases, reaction is precipitated by a move, an accident, a change of teachers, or illness; it may be a medical component of another problem in some cases.

- Separation anxiety disorder, discussed above. This often gets the child what he or she wants, which is to go home.

- Adjustment reaction with anxiety symptoms. A child may experience anxiety as a result of having to adjust to authority, competition, failure, embarrassment, etc. These are big adjustments for a child. An example: Shifting from Christian to secular or secular to Christian schools may generate it.

- Obsessive compulsive disorder. Accompanied by anxiety that is relieved by repetitive compulsive actions. Obsessions (intrusive thoughts) also occur (step on a crack, break Mother's back). Thoughts not wanted, recognized as compulsive, still intrude. Occur as early as ten years. An example: A girl of eight, who straightened her bedsheets over and over.

- Post-traumatic stress disorder. Intense anxiety accompanied by recurrent recollections of a traumatic event, recurrent distressing dreams, feelings of reoccurrence, decreased interest, feeling of estrangement from others, sleep disturbance, guilt, memory impairment, trouble concentrating, avoidance reaction.

A girl, ten, had a recurring dream of a gorilla attacking her. She had been molested by a stepfather but had blocked out memories of the actual molestation.

THE CAUSES, OR ETIOLOGY

Nobody agrees on causes.

"My opinion," says Dr. Minirth, "is that some fears are God-given innate survival mechanisms. When you go beyond that, it's multi-factored. There's not any one cause, but several together. Not all the causes will carry the same weight, but I've found, usually, all are present to some degree. You get in trouble when you concentrate on one and exclude or ignore the others."

The cause may be normal and simply be an innate characteristic, such as the Moro reflex in newborns, discussed in Chapter 2. It's a God-given response to a frightening situation.

Or the cause may be a conditioned response. One patient had been locked in a closet for punishment during childhood. Now, years later, a dark room of any kind arouses an intense fear response. Many unpleasant experiences can trigger conditioned responses: doctors, storms, dogs, or noises, to name a few.

Maturation level is an important factor in fears. Common fear of loud noises in very small children tends to decrease with age. Also, children naturally develop some anxieties as their impulses and desires are met with appropriate restraints. The children have wants, some of which must be thwarted, and that very thwarting may generate fears. Also, when children—particularly infants—become aware of changes in their environment, fears may arise.

Dr. Minirth smiles. "Think about the stress of birth, with the infant's environment changing dramatically. In the amniotic sac, its head is subjected to uterine contractions, then it is pressed through the pelvic canal . . ."

Later, children usually develop a spontaneous fear of strangers. It's age related.

Some fears relate, in some degree, to temperament. Some children are naturally more shy and less outgoing than others, for example. Children with a higher heart rate seem to have more fears, so there is a distinct physiological and biological component to fear responses.

Panic attacks have a definite biological component: heart palpitations, sweating, breathlessness, and, when the blood is analyzed, an abnormally low level of carbon dioxide.

Some fears relate to children's early environments. For example, as we discussed, an overprotective or depriving parental figure can contribute to separation anxiety. Attachment and loss issues cause fears; the child removed from mother becomes agitated and fearful. King Frederick II wanted to see what language babies spoke spontaneously if they were never exposed to human speech (the early church's money was on Latin). Fifty babies were isolated from exposure to language. All fifty died. Attachment-and-loss issues are a life-and-death matter.

Some fears are learned and imitated from fearful parents. Anxious parents produce anxious kids. Fears can be passed from parent to child with no overt awareness in either of them. Some fears stem from unconscious conflicts. For example, painful memories may be displaced to a neutral object, which then becomes greatly feared, as in a phobia, or to a compulsive thought or action, as in an obsession.

Most serious fears probably have multi-factored origins; that is, several of the causes mentioned above may play a part simultaneously.

INHERITABILITY

Can fears be inherited genetically?

Picture four summer cabins around a lake, numbers 1 through 4 on Lakefront Lane, each with a do-it-yourself plumbing system installed by a different nonprofessional. Number 1 has a drain pipe that's too small. The pipe elbows in 2 and 3 are too sharply angled, causing three leaks. Number 4 uses a combination of PVC pipe with other plastics that mutually corrode when connected into the same system. Now picture the four owners going around the lake installing other people's plumbing systems for them.

Here comes Memorial Day weekend. Lots of people descend to stay in lots of cabins. The plumbing systems all around the lake are overtaxed. Stressed out. The drains in cabin 1 back up. But probably, so will the drains in the other cabins plumbed by the owner of 1. Cabin 2 and 3 have water all over, and so do the other cabins the owners of number 2 and 3 plumbed. An so on. The flaws were not evident until a time of stress, and they were, so to speak, inherited along four lines of descent.

Just as the cabins were plumbed according to four lines of descent, people are wired differently according to their genetic differences. The brain is a wonderful system of divergent, convergent, and cyclic circuits. When people are placed under great stress, something happens in their circuitry. Maybe a weak spot gives in. The impairment, then, is not inherited, but the weak spots might be.

The jury is still out on how much weight should be given to genetic and physiological factors, but we do know this: We can make choices and override the weak spots and flaws, if any. There is hope regardless of any genetic tendencies. We can help children make choices that will encourage a huge difference in how well they do in life.

"Do fears of childhood translate to paranoia in old people?" An acquaintance named Nancy asked that question when her seventy-two-year-old mother purchased a handgun. The old woman has three bolts on her front door and two on the back. Inherent in Nancy's question was another: *Will I be paranoid too?*

We find that people may avoid dealing with fears, with intent to resolve them, through busy-ness. It's much easier and less painful to fritter with small surface things than to dig into the big ugly subsurface issues. Eventually, as they age, those persons have fewer things to be busy with. The distractions abate; then the ugly issues surface, unrestrained.

Also, as people grow old they lose autonomy and independence. That's a terrible loss for any active person. Combine those two factors and you have a person unaccustomed and unwilling to become dependent on others, and no longer investing in details in order to avoid resolving fears that should have been dealt with years ago.

The paranoia is not inherited. A healthy balance between trust and skepticism (and common sense in today's violent society) is difficult if old fears intrude.